ENCOUNTERS

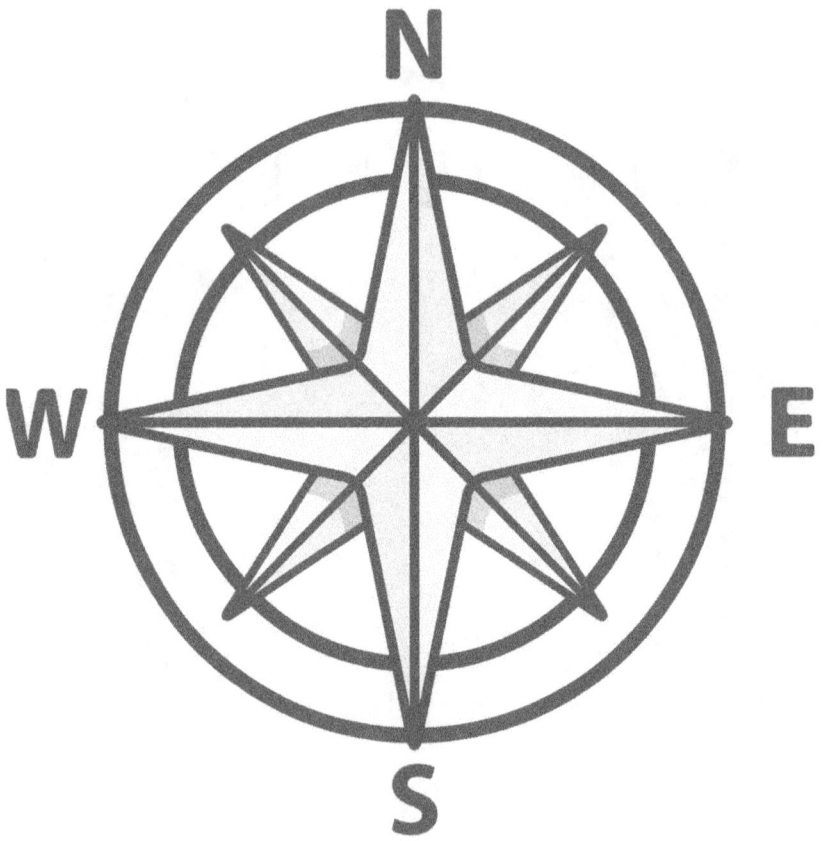

ENCOUNTERS

by
Peter Hilger

Barringer Publishing

Naples, FL

info@barringerpublishing.com

Barringer Publishing, Naples, Florida
www.barringerpublishing.com

Editing by Basil Pettrucci
Cover design & interior layout by Micah Edel; mistermicah.com

ISBN: 978-0-9989069-8-0

Library of Congress Cataloging-in-Publication Data
Encounters/Peter Hilger

Printed in U.S.A.

For my father, who was born 120 years ago today,
October 18, 2002.

As long as I can see, I will keep looking,
As long as I can walk, I will keep moving.

—*Walter De la Mare*

TABLE OF CONTENTS

THE CONSUMMATE TRAVELER

FOREWORD

A Few Words About This Book

All his life, Peter Hilger had both a love affair with wheels and a fascination with people. A storyteller at heart, in later years he collected experiences the way that some collect mementos.

Many of the stories of his childhood and early adult years, driving a wood-fired tractor and then, a beat up Opel while trading goods between the hungry Germans and the needy American soldiers, are included in his first book, *Warn Torn*. Post-War years made car ownership a luxury for many. Our parents took their honeymoon to Italy on a motorcycle, and my dad used it to visit Yugoslavia when I was a toddler in 1953. Most of those trips featured a few photos; one always featured his vehicle.

PETER HILGER, 1935

During our childhood in the suburbs of New York City, Dad wore the buttoned-up, tightly-wound life of a career in corporate 1960–70s America. Even still, magic cars would show up. The classic Thunderbird. The Corvette. Always with a hefty dose of speed. One of them resulted in a 30-day suspension of his driving privileges, where much to his chagrin, our mother had to drive him to the bus station for the daily commute into the City. We tagged along, too young to stay home alone. She rarely drove him anywhere, even on long trips, as he always preferred being the one behind the wheel.

Later there was the company car, a big dark sedan that my dad drove to work for all the odd corporate hours he had to keep. After taking the step to resign, he packed us into that car for a 5-week trip around the US, a vacation we'd not been able to take previously. As the only campers in Swan's Creek Campground near Yellowstone, my mom cooked breakfast pancakes with fruit syrup on the Coleman stove, and we were all sleepless from listening to prowling bears during the night. We ditched the roof rack along side the trash cans. He did not photograph that. Eventually we returned to New Jersey and he started a new job, but the memories of that trip persist.

Our family cars were always spotless and looked new despite being several years old. As kids, we did not dare to eat and leave crumbs in his cars or kick our feet under his seat. He also let my brothers buy a 1961 Fiat convertible for $150 from neighbors across the street. They took it to another neighbor, a racecar driver, and gave it a valve job.

In the early years of my own courtship, my husband John, ever the argumentative journalist, told his future father-in-law that he was a closet hippie and that one day he'd ride a BMW.

It was 1974 and my father was not amused. John was right about the BMW.

The retrofitted van and later, a blue Geo Tracker sustained my parents during trips north and west, like the one to Newfoundland, where they rolled down an embankment, scared but unhurt. Because it could not hold a wheelchair, the beloved Tracker had to be sold in order to accommodate my mother's ever increasing frailty from Multiple Sclerosis. My father agonized and purchased a pedestrian sedan. The wheelchair was used only once, and the Tracker and its adventures became a distant memory.

But not for long. Although at 77 years of age, my father was no longer riding a motorcycle, he soon acquired a Jeep while also continuing to ride his *Lightspeed* titanium bike. And then came the Saturn Sky, a sports car blaring "techno-music" that restored the thrill of the ride.

Peter's final ride ended on January 2, 2015, with the Saturn Sky and his dreams of travels to Chile or Colorado still intact. But as storytellers love to do, he had one set of stories left to tell. This book is the result of that final request. To all of you who contributed as the cast of characters to his Encounters, he would surely grab his daily bourbon cocktail, raise a toast and say "cheers!"

—*Astrid Hilger Bennett, with Peter and Steve Hilger*

PREFACE

Already during in my twenties, Jack Kerouac's book *On the Road* lay on my night table. I must have read it a dozen times from beginning to end, soaking it up and admiring the author's philosophies, which I intended to make my own when I had a chance to travel as he did.

In subsequent years, the book enticed me to journey near and far but mostly to distant outposts. Many of these excursions were made on a motorcycle to which I strapped the essential things I needed—a tent, sleeping bag, one set of extra clothing and food-stuff—mostly cans of food to be cooked over my backpacker's stove.

Other journeys were completed in my GEO Tracker four wheel drive, with identical supplies loaded into its cramped quarters. Still other trips were done via airplanes, ships, trains, buses, bicycles and by hitchhiking.

I have cruised the highways of the North American Continent ever since. I have also traveled extensively through Europe and Japan, either as a student or, in later years, to recapture the spirit of early wanderings.

On these journeys, I have had encounters with many fascinating people—old and young, rich or poor, male and female, black, white, Asian, Indian and Hispanic. This series deals with some of those encounters.

So, come travel with me. Be prepared to meet the most pleasant and interesting people on this globe, although some of them may turn out to be bizarre types.

OPPOSITE PAGE, FROM TOP TO BOTTOM:
PETER IN CHILE; PETER AND HANNA, 1980S

ACKNOWLEDGEMENTS

The events in this book are actual happenings
and people are real. Their names were changed in some
instances to protect individual privacy. The author wishes to
extend his sincerest gratitude to the Island Writers Group of
Sanifbel, Florida, for their encouragement and oustanding
support in writing this book.

PETER AND HIS FAMILY IN PRE-WAR GERMANY—OBVIOUSLY,
HE WANTS TO DRIVE THE FAMILY CAR. HE'S THE YOUNGEST.

Chapter One:
ADOLESCENCE

1925 CHILDHOOD FOLLIES

My grand-daughter, Laura, was enrolled in her senior year at the University of Brighton, England. She sent me a book with the title *"DEAR GRANDAD, FROM YOU TO ME; Journal of a lifetime."*

The cover shows a tree with bright red and brown leaves projecting fall perhaps, because after all that's the season grandfathers are normally in — their autumn years. Inside the tree are several photos of kids small and not so small, or grown, not so old, or older.

I found the title intriguing but did not quite comprehend why she sent it until I opened it. There it was: page after page of blank paper, except every page had a short message on top:

– What are your earliest memories?

– Please detail what you know of our family tree,

– What sort of pets did you have when you were young, and what were their names?

– Tell me about the things you DID as a child that are different for today's children.

– Did you have an idol when you were young? Tell me who and why?

...and hundreds of more questions like that, to the end:

– Given your experiences, what advice would you like to offer me?

Then finally the last:

– And now, your chance to tell me some other personal stories that you want to share…

Leafing through this exhaustive book to the end made me nearly faint, sinking into my favorite easy chair. Laura, what are you doing to me? I love you dearly, but the questions and answers would easily fill 2000–3000 pages—maybe more. And here I am still laboring on my fifth book about my teenage years living in a dictatorship regime. This 300 page book is in fact a life-story in itself and would answer many of your questions in detail. And there are four other ones I wrote and finished earlier in my life.

One question in the Laura's book triggered my mind. It was a subject I have never thought of writing about: *What are your earliest memories?* I started to scratch my head. Nothing came out at first.

Then I had one. It happened very early in my life, maybe before I was two. We always ate our main meal at noon. My Dad would come home from the office at about one o'clock, for a meal and possibly a three-minute nap.

Before that, my nanny had picked me up from my highchair at the dining room table to bring me up to my room for my nap, which was expected to be much longer than my Dad's. But I did not fuss about it, except when they forgot to give me my "Bana", a banana which I wanted, received every day and—resting on the solid arm of the servant—carried like a gun over my tiny shoulder up to my room.

But on the day I remember, I did not want a nap. So I must

have gotten out of my bed, wearing my pants with my diapers bulging inside and a much shorter shirt above that only reached to my stomach, climbed down the stairs, got out on the street and walked a block and a half to the large fountain in the park. I knew this fountain from afternoon walks when my nanny pushed me there in a stroller. I always wanted to explore the magic it held for me but the nanny never allowed it.

This time, there I was all by myself, toddling along, crossing a busy street by the edge of the water, with streetcars and automobiles going to and fro, ready to fully explore that intriguing invention the adults had built. The water looked cold. So I stuck my hand into it to see how cold, then plunged right in.

That's when I heard my name. My dad was standing at the edge of the basin. He had been delayed at the office and was later than usual coming home for lunch. He first went by the fountain. But then—he told me much later—he remembered: "Was that my young son in the water perhaps?" That was happening when I was about two years old. But it stuck with me forever.

Now, as I write this down, I think of the life-sized painting of me that my parents had commissioned an artist to paint. It must have been roughly at the same time.

We lived in a brownstone—a three-story house in Oberkassel. The third floor contained only two very large rooms, with attic areas on both sides as a crawl space for storage. One of those rooms was our playroom, first for my three older siblings, then for me. The other was rented out to a painter. Why? The room's window faced north, creating ideal light for painting. The painter had no money and could rarely, pay the rent. My parents were obviously okay with that. I don't think they rented the space out to get rich. I think they did it more for philan-thropic reasons.

When the painter was again behind on rent, my Mom sug-gested that he do a pastel sketch of her youngest son. That was me, age two. So he made it life-sized: me, with big, happy blue eyes, dressed in blue, the upper part looking like a frock over short pants, wearing my older sister's shoes. I had the reddest hair that I have ever seen on a human being. It was curled into dense, long locks all over my head. I was reach-ing up to a table which was taller than me, to play with my beloved wooden railroad cars my maternal grandfather had made for us kids, and I had a piece of melting chocolate in my other hand. To make it genuine, the painter had it diagonally signed in one corner: "Reusing 1925."

After my mother, who survived my dad by eight years, died, my older siblings decided to send this 'work of art" by freighter to me in the US. And there it stood one day, four feet high, three feet wide, enclosed with a gilt wooden frame, leaning against the living room couch. Where to hang it? Han-na loved it and wanted to put it up in our bedroom. I revolted. I was so ugly as a child. I just could not bear to see my coun-terfeit while waking up every morning.

So, it was finally hung in the entrance hall in such manner that when the front door was opened all the way, it would cover the wall where the painting hung. We almost never used this en-trance. So nobody really noticed it there, which suited me fine.

Its secret hiding place lasted a few years. I was happy about that. Then Hanna died. In her memory and as we had done together for so many years, I threw our traditional neighbor-hood July 4th party later that year. It was inside the house and outside on the covered patio facing the Blue Ridge Mountains.

Some of the ladies among my guests accidentally moved the otherwise open front door and discovered what was behind there. "Oh look," they shrieked, "wasn't he cute. See that outfit. Oh, that's darling, he looks like a girl. And these locks. Heavens. I wish he would still have them." And so they went.

From that day on, when I have outside parties or even just dinner guests, invariably one of the ladies will whisper to another and they will quietly disappear into the front entrance hall. I would hear them giggle and the word "cute" again and again.

So, I normally go into the kitchen to start the dishwasher.

1938 THE KAYAK KID

When I was in sixth grade, in the *Unter Sekunda* as it is called in the German school system, I met Helmut. He also attended high school when I did, which turned out to be a milestone in my life. We were both in our mid-teens. I was taller than him, but he packed more muscle on his broad frame. He had dark brown hair with brown eyes almost the same color. I was red-haired, blue-eyed and freckled.

We saw each other often, going from class to class. At some point during this period when we crossed the halls, I nodded. So did he. Soon thereafter, we talked to each other. But we both had a different set of friends in school, so I did not see or speak to him at length, until the following year.

That was when I found out he was an experienced kayaker. He didn't tell me that, but I watched him at a kayak event in Bavaria, in the summer of 1938. I happened to be vacationing there with my folks. On a white water stretch, I witnessed his expertise in negotiating tight spots and thundering water cascades. I knew then that he was a master of the sport even at his early age. Some years before, I began to be interested in kayaking but never became experienced in the sport. Here was Helmut, a classmate so to speak, even though he was older. He was seventeen; I was fifteen. To teenagers, two years make a lot of difference!

After the event, when he had beached his kayak at the finish line, I went over to him and congratulated him on his run. He grinned and said: "It was fun. You should try it some time."

"I would LOVE to," I instantly blurted out.

"Good. When we get home, I'll show you a few moves and tricks. The first thing you'll have to learn is the roll."

"What's that?"

"We call it a 360. It means you have to roll the kayak once around through the water to learn to come up again."

"Okay, got that. What then?"

"Then I'll show you your best paddling position, stuff like that. We'll go out on the Rhine first, to give you an introduction. We can take a smaller, faster river after that."

I was in seventh heaven.

Soon after we returned home, we went out in his two-seat sea kayak. They are wider than white water kayaks. He taught me my seating position, my forward stroke with each side of the paddle. He showed me how to handle currents, especially around the river's numerous jetties. He guided me through some of the rapids.

In October, my Dad found an inexpensive, used kayak made out of wood. I needed—and built myself with Helmut's help—a two-wheel cart to roll it to the river some three kilometers one way. Weighing a ton—or so it felt—it was nevertheless a good tool to learn on.

By fall, I had learned a lot about the sport! By fall, I had my sea kayak. When we went out, we each had our own! By fall, we had become kayaking buddies!

Realizing that I was hooked on a new sport—and likely also approving of their son's new friendship—my parents gave me a new Klepper single canvas type kayak like Helmut's for Christmas that year. They were made for white water rivers; narrow, sleek and fast. They were equipped with a spray skirt to prevent the water from entering the kayak in a roll. Helmut's rig was faded green and well used. Mine was new and still dark green in color.

During the winter, we often met after school, walked down to the river, talked about kayaking and dreamt about next spring when we could go out again.

The following summer of 1939, we set out together for almost three weeks of kayaking white water rivers in the European Alps. I was still a minor at sixteen and needed the permission of my parents. But they had met Helmut. By then, he was a frequent visitor to our home. My folks approved of him.

Both kayaks could be folded into a backpack and checked on the train. At the river, we assembled them in about twenty minutes. They were light enough to be shouldered in portage areas. In contrast to today's white water kayaks, they also had storage space for camping gear and food.

Helmut taught me white water kayaking that summer—the REAL stuff! He was superb in handling his rig, showing his great expertise but also outstanding courage and sometime dare-devil quality. He was a master. But with me, he was always cautious and concerned for my safety. He would not allow me to do the things he did, until he felt sure I could master them.

I learned my first rolls in real surroundings; I learned to negotiate the rapids around great boulders and through cascading masses of water without needing to roll. And when I finally achieved the necessary skills, he led me down the next river at full speed, both of us screaming in joy when we had negotiated the tight spots or wild rapids, then laughing all the way to the next one.

At night, we would find a spot on the river's edge and set up our tent. We always picked locations near a village so we could climb up the river bank and walk to the next eatery for food and beer, lots of beer, usually the dark stuff. And nobody asked us for our ID to see if we were eighteen. After that, we would sit in front of our tent, listen to the water burble past and talk endlessly about our lives, about girls and forever about the sport of kayaking.

We also made plans for our next trip together the following summer after Helmut graduated and before he was to enroll into the University at Munich.

That never happened. As soon as we were home again from our journey down the fast rivers in late August, Hitler invaded Poland.

Two months later, Helmut was drafted into Hitler's Wehrmacht. Another month later, in December, he was hit near Warsaw by a Russian-made hand grenade. He didn't live long enough to be home for Christmas. Eighteen years old!

Knowing him, his outstanding courage, his sense of duty, he probably went beyond the limits to serve his fatherland. His death created a void in me.

I was only sixteen. He was my role model. I wanted to be like him in my life. Our friendship would have lasted well into our adult lives as so many others did.

The next two summers while I was still home, I went to the river often, alone, either sitting on my favorite jetty when it was too cold or in my kayak when it turned warmer. The war went on, became more vicious and ultimately ended in chaos.

* * * *

During subsequent postwar years at universities in Germany and France, I found no time or chance to kayak. Then I married, we moved to the US and I became a father. Hanna thought the sport might be a bit too risky for the head of the household. So I gave it up.

But in 1985, when Hanna was in Europe and our children had grown, I had a chance to kayak twenty-two miles down the Green River Canyon Gorge in Utah in a rented, superlight, fiber-glass rig.

The rapids were not wild that day but just curly enough to pump up my adrenalin. I screamed with joy "yippee" and the canyon echoed back my "yippee, yippee" outburst a few seconds later. To me the sound seemed to be familiar. Was it Helmut's voice answering? Was it the screaming of the two of us when we sped down some European rivers so many years ago?

I was sure it was. My thoughts were intensely with him then. And always it seemed that he was there with me!

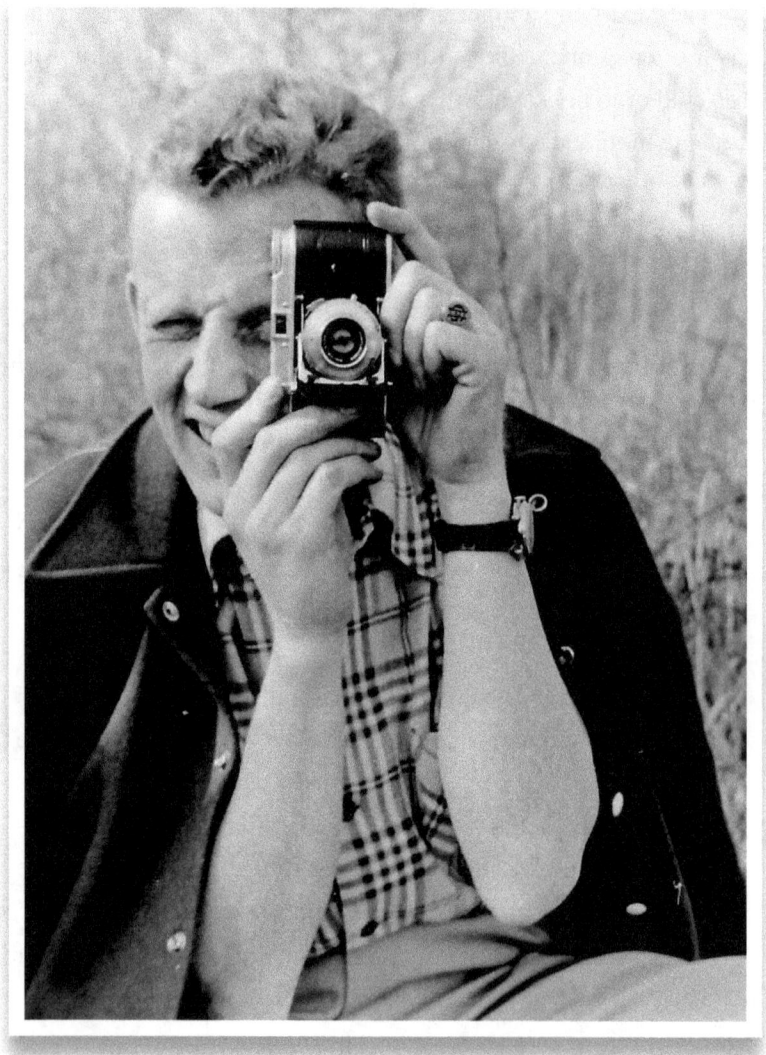

PETER HILGER AS A YOUNG MAN WITH HIS
VOIGTLANDER CAMERA. *PHOTO BY KLAUS REESE.*

Chapter Two:
STUDENT YEARS: FREIBURG

1944 TAKING A BATH IN FREIBURG

During the summer of 1944, I was enrolled in my third semester at Freiburg University Medical School. A bunch of guys, nine of us, had spent the night drinking beer in the cellar of the old Rathaus, the "house of counsel," in the true translation of this German word. Built in 1235, it was the sandstone city hall with religious paintings adorning its side walls. It stood right opposite the tall, gothic cathedral and had done so for centuries.

But we students weren't that much intrigued with history. What did interest us was the fact that in its cellar, the "Rathaus" had a tavern. It was a fitting place for get-togethers with pals devoted to having a good time. It was cool and rustic, with wine barrels lining the rock walls and the heavy smell of fermentation in the air.

We had consumed a fair share of spirits when, at three a.m., the place closed down for the night. We were "encouraged" to leave, which we did. We headed home to our quarters, walking north on the city's main street. It was a starry, mellow, warm night in June.

Then, one of us had the thought to take off our shoes and socks and walk barefoot, in those little riverbeds which ran in cemented ditches between road and sidewalk. We thought this would cool us down, both physically and in our foggy minds. Great idea!

Thus we arrived at a fairly large fountain. It was a monument well known to us, dating back to earlier times. When the Dukes of Baden, then the state for which Freiburg was the capital, needed to document their power and status, they built mansions, fountains and other expressions of wealth.

This fountain featured several oversized statues of men, with sinister faces and long beards, holding monumental swords and guarding the activities of the citizenry below.

But at fifteen past three in the morning, none of that was on our minds. We had all seen these old men on top of the fountain before. They did not bother us now, with our feet nice and cool. We decided to rip off all our clothes, drop them on the mosaic sidewalk and go swimming in the fountain's bubbling water. Loudly carousing, as we had done since leaving the tavern, we chanted student songs and anything else that came to mind.

Alas, we heard the sirens. Warning of an approaching Allied air raid? No, police cruiser sirens! The sound penetrated even our beer-fogged minds. We bolted out of the water but had no time to grab our clothes, get dressed and escape. So we stood, all nine of us, stark naked, motionless, trying to pass as part of the fountain's mighty statues depicting some distant water god or goddess. And so we hoped for the best. But, in our condition with that many liters of beer aboard, no one could stand motionless for very long. The *Polizei* knew at once what was going on.

We were taken to the station and fined one mark each, then freed to go home. At ten the next morning, we paid the fine in the same police station, headachy and hung over. We had chosen to pay in *Pfennig*, all nine of us, slowly counting them out individually on the policemen's desks, nine hundred pennies in all!

"Get out of here, fast," they called after us when we were done and started to bolt out of the station, "and BEHAVE!"

1947 EVA

During the winter of 1947/48, I met Eva while cross country skiing in Germany's Black Forest. A mutual liking let us become good friends soon thereafter.

During the following summer of 1948, while I took summer courses at the University of Freiburg to prepare for my approaching graduation, she had no such schedule. She needed to augment her financial coffers to finance her next year's semesters.

Hence, Eva took a summer job as an *au pair*, or "house daughter," as such positions were called in the German language. It meant a mother's helper for the family, to watch the kids, wash the dishes, mop the floors.

The family that chose her for the job were wealthy Swiss, living in a large, patrician home on the east side of Zurich, near the lake. The house faced a square which included a small, well-kept park. Many European cities feature such parks in residential areas.

I had a chance to sell my Opel that summer because I would not be taking it with me to Paris, after graduation later that year. So, I hitchhiked to Zurich one Saturday morning to be with Eva for the weekend.

We spent Saturday afternoon and early evening together, walking through the city, watching the sun set over the lake, eating some spiced sausages on a bun with sauerkraut, and washing the food down with a bottle of inexpensive but excellent Swiss country wine.

Eventually, we found a garden restaurant where the proprietors had set up a small, wooden dance floor, in front of an equally small bandstand. A five-man band, consisting of brass instruments and an accordion, was going at it with lots of *hummtata, hummtata*. There, we occasionally heard some yodeling. Between sips of beer, I twirled Eva around until ten. The bandleader then pronounced that the place would close down for the night.

"Why?" I asked Eva.

"Because the *Zuricher Frauenverein* sets the rules. And according to that bunch of old women, everyone should be in bed at that hour."

"Is there actually an association of ladies of the city of Zurich?" I asked again.

"Sure is."

I brought her home at ten thirty, since it was the hour of the curfew imposed by the family. I waited outside, until she was in her third floor bedroom. The house was of traditional Swiss design, with living and dining rooms, kitchen and pantry downstairs, bedrooms for the family on the floor above, guest bedrooms one more flight up and the maid's quarters in the attic.

Eva occupied one of the guest bedrooms. Once up there, she opened the window to let the mellow summer air in and to lean on the window sill to talk to me down on the street. We tried to hush our voices, so as not to disturb anyone in Eva's house, or the neighbors surrounding us.

It did not last long. I heard the lady of the house calling Eva, from the door of her bedroom. I then saw Eva resolutely begin to close her window while I quickly ducked behind some bushes. Never mind my attempts at hiding; Madame still shouted down into the plaza for me to go away, NOW!

Of course, I didn't. I had no place to go anyway. I had planned right along to stretch out on some park bench for the night. It so happened that the park in front of Eva's house had one, long contoured bench, so I could not roll off in my sleep.

I was still sound asleep the next morning when her tall, grimfaced employer rudely awakened me, shaking me by my shoulder. Then, he rendered a long lecture, so early in the day, about such sinful things as sleeping outside in the open, the judgment of disorderly conduct and vagrancy this fact might have earned me from his neighbors.

Well, to be truthful, I hadn't thought of that.

I rubbed my eyes and said: "Good morning, sir." Beyond that I said nothing.

This made him even madder. He carried on, snorting like a bull in a Spanish arena, being readied for the fight.

When he ran out of things to say, he stared at me for a long moment. Then he snarled,

"Well, I have said enough. You must be hungry. Come up and have breakfast with us. But wash your hands first."

"Yes sir! And thank you, sir."

When Eva came into the dining room to bring me my boiled egg and toast, I winked an eye at her and we both barely avoided grins. But any smile would have soon disappeared when our host abruptly continued his moral sermon. Breakfast had obviously given him a second wind.

"Why did you not book yourself into a room at the inn? It is only two blocks away from here."

"It just did not seem that I had the time to do that, sir.

Actually, they were already closed at nine when Eva and I came back here."

I knew he did not believe me. It was too lame an excuse anyway.

"In Switzerland," he continued, as if reading my thoughts, "one either has the income to travel or one does not travel at all. Did you come by train?"

"No."

"By car then?" he continued probing.

"No, I just sold my car."

"How did you get to Zurich then?"

"Hitchhiking."

There was a long, awkward pause. It felt as if a bomb had exploded in the room. My host drilled his piercing eyes into me. I responded by looking at him with the best, most sincere smile on my face that I could muster. But I knew I had to get out of there soon. I knew I would blow my top if this continued and that would not have done Eva any good.

Then my host finally spoke again, and he said these unforgettable words:

"Do you not have any income from your capital?"

"No, sir."

"Well, why then do you not see the necessity to sell some of your, how do you say in America the word for capital, —assets, is it, no?"

"Because I do not have any assets, sir."

But now, I had to laugh out loud, in spite of my deep frustrations with the entire course of conversation. I couldn't keep it back anymore, which now infuriated him no end. Yet before he could catch his breath and go on, I swallowed my last bite of toast quickly, washed it down with the remainder of my coffee and thanking both my hosts for breakfast, asked the lady of the house if Eva and I could be excused. She nodded gracefully.

It was a beautiful Sunday morning. Church bells rang out all over town. People walked to places of worship wearing their Sunday best. It was Eva's off-duty day, after clearing the breakfast dishes, that is. Our hosts had taken their Chevrolet and driven to church with their children.

We walked down to the lake to go swimming at one of several public beaches. After paying our modest entrance fees, Eva went right, I went left, into our respective changing rooms. But as I came out onto the sandy beach, I noticed the high wooden fence running down the middle, dividing it into male and female sections. I could fathom such rules for changing of clothes but found the continued segregation of the sexes old fashioned.

The dividing fence extended far out into the water, as I probed for ways to get over to the female side.

"Eva, you there?" I called at the wooden divider.

"Yeah, I am almost right across from you. This is stupid, don't you think?"

"Very stupid. Let's swim out to the end of this thing so we can do some talking."

"Okay, seems that's all we can do."

So for Eva and me to see each other and talk meant swimming far out each time and treading water, while carrying on any sensible conversation. All of Switzerland was very strict then, with moral standards set unreasonably high.

Eva and I remained good friends all the years after my journey to Zurich. She came to my home on Sanibel, Florida, one recent winter to visit and have lunch with us. As we walked the short distance to the beach, many a male head in my neighborhood turned to take another look at her elegant stride and gracious face—older now but still beautiful.

After a long battle with leukemia, she bade her final farewell to us on March 7, 1999.

1948 ANTOINETTE

In late October of 1948, I was supposed to prepare for my MBA written and oral exams at the University of Freiburg. They were scheduled for November and December respectively, with graduation planned in time for Christmas. I was nearing the end of many years of learning and eager to get it over with.

Besides, on New Year's Day, I would take the train to Paris to attend the Sorbonne's Law School for postgraduate work.

But one day, a young lady I knew, who was from Neufchatel, Switzerland, walked into my room at a boarding house where I lived. I had met her briefly before through a mutual friend. Her name was Antoinette. She was determined to spend as much of her father's money as possible. I was sure her father was hard at work keeping up with her spending habits while manufacturing Swiss wristwatches.

She was also quite attractive.

But what impressed me most about her at that point was her beautiful, shiny, snow-white Mercedes Benz convertible, with red leather seats.

She swept me off my feet by persuading me to come along on a little fall trip through the Alps in her sporty roadster. I succumbed.

In Switzerland, which has plenty of Alps, she couldn't travel with a male friend. Such unheard of things were done in France. Switzerland then had even more of a moral code than now. Sort of dull, I thought.

I didn't have a dime to spare. She did, though, plenty of them. We took many detours to reach Salzburg, Austria, our eastern-most destination. We checked in for three days at the Grand Hotel, opposite the Mirabelle Palace. There, the Dukes of Haps-burg entertained their lady friends while their wives and families stayed in the confines of their grey fortress on the mountain top above town.

And we went to hear the Vienna Philharmonic Orchestra at the *Festspielhaus* every night to hear Karl Boehm conduct Mo-zart. All Mozart, of course. Mozart is everywhere in Salzburg. It was Heaven on Earth!

I was exhausted when I returned. But I graduated, though I never did get good grades during either exam. And my loving Mother scolded me good and hard when she phoned my boarding house and could not find me home.

DAD AND THE BOYS; SORBONNE '72

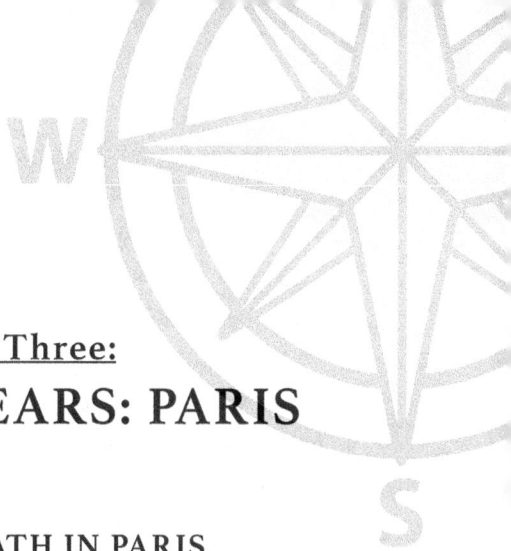

Chapter Three:
STUDENT YEARS: PARIS

1949 TAKING A BATH IN PARIS

New Year's Day, 1949! On that day's cold and wet afternoon, I arrived in Paris by train at the city's *Gare de L'Est*. I had never been there before. I knew where my school was located in town because I had studied city maps for weeks before my arrival. So, without delay, I rode the old, clunky Metro to the intersection of Boulevard St. Michel and Boulevard St. Germain, on the left bank of the river Seine, near the stately Cathedral of Notre Dame.

Not yet four years after the end of World War II, I found Paris undestroyed, magnificent and unchanged from what my parents had told me about the city.

Life was pulsating, traffic roared, meat and vegetables were stacked in heaps. The tables took half of the sidewalks in front of their stores, luring customers with delicious sights. The sidewalk cafes were crowded and students from all over the world walked the streets and parks, lounged on riverfront benches and sat on steps of numerous monuments.

Peace and abundance had returned to France.

I checked the quieter side streets for places to stay and stumbled onto a *pension de famille* at 29 Rue de Buci, off Boulevard St. Germain and not far from the Sorbonne. It looked decent and not too expensive.

I walked through the unlocked door and found the owner's apartment immediately to the right.

"*Bon jour, Madame.* Do you have a room in which I can stay while I go to school here?" I asked.

She looked me over, checking me out. My carrot-topped six feet towered over her and my distinct Teutonic Anglo accent broke through my halting French.

"*Mais oui, Monsieur,*" she replied encouragingly.

"And how much will that be per month?"

She looked intensely into my freckled face, as if she wanted to size up my material wealth. "Four thousand francs," she replied, matter-of-factly, apparently satisfied with what she had seen.

I conducted a swift mental calculation: the dollar bought about three hundred fifty francs in 1949, so this would be $11.42 a month. My scholarship to the Sorbonne would provide tuition free attendance at all classes of my choice and a monthly living allowance of $40.00.

"*Bien sur*, I will take it."

I was shown to my room, five flights up. It faced the inner courtyard. Measuring only eight by ten feet, it contained a double bed, a small table and chair, a wash stand with the smallest bowl and water can I had ever seen, and a pint-sized closet for my clothes.

That fact didn't bother me much because I didn't own any clothes to speak of anyway. What I did own would easily hang on the narrow rod provided. A small shelf above the coat rack held my underwear, socks, handkerchiefs and shirts. My backpack fit snugly under my bed for storage.

Then I found a faded note pinned on the door, which I deciphered to say that to take a bath in "*la salle de bain*" would cost forty francs, meaning eleven cents. Affordable, I thought.

A toilet was located on each landing between two floors. The view from my room's window into the courtyard revealed another toilet, this one on the ground floor and designed in the then traditional French way—a stand up situation with a solid grab bar on each side to hold onto while conducting one's business. Madame would clean it every day, by hurling two or three buckets of water into its cavernous, walled confine. It turned out to be the most hygienic of these establishments in the pension, and the one I would henceforth use.

When I had unpacked, I looked for Madame and asked her if I could take a bath for forty francs, "*naturellement.*"

"*Certainement,*" she answered with a totally bewildered look on her face. "How about ten o'clock tonight?"

Why so late, I thought. I wanted to freshen up, clean off the train's smoke and grime before setting out to find a place to eat a cheap meal. Instead, I went out to do the latter first. On the way to the staircase, I noticed that Madame and one of her maids were starting to empty a room, with some of its furniture already stacked up high in the narrow hall. I said "*bon soir*" in passing but had a chance for a glimpse into that room they were clearing.

It was *la salle de bain.* The tub was still filled to the ceiling with excess furniture. I took my eleven-cent bath that evening, but never used it again. Instead I decided to visit *le piscine* a few blocks away, the public indoor swimming pool owned by the city. It featured not only open stall hot and cold showers but also an Olympic-sized pool for my daily dose of exercise.

I found out from Madame the next morning that in all the many years she owned the establishment, the *salle de bain* had never been used.

Later that day, the furniture was removed from the hall and returned to its traditional resting place in the bathtub.

But a few days later, I found a faded poster from an art calendar down at the book stands on the river, Seine, and pinned it over the equally faded "*salle de bain*" sign on my door.

1949 RODIN

It was in early 1949, January 2nd to be correct, when I enrolled in classes at the Sorbonne's prestigious *Ecole du Droit* in Paris, its law school which only taught the "Code Napoleon." Anything else that might have been mentioned was considered outlandish.

Whenever such classes were held in the university's large auditorium, I soon exchanged greetings with a guy I always sat next to. His name was Rodin and he was born and raised in Paris. He witnessed my daily struggle with his language. Because I basically knew only grammar.

"Pierre, you want to know how to learn French?" he asked one day.

"*Certainment*," I replied eagerly.

"Well, then, get up an hour earlier every day," answered Rodin, "and buy *Le Monde*, our leading morning newspaper. Then take either the left or the right column and read it aloud. Hear yourself pronounce the words, listen to your accents. Place your dictionary next to you. Keep it near and handy at all times. Stop at every word you do not know and look it up. It will help you learn my language quickly."

I did as Rodin suggested. It took me much more than an hour at first to translate a column. After a month had passed, it took ten minutes. In two months, along with what I had learned in daily use and at school, I was fairly fluent in French.

Rodin was beaming.

One day when I had mastered the language, he asked me to come to dinner at his house on Thursday of that week. "Because now you can converse with my mother who does not speak anything but French," he added.

I went there Thursday evening, spiffed up and shaved, arriving half an hour late, as is customary in Paris. As soon as I had entered my host's spacious, elegant apartment near the *Bois de Bologne* and exchanged the customary formalities applied when meeting the lady of the house, I found out why Madame did not speak any other language. She strongly disliked anything non-French, starting with the Germans and, somewhere along the line, also including Americans.

"But Madame, they liberated your country, *les Americains*. Without them, Hitler would still be here to terrorize you," I said after dinner over cognac. She must have known that I was American. Rodin had told her, I was sure.

"*Mais non, Monsieur Pierre,*" she burst out. She looked as she was really furious. "It was Le General de Gaulle who liberated France!" she exclaimed.

Rodin cringed. I just shrugged. I had heard this before. No use to argue with this feisty lady, she would never give in.

But I knew it was a great honor to be invited to dinner at her apartment. Because in France, entertaining is done outside the house, in cafes or restaurants. Only family and intimate friends are ever invited home. And even that does not often happen.

Rodin and I remained close friends. We saw each other every day during semesters.

During vacations, he would travel to the family castle in the country, near the Loire River, while I hitchhiked through Europe.

He married shortly after he graduated. I was invited to be his best man. But I had left Paris two weeks before. I would have felt greatly honored to be there for him.

1949 FRENCH TRUCK DRIVERS

What I remember most of Lyon, that large industrial city in central France, was *Les Halles*, a sprawling complex of open-sided halls where produce, meats, poultry, fish and an assortment of other vital food items were traded, from about three until after seven o'clock every morning. We would call it an exchange, a market where farmers and producers offer their wares to the buyers who traditionally purchase foodstuffs for one day only, to ensure its total freshness.

Those buyers were mostly from local restaurants, but quite a few were individual shoppers who rose early to buy the best, in spite of the customary late night hours.

It was early July, 1949. The Sorbonne had closed for the summer. I was now free to do what I pleased. There were no summer courses to interfere with plans I might have had for traveling and getting to know my host country.

My scholarship at the Sorbonne provided for free tuition to any course I wished to take. I had chosen Law and Political Science. Beyond that, it paid a modest amount for living expenses—forty-five dollars, to be exact—which were automatically transferred to my bank account in even amounts throughout the year. So it did not matter much whether I stayed in Paris or not.

Throughout my student years, my living allowance barely covered the minimum even in those days of better exchange rates and lower prices. So it made no difference where I was while I was living frugally. But I wanted to see the Mediterranean and the only way to get there was to hitchhike. And that I did for the whole summer—to the Cote d'Azur, to Marseille and Barcelona, Spain.

Hitchhiking in post-war Europe was an accepted and common mode of travel for young people in most countries of the continent. I gave myself two months and established a very tight food budget consisting of one baguette, one bottle of milk and one bar of chocolate, as my daily allowable intake. An even tighter budget was applied to accommodations during the night, by stretching out my sleeping bag somewhere out of the weather for a secure shelter from the elements. Daily showers would have to be rivers and lakes wherever I could find them.

One beautiful morning, I took the Metro, Paris' subway, to *Porte d'Italie*, the city's exit to the southeast, towards Lyon. To this day, it serves as a busy gateway out of Paris.

Not many cars stopped at first. But eventually, I caught several rides to a point out in the country, almost midway between Paris and Lyon. There, I stood for a long time. Previous experiences on the road had already taught me the lesson of waiting and the virtue of patience.

Ultimately, in the evening, a *routier*—French for truck driver—took mercy and hauled me into the cab of his huge truck. Following the etiquette self-imposed by most hitchhikers, I immediately introduced myself:

"Bon soir, Monsieur, je suis Pierre, un etudiant a Paris."

"Bon soir, mon garcon. Tu vais a Lyon?"

"Oui, Monsieur."

"C'est bien," he said.

He was much older than I, surely over forty-five, and very friendly.

"You are going to Lyon to live, Pierre?" he wanted to know.

"No, I am going to Marseille," I replied. I did not want to imply that I was rich and reaching out for the glamorous resorts like Cannes or St. Tropez.

"*Tres bien*," he said again. Then he started to talk, to tell me a long story about his family, down in Grenoble where he was from.

I had already suspected that much, judging from his broad, southern accent.

"My father was a fighter in the Resistance, an underground member organization of those opposed to the German occupation during World War II. I was too young for service."

"How old did you have to be, to become a member?"

"Eighteen."

I started to count. Eighteen in 1941 would make him twenty-six now. How wrong can one be? He looked over forty to me. Maybe it was his size, his belly, his baldness.

"But we are all very thankful to America to have helped us in some small ways to win the war for all free nations." What a very French statement that was!

Two hours later, it must have been after nine o'clock in the evening, we stopped for dinner at a roadside restaurant, an *auberge* which looked very inviting to bed down in. But I knew that was out of the question. There were plenty of other trucks parked in front and on the sides of the establishment, indicating the nature and purpose of it as an early version of an American truck stop.

As we walked inside, another truck pulled into the last

available slot next to the *auberge's* front entrance, letting out that familiar hydraulic hiss.

Behind the bar, full and loud, its polished countertop damp from the wet rags used by Madame to wipe off the remainder of beer and foam, she would reign, cuss, tease, and scold.

She was resilient alright. The *routiers* loved her, I could tell.

She had to be like she was, I guessed, dealing with big men, big beards, big mustaches, big bellies, big voices. But they were friendly and gallant to Madame and the waitresses. Even so, I would always try to be on their right side, any other way could be a crucial mistake.

We found a table and sat down. My friend and savior of the road asked me what I would eat, and I said:

"I am not very hungry. I will just have a glass of water."

The waitress came and placed the obligatory basket with two baguettes on the table. Then she was ready to take our orders.

"I will have," started the *routier*,

* "Soft boiled eggs in mayonnaise, garni with moist pieces of *celeri remoulade*,

* two short *saucisson* well spiced with red peppers and rice, carrots and peas,

* chicken and gravy with tiny potatoes roasted with herbs, and tomatoes stuffed with garlic and parsley,

* *frommage blanc*,

* *creme caramel et cafe noir, avec un calvados, s'il vous plait, Madame."*

My mouth watered.

"Et pour vous, Monsieur?" It was my turn. I swallowed and said:

"Un verre d'eau."

Both the truck driver and the waitress stared at me in disbelief and shook their heads. Nobody drinks water in France, he must be sick, or from an outlandish country, they both probably thought.

But, automatically, throughout the long process of first discussing then ordering the evening meal, a ritual strictly observed in France, I had quietly munched away, without realizing it, most of the fresh bread in the basket.

The *routier* signaled the waitress to come back.

"*Oui, Monsieur?*" she said, not looking at me.

"Give this man to eat what I have ordered, just double our dinner."

She smiled with a shining eyes, looked at me again with that satisfied face which often comes to well-meaning mothers when they have won their children over to eat.

"*Oui, Monsieur,*" she replied and scurried away to order our dinner.

"But I am really not hungry, *Monsieur, merci beaucoup,*" I said, in a faint attempt to sound plausible.

The waitress had heard it and stopped walking.

"Do what I told you," the truck driver called after her.

"But I don't have the money to pay for my food," I said in desperation.

"I know that."

I wolfed down my dinner, I thought it was the best I ever had. In between forkfuls, I looked across the table to my benefactor, who by now had opened the top buttons of his shirt, to let the heat generated from the process of eating escape. His hairy chest was adorned with a golden crucifix attached to a golden chain. He was busy now talking to another *routier*. They were rapidly firing words back and forth, a friendly banter. When he stopped and turned toward our table again, I said in a very low voice:

"Merci."

He laughed. I did not think he had heard that, but, obviously, he did.

We left shortly before eleven, with my truck driver friend having consumed a whole bottle of red wine with dinner, before enjoying his *digestif* with his coffee. To Frenchmen, this is equal to drinking coke, 7-up or milk with their meals.

I had stuck to my water, several glasses of it.

We hit the highway again, towards Lyon. I could not go to sleep. My companion had fallen silent, concentrating on the dark ribbon of asphalt ahead of him. It was another item of the etiquette of hitchhiking, never to talk to your host unless they ask direct questions.

About four hours later, at ten minutes to three in the morning, we rumbled into the outskirts of Lyon. The *routier* was busy winding his big rig with its trailer behind, through the city's narrow streets. But somewhere in between, he asked:

"Pierre, where to you want to get off?"

"At Les Halles,"

"But that is out of your way." It was, way out of my way.

"No, it isn't," I said affirmatively.

He looked puzzled for a moment. Then, the by now familiar winning smile came over his face again, the same smile he had displayed when he had managed to order food for me.

What I remember most about Lyon, that large industrial city in central France, was "Les Halles", a sprawling complex of open-sided halls where produce, meats, poultry, fish and an assortment of other vital food items were traded every morning from about three until after seven o'clock. We would call it an exchange, a market where farmers and producers offer their wares to the buyers who traditionally purchase foodstuffs for one day only, to ensure its total freshness. Those buyers were mostly from local restaurants, but quite a few were individual shoppers.

Les Halles of the city of Lyon were scattered around a large area. They were actually roofs with all sides open, like carports in the United States. They were not quite as large as those of the city of Paris by the same name. Their interiors featured a good number of *etaux*, stalls of varying sizes to serve vendors for displaying their wares. Wide passageways separated them from each other.

We arrived early enough to witness the confusion, noise, sweat and commands barked out by people unloading their stacked crates from the trolleys made available by the managing authorities. Others, those who organized their loads for display at their stalls, hollered for "*cafe et croissant*" to the page boys scuttling back and forth.

The passageways were littered with crates, cardboard and paper straw. The floor was adorned with lettuce leaves, squashed fruit, tomatoes and other items during the chaotic stage of delivery.

I had jumped out of the truck's cab as soon as the *routier* had maneuvered his rig into the unloading bay assigned to him. He came out on his side, went to the rear of the truck and opened the wide hatch. Inside were stacks and stacks of crates filled with fresh vegetables from the country. They reached to the truck's roof.

The truck driver climbed up, bellowed out a command to me down below to run and secure one of the large trolleys and bring it up alongside the rear hatch. I scrambled to do this, like I had seen the page boys do.

Then came out crate after crate. With close guidance from my companion, I learned quickly how to stack them securely enough for the rapid trip inside. When the cart was loaded I ran into the halls with it, pushing it to the stall number given to me by the driver. Page boys would help me unload before I rushed out again to the truck for the next batch.

When the truck was done delivering its last load into the halls, the *routier* maneuvered the trailer into the bay. It was unloaded in the same manner.

I was soaked with sweat. I had not worked physically that hard in a long time. But I was laughing because it was fun and I could pitch in, help my savior on the road and be accepted by everyone as "one of theirs."

When all was done, we had some coffee and hot croissants. I was again invited. This time I accepted without fuss.

The halls began to look presentable. The crates had been stashed, the carts parked, the floors swept by an army of helpers.

Les Halles de Lyon was open for business. It was four-thirty in the morning.

I never saw so much fresh food in my life. One hundred and ten stalls were filled to the brim with olives, anchovies, cabbage, salad, beans, peas and carrots. Others contained heaps of chicken, plucked of course, capons and ducks. Still others had fish laid out gill to gill, row after row—clams, mollusks, shrimp, lobster, halibut, eels. Men with deft hands and long, thin knives were cutting filets, the noise of rubber boots ringing from the wet floor below.

Then I called out to the *routier*,

"*Je vais sortir, Monsieur,*" signaling my imminent departure. "*Et merci, merci beaucoup,*" I added, stretching out my hand to him.

"*A ton service, mon garcon, et bon voyage.*" he said, shaking mine.

Sweaty and dusty, I headed out of the complex with the backpack on my soaked back, bedroll tied to its underside and mess kit dangling from its left flap.

I sniffled myself and did not like what I smelled. But, it was a three kilometer hike from there to the road and the river Rhone.

I decided, smell or no smell, that my daily cleansing process would have to wait until an occasion presented itself.

1949 MONSIEUR ET MADAME DES GAYETS

It was now an hour after I had left Les Halles at six in the morning. I was still soaked with sweat from the heavy work unloading my truck driver's cargo of vegetables from the country. I stood on Lyon's road south to Avignon in southern France, thumbing a ride.

It was a radiant summer morning, full of promise for new discoveries, perhaps adventures not experienced before. I was whistling while waiting for a car to stop:

"Sur le pont "On the bridge
d'Avignon,   of Avignon
on y dance   there one dances
toute en ronde..." all around..."

Maurice Chevalier sang it so well. It refers to the famous bridge in Avignon, built by the Romans about 1,900 years ago. It had crumbled over the centuries and now spans only half of the Rhone River.

I hoped to hike down to Avignon that day, to sleep under the bridge's shadow in my bedroll, hidden by the tall river grass near the river's edge.

The highway south to Avignon and ultimately Marseille was very busy that morning. Heavy traffic prevented many willing drivers from stopping for me. It would be too dangerous to undertake such a maneuver. The morning rush hour was in full swing. Its vehicles virtually rolled right by my toes.

Eventually, when traffic eased somewhat and there was a gap in the line of cars, trucks, motorcycles, Vespas and bicycles, a sleek, grey two-seater Citroen convertible came to stop a bit further up the road where the driver could find a safe spot on the shoulder. A young couple drove it, top down. I had seen it pass by, her hair flying in the wind, taking a glimpse of the red leather interior. A nice car, I thought.

Now the car stopped. I grabbed my backpack and ran up to them, using my well practiced hitchhiker etiquette again, of introducing myself. Then I asked:

"Vous allez a Marseille?"

"Mais certainement," said the man who had stepped out of the car, "we are going that way. But we do not have much room. Do you think you will be comfortable in our narrow car?"

I took a good look at Madame in the right seat and decided I would be very comfortable indeed.

My backpack barely fit into the extremely tight trunk space, which was loaded with expensive looking luggage and tennis rackets.

Madame moved over towards the center and its gear shift lever. Then I squeezed myself into the narrow space between her and the right door, forcing her even more towards the gear shift. She looked terribly uncomfortable.

"Are you comfortable, Madame?"

"Very," she replied, in a mellow voice which made my spine tingle. *"Vous etes Americain, n'est ce pas? Ou Allemand?* We are Monsieur et Madame des Gayets, from Lyon."

"*Enchante, Madame, Monsieur*, and yes, I am American of German heritage. My grandfather came to the United States from Germany. So you are right."

They were a young couple, perhaps a little older than I was, but obviously with much more money at their disposal.

"We were married yesterday," said Monsieur, "and we are now going south to Rome, on our, how do you say in English, honeymoon?"

So, they were married. Hmm! Only yesterday. I stole a glance at Monsieur. I wondered what made her choose him as a mate. After all, he was short, much smaller than I was, which I found out when he stashed my backpack into the trunk. He was attractive, his dark hair combed straight back with the help of lots of Vitalis or whatever the French used to achieve that look. I was sure he did not weigh in at much more than 125 pounds.

I felt almost clumsy next to him, towering over him, with my frame well-toned from swimming hundred meter sprints on the school team, my head full of curly red hair. But I had freckles, lots of those. Maybe Madame didn't like freckles?

Stop this nonsense, I said under my breath. Nevertheless, painfully aware of the lack of personal hygiene that morning, I kept my arms pressed tightly against my sides. If my odors bothered Madame, she certainly did not say so. Maybe the wind swept most of them away.

I traveled with them all day. They invited me to a luxurious lunch in a roadside restaurant so elegant that I was hesitant to accept their invitation because of the way I was dressed. But they insisted that I come. I had fewer problems with being treated to a sumptuous lunch. I knew they could afford it.

In Avignon in late afternoon, they asked at which hotel I had reservations, as they assumed I would also stay overnight.

I said "none", but would find accommodations, *merci.*

Next morning, after my night's sleep under the famous bridge, I went for a refreshing, long swim in the Rhone river. The water was cool and clean looking although one never knew what its consistency was in those days of complete lack of environmental awareness. While munching on a piece of dry baguette, I tried to figure out when newlyweds on their second day of honeymooning would rise and hit the road. Nine in the morning, maybe?

I stood at the curb on the road south to Marseille, about one kilometer out of Avignon, precisely at five minutes before nine. I combed my unruly locks again, using some saliva to wet them down. But like this morning when they were wet from swimming and I had tried to flatten them out with a small brush, my efforts were again to no avail.

Shortly after nine-thirty, a grey dot appeared in the distance. The Citroen! By then I lost all my courage to flag them down again. It would be too imposing, impolite. Instead, I turned my back to the road and pretended to look intensely into a tree above my head where a bunch of starlings had noisily gathered.

"Hallo, Pierre," exclaimed Madame des Gayets from the stopped two-seater, in her mellow voice, opening the car's right door wide.

"*Bon jour*, Madame, how are you this beautiful morning?"

"*Tres bien, merci.* Are you coming?"

Monsieur had already unlocked the trunk lid from the inside. I did not hesitate to store my backpack there. They had obviously left some room for it when they packed that morning, probably figuring they'd see me again.

I rode with them a second day. All day. I was again royally fed, this time from an elaborate picnic basket. We had found a bench and table out in the country of Provence, northwest of Aix-en-Provence. The smell of warm, dry cedar hung heavy in the air. Our shoes slid on thick groundcover of pine needles.

The basket produced such marvelous things as fresh baguettes, crisp black bread rarely baked in France, butter, six different sausages, seven varieties of cheeses, miniature tomatoes, artichoke vinaigrette, thin slices of cucumber in a creamy sauce, Norwegian sardines, fresh oranges, tasty apples from Provence, and lastly a superb, light, springy *Cotes de Rhone Villages* to accompany the delicious list of lunch items.

Later in the afternoon, we arrived at St. Tropez on the coast of the Mediterranean. At that time, it was a small, charming town with an ancient history, on the shores of the blue, warm water. To me, it looked like it came out of a fairy-tale book.

In the heart of town, the old castle's stonewall provided an excellent setting for watching the sun descend over the emerald sea and seeing of what I had never witnessed before, *les nudistes!*

I stood in awe. I even blushed. I could feel the blood rush to my cheeks and ears. Madame had noticed it. She looked at me with a veiled glance in her eyes. That made me blush even more.

Nowhere had I ever seen anything like this on a public beach, right in front of the town's center, with everyone parading back and forth. Nobody around me seemed to be bothered by this display, though. I was not bothered by it, either. I was raised in the country where, as teenagers, we always skinny-dipped in the Johnson's farm swimming hole, boys and girls, without ever thinking anything of it.

But this was a public beach! Wait until I tell my pals in school about it!

"Oh, my God," I said without realizing it. Madame had continued to watch my reaction to the beach scene with great interest. Now she just smiled and we all moved away.

We walked back to the Citroen in the brilliant late afternoon sun. I knew the moment of departure was approaching. Monsieur sensed it also and spoke:

"Pierre, we know you do not have any money. But it would give us great pleasure if you would accept our invitation to be our guest at the Hotel d'Azur tonight. We have booked a room for you by *telefone, ce matin*, so all "is set" as you say?"

"*Merci, Monsieur, Madame, merci beaucoup.* But I want to break away early tomorrow morning for Spain. Besides, I have imposed myself on you enough to last a lifetime. *Alors, merci, bon voyage*, perhaps we meet again, one day, one year."

Before I knew it, they both rushed up and gave me a hug. No more was said.

I turned swiftly, feeling terribly alone all of a sudden, hiding my eyes from them, because they had turned somewhat moist with all their kindness.

But a friendship had begun. We wrote Christmas cards to each other for years.

Hers were perfumed, full of mystique, as was she. The French are kind people.

They are very polite and have a lot of heart!

1949 THE MONKS OF REUS

In the hot summer in 1949, I wandered through Europe, during the Sorbonne's recess. In June, I headed south out of Paris.

I longed to go to Madrid and on to Seville. But instead, I got stranded in Reus, a village near the Mediterranean.

Traffic was light on the coastal road from Perpignan, in southern France, to the border. But once in Generalissimo Franco's paradise in Spain, not many cars were operating anymore.

Hitchhiking out of Barcelona southwest, I aimed for Madrid as my next stop. After that, I thought, I would go on to Gibraltar via Cordoba and Seville, then return along Spain's Costa del Sol and Costa Brava to Paris. I figured that once in Gibraltar, I might just as well skip over to Tangier, Morocco on the ferry. Yet I had heard that hitchhiking there was not advisable, so I abandoned that plan. Anyway, I still had almost four weeks until school started again.

On the outskirts of Barcelona, I found a ride with a Spanish priest driving an aged and feeble 500cc *Topolino,* the smallest car Fiat then made.

Padre soon found out that I wasn't at all fluent in Spanish. So he smiled and resumed reading his prayer book while rolling southwest along the magnificent coastal road. He drove with one hand, holding the sacred writings in the other. Once in a while, he would look up and out to check the road. Did he perhaps need a prayer book? Yet, I was not much alarmed by his strange habits because the car could barely travel more than twenty five miles per hour. First, it was old. Second, there were numerous curves.

I had no idea how long I would travel with the priest, because when he told me where he was going, I did not understood him. As soon as we entered and passed through the medieval hamlet of Reus about two hours later, he suddenly slowed and gestured to what appeared to be a small monastery. He steered the *Topolino* up a narrow, unpaved driveway. Once up on top, he stopped in front of a stone-arched gate and pointed for me to go through into the simple courtyard beyond.

Paying absolutely no attention to our arrival, some fifteen other brothers paraded slowly in the shade of the arcades, prayer books in hand, deeply submerged into their religious ritual.

"*Buenos tardes*," I called out to the monks. No answer. They did not even look my way. Then the padre who had given me the ride and was parking the *Topolino* somewhere, reappeared and guided me through a heavy, wooden portal into a stark, rectangular room with whitewashed walls and a long table flanked by two equally long benches. It was a marvelously simple room.

Padre said only one word to me: "*Mensa*." And from my years at various European universities, I knew this to be the Latin word for table but also for a place of eating.

The other padres folded their prayer books and entered the room behind me. They walked around me to their respective seats on the benches and I was motioned to sit down where two of the *Men of God* had left room for me.

Now I wondered what would happen next.

Sixteen monks and I sat down to eat. Nobody spoke. Everybody was silent. They could not or would not communicate.

I was handed a large wooden bowl of spicy soup with freshly baked bread. I was offered a second bowl and more bread and accepted both gratefully.

After supper, I stepped outside and climbed the short distance to a nearby hilltop. There, I sat on a boulder for a while to watch the sun set over the distant blue of the Mediterranean. The brothers had gestured to it. They probably used this spot too, for the same reasons I did. Except they had their prayer books to find solace, whereas I drew inspirations from my surroundings.

This, I concluded, must be a group of silent monks. I had read about their order somewhere but never encountered any of them. I couldn't ask them either. They weren't allowed to talk to each other or to strangers. Except the priest who would show me to my cell later. He must have had permission to explain my lodging to me. And, I imagined, the padre who had picked me up. He talked to folks outside the monastery. He was probably their liaison.

But I was thankful for their hospitality. It seemed to come natural to them. I was even more thankful because I realized that they must be very poor. Yet they shared their bread with me.

As dusk fell, I returned. The padre assigned to show me my cell had waited for me at the gate. He spoke three words of French. He led me through the arcades, dark by now, to my sleeping spot. I would have it to myself. As far as I could gather, the brother who occupied it was away. He opened the cell's wooden door, which was unlocked, nodded, then slipped quietly away into the dark corridors of the monastery.

There was no light in the cell. In the glimmer of a starry sky filtering through a narrow window, I found my crude wooden bunk and ran my hand over its straw filled mattress. A small pillow for my head was similarly filled with crunchy straw and the blanket proved to be coarse, from the horsehair it was made with.

I parked my hiking boots under the bunk and dropped my folded jeans on the prayer stool. They had never been folded as long as I owned them but I felt their resting place for the night demanded the respect of an orderly storage.

My wrist watch said it was not even ten o'clock. I was not used to retiring so early. But the entire building was quiet. I instantly fell asleep.

The next morning at five o'clock, the padre from the night before shook me awake, waited until I had dressed, then guided me to the *mensa* again for dry farmer's bread and still-warm goat milk.

Then I retrieved my backpack from my cell and started to bid my farewell to the brothers. They were again marching slowly and in single file through the arcades, reading their morning prayers. I stretched out my hand as a sign of gratitude for what they had done for me.

But the friars did not shake it. They just nodded silently without showing any emotion, yet I thought I noticed a very faint smile come over their faces when I bowed before turning away.

The unpaved, steep driveway I drove up the night before, was shorter than I had thought. I strode down and walked to the intersection in the village's center where the road to Madrid branched off the coastal highway.

It was the road I should take, the one leading into the interior, into the hills, unpaved, curving up to Spain's high plateau at Zaragoza.

I had studied my map of Spain so often that it was almost in total shreds. I walked up the road one hundred meters to make sure people would see me from a distance. It started to rain soon thereafter. As a matter of fact, it rained all day.

No cars either—all day.

At six in the evening, I went to the beach to camp in pouring rain under a rock. I didn't have the heart to go back to the monks. Dinner was a stale roll.

It turned out to be a miserable day in the life of a hitchhiking nomad!

1949 NEIL

All day I stood on the road to Madrid. It also rained the entire day, heavy at times and throughout the following night, even heavier. Not many cars came by. And those few that did, passed up the soaking wet hitchhiker hunched by the edge of the road.

The water running off his parka would have spoiled the seat fabric.

It was a hitchhiker's nightmare.

By evening I gave up. As a rule, I never hitchhiked at night. I was not about to start that habit now. I bought a bar of chocolate and some milk in the only store in Reus and went to the beach.

I did not have the courage to return to the padres up the hill. I was sure they would have silently taken me in and let me share another quiet meal again. But that would be intruding, overstaying one's welcome.

I spent the night sleeping on the sand, spreading my sleeping bag under a huge rock cliff.

Sinister looking clouds the following morning convinced me that the weather would not change for several days. The sky to the southwest remained a slate-blue wall of rain-bearing clouds. Along with the grey hanging over my sleeping spot and elsewhere in a wide circle around me, the sun would neither be seen today, nor, I suspected, tomorrow.

If I waited there too long, I would run out of time. Madrid and Gibraltar would have to wait. Tangier, in Morocco, would have to be skipped altogether. I would never make it back to Paris in time for school. Traffic in 1949 was just too thin in Spain.

Maybe, I thought, I should go back to the Cote d'Azur, then

up the mountain roads through Grasse, then across the Montagne de Cheval Blanc and Montagne de Ians to Grenoble. It would be just as nice.

I awoke at dawn.

I was all alone on the beach, so I dropped my clothes and went swimming in the Mediterranean—naked, cooling and cleansing myself. I even tried using my brown soap which I carried in my backpack. To no avail, as it would not foam in the salty water. When I emerged onto the sandy beach, the rain started again. But my sheltered sleeping spot remained dry enough for me to dress and pack.

Munching on the rest of my chocolate, I set out for the road back to France, the road to Barcelona where I had come down with the padre two days ago. It was seven o'clock in the morning. As during the day before, there I stood again, in the pouring rain, for several hours. No car came. No cars were even visible for those several hours. The rain did not encourage those which eventually did come to stop and pick me up. In my poncho and backpack, with rain dripping out of my unruly red hair, I didn't look particularly inviting anyway.

I began to think of alternate plans. There were not many alternatives. I did not have money for train fare. Hopping on a freight train as a stowaway was not my idea of a summer vacation in Spain either. I thought of only one not really appealing escape out of this mess—go back to the padres up the street, to see if they were going back to Barcelona any time soon.

I knew the rain would end sometime. But when? Patience had never been my virtue.

Towards noon, after I'd stood five hours on the side of the road, a small car appeared from a distance. A Morris Minor, I saw as it approached. Black as usual. They all seem to be black. The English must have copied that idea from Henry Ford. Undoubtedly from Britain, but I could not yet make out its license plate.

But yeah, it slowed down!

Like all British cars, it was built for left hand driving. Its steering wheel was on the right side. So, of course, was its driver. I could see only his face and hands which looked broad and powerful, like he'd played a lot of rugby. His brown eyes and reddish blond hair made him look like an Englishman.

He stopped in front of my toes, rolled down the window a crack and asked:

"Are you going my direction?"

"I don't know, Sir, because I don't know where you are heading."

"Well, I do not know that either. Do you know anything about Spain?"

"A little."

He had an English accent. But somehow his accent did not sound like pure English, never mind Oxford. Some other, vaguely familiar twang made me wonder.

His license plates were from Britain, though. I had looked at the front one when his car was close enough.

"Are you British?" he asked.

I told him that I was not, that I was going to school in Paris.

"But you speak my language well?"

"I am a US citizen."

"A Yank," he exclaimed happily. "Well, mate; I have got this problem here. You see, Thomas Cook, you know, the travel agency in London, you know them? Yes? Have you indeed heard of them? Good. They are very fine folks, nice, competent people. They mapped out this here itinerary for me."

He pointed to a fat red line on the thick travel book's sectional maps displaying the Gold Coast of Spain. Inscriptions on the side explained things to see, history, places, geography and the like. It was obviously a masterpiece of travel literature.

"But I am sick and tired of traveling the prescribed route," he continued, slapping his fancy maps with the back of his hand. "I am really bored with it. So I thought maybe you would know some more interesting things to see and do."

By now, in his excitement, he had rolled down his window all the way.

"Your map is getting wet, Sir," I said while pondering his remarks.

"Oh, thank you," he replied and rolled up the window one inch. The maps were still getting wet. I said no more.

"Well, I could try," I volunteered after a few seconds. The idea of hitching a ride with this guy, along the route I saw on his map, was absolutely appealing, because if I played it right, it would take me back to the Cote d'Azur and up to Grasse and Grenoble to Paris, for about the three weeks vacation he had left.

"My name is Peter and I would be glad to be your travel guide."

"Hop in, Peter. I am Neil. I live in England right now, but I am from Australia."

Neil was two years older than I. He possessed all the uncomplicated, easy manner of an Australian. He had a great sense of humor and was a master in understatements. Sturdily built, he nevertheless had developed the beginning of a paunch. "All the English tea and sweets, not enough Scotch," he would say later when we had gotten to know each other and I kidded him about his small potbelly.

So we headed for France, the two of us. It didn't take us long to become buddies. In many small ways, we were so much alike. Thomas Cook hadn't and—now knowing Neil better—certainly couldn't turn him on to some adventure. But obviously I suceeded. Or, perhaps it was the easy banter between us that did.

We camped using Neil's tent and cooking gear. We shared meals, and often stayed in *pension de famille* establishments in small Spanish, then French towns. They were an early European version of Bed and Breakfasts, except the breakfast in those countries was always skimpy, too skimpy for an always hungry student living on a meager stipend.

We did a lot of girl watching and we drank a lot of wine or even beer, which Neil liked better.

I took care of all the logistics, like finding accommodations, planning routes, suggesting diversions. Neil drove most of the time and added spark and excitement to our journey.

We complemented each other well. Traveling with him was great fun.

For most expenses, I did not have to pay. I couldn't have anyway. I did not have the money for it and Neil must have known.

"Consider it my contribution to your guiding me around to all the fun we are having," he said when I told him of my acute shortage of funds.

I showed him Barcelona first, somewhat drab under Franco's rule. Later, back in France, we rolled into Marseille one afternoon, the largest French port on the Mediterranean coast. We had big bowls of bouillabaisse and baguettes in the evening, along with some excellent wine from Provence.

Later that night, we tested the bars near the harbor, rubbing elbows with sailors from all over the globe, to talk, drink, jibe and womanize.

In St. Tropez, I did not mention the beach of "les nudistes" to Neil. Instead, I just took him to the spot where Monsieur and Madame des Gayets had introduced me to the sight some ten days earlier. Now I could watch Neil's face when he saw what was going on, like Madame had studied mine. Except, Neil's ears didn't turn red like mine had. But he nevertheless stood motionless, silent, with his jaw dropped.

"Ain't like that back home in Australia," he finally said with a grin, licking his lips.

We leisurely drove along the lower Corniche through Cannes and Nice. There, we found a fifth floor room, in a small hotel near Boulevard d'Anglais. No elevator. It was no problem for me, but Neil had broken his leg once while playing rugby and was limping under the strain.

The reward for his labor came when we discovered that the attached bathroom had its bathtub running alongside a wide window which opened to the south, offering a superb view over the rooftops to the blue Mediterranean Sea beyond.

"Ain't like that back home in Australia," said Neil again while he lounged in the hot bath.

In Monaco, Neil wanted to see the Casino and gamble. I could not go with him. My rough, outdoor attire did not meet the Casino's dress code. He lost forty-five dollars, as much as I lived on all month. That settled his gambling for the day.

He wrote it off: "Heck, I only lost forty-five bucks."

From Cap d'Antibes, near the French Italian border, probably the most luxurious area on the Cote d'Azur, we turned west on the upper Corniche, then headed north into the mountains.

A stop in the town of Grasse, perched on a hill along the way, was a must because I had told Neil of its reputation as the perfume capital of the world. It was late in the afternoon and we found another one of the small hotels to stay the night. But as we opened the window to let the night air in, we sniffed the various grades of the alluring scent all night. It just hung around the town as a permanent fixture.

"Ain't like that back home in Australia."

Nevertheless, Neil insisted we stop by one of the many stores the next morning, to buy some of the stuff right there at the source, to send home to his mother in Australia.

The road to Grenoble led us through pristine forests and remote, rocky mountain stretches. There, we mostly camped and used the rushing, cold streams for our daily bath.

Almost three weeks after I had met Neil in Reus, about one hundred sixty kilometers southeast of Paris, near Dijon, the Morris Minor gave out. A part was needed which no one in France had in inventory. It had to be shipped from the factory in England. I could not wait that long.

"I am going to try hitching a ride back to Paris because school will start the day after tomorrow," I told Neil.

"Go ahead," he replied, "I'll stay here and wait."

"But when you are done and ready to roll, come to Paris, go to the left bank and look for 29 Rue de Buci. That's where I live, in a small *pension de famille.* My room is tight, but we will manage."

"I cannot accept that, unless you let me share in the rent."

"Nonsense, Neil. You have enough expenses with your car as is. Besides, you paid my way for the last three weeks. Now it's my turn."

"Right, mate, it's a deal."

"If I am at school when you get there, Madame will show you where my room is. She has got a key. Her name is Philippine," I shouted back to him after I had started to walk towards the highway to Paris.

Neil arrived five days later, broke as I was save for gas money back to England. The Morris part had been specially ordered and flown in to Dijon. It was sinfully expensive.

He stayed with me for three more days. I skipped some classes in order to be with him. I showed him Paris. Neil loved it. He forgot his worries. Once again he was his own self.

We, too, wrote Christmas letters to each other for years. A friendship had been built on solid rock.

1949 EUROPEAN UNITY?

Picture Paris, on the left bank of the river Seine. At the Cafe de Fleur on Boulevard St. Germain, we would gather to discuss our favorite subject, the future of Europe. All of us were enrolled at La Sorbonne. Our group of as many as twenty-two students varied in number, but remained consistent in lasting friendships. It included about eight Americans and fourteen Europeans, the latter mostly French, Swiss, German and Swedes. I still have contacts with some of them.

World War II had ended a mere four years before. Its wounds were still evident throughout the continent. We as students felt strongly about never letting it happen again.

Our European friends eagerly asked us how America became what it is, how true democracy really works. They wanted to unite Europe, and so did we, especially after the great postwar French Prime Minister Robert Schumann called openly and publicly for a Europe united and had sponsored legislation to create a European Union in late 1948. Thus he became her first true leader. If he would have called for it, we would have jumped the barricades for the cause.

"*Vive la France, vive l'Europe,*" he would shout over the radio or off the speaker platform in the halls of the Assemble Nationale, the great parliament of France. He was then fifty-eight years old.

"*Vive l'Europe, vive la France,*" my friend Rodin, a prince of Bourbon, from Paris would proclaim during our fierce discussions. He was twenty years old.

"Europe united," Antoine from Grenoble would greet the group when he approached the cafe. "We should never be separated again, never again go to war against each other."

"How did it happen in America that you are free, united?" Francoise from Orleans asked. She and Wendi from Stuttgart were the only women in the group. Wendy ended up in Washington at the German Embassy for a number of years.

"It was not easy, it did not happen without severe blood shed," replied Chuck from Albany, before he set forth explaining our turbulent history.

"But we have shed the blood of millions during the six years of war as well," said Rene from Biaritz.

"Never again," repeated Jorge from Goeteborg, never much one for wasting words.

"Are you Americans first, then from your home state?" asked Christoph from Zurich.

"Yes, we are," replied Dick from Montana.

"So we want to be," said Horst from Tuebingen.

But then Stieg from Upsala interrupted: "your Gary Davis, he did not even want to be American anymore. He volunteered to be a "citizen of the world" last year?"

"He will be sorry he did," I mused aloud.

I knew of Gary Davis. He had shortly before surrendered his American passport at the Embassy in Paris, by that act losing his American citizenship. Instead, he proclaimed his status as a world citizen who no longer needed a specific nationality, someone who would freely move around the world without boundaries.

Gary soon found it difficult to cross even the French-Swiss border because he was now declared a "stateless citizen." As such, he had to apply for entry visas everywhere, carrying large legal documents with him wherever he went. It involved a long, frustrating waiting time for visas to be issued. Border guards had to check with higher authorities in their respective capitals.

As expected, he reapplied for his American citizenship and passport at the Embassy in Paris in the late fifties, but was told he had to wait a minimum of a year.

But never mind Gary! We students were ready for a united Europe. But Europe was not ready for us and our revolutionary ideas.

And as I write this down, in 2014, the European Union created in 1948 has twenty-eight member countries now. Europe is still not ready to unite, to establish one nation for all, to acquire statehood, so to speak. Many diverse cultures and multiple ethnic origins need to be merged before she does.

But a lot of progress towards unity has been made in those five decades. Belgium's Brussels was selected as the Union's headquarters; a Parliament in Strasbourg, France; a Central Bank in Frankfurt, Germany; a High Court in the Haag, Holland were created. Europe's member boundaries are still in place but no longer patrolled. Customs and immigration inspections are abolished save for those entering Europe from countries outside the Union.

On January 1st, 1999, a new European currency, the Euro, was introduced. Coins were issued for circulation, bills would follow within the following two years.

Forever neutral Switzerland abstained. And the UK joined the Union but kept her currency.

Now in my nineties, I still witness the world's progress, as I observed Scotland's recent vote to stay, or leave, the United Kingdom.

But I also believe that we as students in 1949 Paris are due some credit for an idea whose time has come sixty-five years later!

1949–1950 UNCLE HERMY

Spring 1950!

"I love Paris in the springtime" was the theme of a song made famous by Maurice Chevalier. He intoned it with such charm and lent it French authority with his accented English, making his version much better than the original American production.

Maurice sang of love and the city of "*l'amour.*" I lived in Paris and I was in love, again. Her name was Bambi, and she did not know that I was in love with her. She had formidable, almost forbidding beauty.

Like me, she attended classes in law at the Sorbonne. When I sat near her I observed every move she made. My mind then would not be on the "Code Napoleon" which I was supposed to study and write a thesis upon.

"Your mind is on *l'amour, non*, Pierre?" said my buddy Rodin who sat next to me. I just shrugged and smiled. But he was right.

One day, our mutual friend Erique introduced me to Bambi. Beyond a casual friendship, Erique did not show much interest in her.

But she turned my eyes around in my head, swiftly and surely. We began to spend some time together, walking, taking a picnic lunch into Les Tuilleries, visiting a museum or two, nothing more. But it raised my hopes. Maybe one day, I thought, I would get to know her real well.

Then Uncle Hermy breezed into town. He was my father's first cousin. Born and raised on Long Island, he never did an honest day's work in his life. He didn't have to. He had inherited a tremendous fortune. He was rich, and famous because of his experience and reputation as a breeder and judge of Dobermans.

Like others of my expatriate relatives, he lived in Europe.

"I cannot stand the frozen food they serve in America," he would tell me when I asked him why he didn't live there.

"But you go back to the States once a year, do you not?" I asked again.

"Sure," said Uncle Hermy. "You know that I am one of the judges at the New York Dog Show. I never miss the exhibition. It is fabulous."

"I have heard of it. Do you take any of your eleven Dobermans with you then?"

"Some," he would reply. "I always take the Queen Mary. They have great kennels for the dogs. They are really happy there."

"Why don't you come more often?"

"Once a year is enough. It will suffice to meet the requirements of Switzerland's residence laws. Because I don't want to lose my visitor permit and endanger our house in Locarno."

That was an angle I hadn't heard yet. But I liked Uncle Hermy.

He had four cars. And I had always loved cars—especially fast ones. One of the four was an early version of the station wagon, with wood panels on its sides, a 1949 Buick to be exact. It was used solely to take the dogs out for a walk. I don't remember what car Aunt Amelie drove. But I do remember that another of the four was a fast one. A Ferrari two-seater convertible—fire engine red! It was Uncle Hermy's car. He drove it to Paris from Switzerland in five hours, 550 kilometers. No Auto Routes then.

He also had a keen eye for pretty women. Although married to Aunt Amelie, for I didn't know how many years, he would let those he saw or met know of his admiration. He was also tall, six foot-two, sort of good looking, especially when he drove the Ferrari, with his silvery hair blowing in the wind.

He called me soon after he had checked into the George V. A month before at my *pension de famille*, Madame had splurged on a telephone. It was installed downstairs in her apartment, five flights down from my room. She positioned herself at the foot of the stairs and hollered up through the cavernous tube of the narrow staircase five floors up:

"Pierre Pierre P i e r r e! *Telefone!*"

"Can you come to dinner tonight?" Uncle Hermy asked.

"Sure, I will be glad to, Uncle, but I have a date. With some-one I have been trying to have a date with for a long time."

He totally ignored my response, in a manner typical for him, and said: "I will come by your place on Rue de Buci after eight and pick both of you up. What is your date's name?"

"Bambi."

After he hung up, I realized I should have known better. I should have turned him down and taken Bambi for a bite to eat at a student hangout on Boulevard St. Michel called Closeries des

Lilas. Considering my meager budget for such purposes, I could have entertained Bambi royally. And I would have had her all to myself, all evening.

Now, knowing my Uncle Hermy, I wasn't sure what would happen.

The red Ferrari pulled up narrow Rue de Buci at close to nine o'clock. I hadn't really expected it any earlier anyway, knowing Uncle Hermy's terrible habit for tardiness.

When he saw me standing there with Bambi, waiting on the narrow, busy sidewalk, he stopped the Ferrari in the middle of the equally narrow street. Cars honked wildly, wanting to pass. A second later, he jumped out and came to greet her with a gallant kiss on the back of her outstretched hand. The waiting cars continued their honking chorus, increasingly incessant now.

He was elegant, slender, impeccably dressed.

To me, he said only: "Hi, nephew, you are wearing my father's suit." Bambi looked back and forth between the two of us, somewhat bewildered. I only laughed because his remarks amused me; I was used to them.

"Yes, fortunately Uncle Freddy, your father, gave it to me because he couldn't use it anymore and I did not have a suit. I am grateful to him," I shot back. I knew that would quiet Uncle Hermy down. And it did.

It was an expensive, hand tailored, wool suit. I had it altered to my measurements in Lucerne, near where Uncle Freddy lived in retirement. Its color was an ugly mauve. It also had a vest and looked totally elegant. Uncle Freddy's tailor lived in London. He had all his suits done there. This thing would last me forever. It was the only suit I owned.

But looking at Hermy and Bambi now, I knew I was in trouble.

Bambi reacted to him like any charming, beautiful woman would.

We all hopped into the two-seater, Bambi between us. Uncle Hermy started the engine, let it roar up through the revolutions a bit, then raced off, back to Boulevard St.Germain and west on that busy thoroughfare towards the Assemble Nationale. He expertly wove in and out of traffic that was already moving at a fast clip. He was a superb driver. He applied the brakes only when absolutely necessary, and then rather abruptly.

Bambi loved it. She was all ears and eyes for Hermy. Her coal black hair, free falling down her entire back, blew in the wind like a flag at sea. She threw her head back and laughed playfully, her snow-white teeth radiating her abundance of joy.

She looked absolutely marvelous.

Uncle Hermy smiled expectantly. His manicured hair was slightly ruffled from the wind. Mine wasn't. I just had a crew cut. It was cheaper in the long run. My unruly red locks were temporarily gone. My hair didn't budge. I didn't even carry a pocket comb when Bambi asked me for one.

Uncle Hermy took us to a splashy restaurant on Rive Droit, on Avenue Foch. It was called L'Horizon. Its entire ceiling could roll back into the building's sides, to let the stars gaze in.

That night, it was rolled back. The restaurant's lights were dimmed. The table's candles threw a warm glow over Bambi's face. I could not say much during the evening. Not that I didn't have anything to say, but I was not given much of a chance.

A few days later, I met Bambi again at school. She sat in front of Rodin and myself. As usual, she was as charming as ever, but when she talked about the evening with Hermy, a special, mysterious look spread over her face. Rodin's eyes rolled.

"But his car, *il est vite, tres vite*," she exclaimed. "Erique saw us go by on Boulevard St. Germain. He was also very impressed. *Tres chic, ton Oncle Hermy, oh, la la, tres chic. Il est jolie, n'est ce pas, Pierre?"*

To this, I did not have anything to say. I had always liked my Uncle Hermy. He was nice. But jolie? Naaa!

Rodin's forehead was deeply wrinkled now. He looked back and forth between us. He had gone through the motions with me in securing a date with Bambi. Now that all looked threatened. He was worried, I could tell.

Bambi and I remained good friends, during my school years at the Sorbonne. But Erique's attention was obviously aroused with the sight of the silver haired, tall gentleman from Locarno, Switzerland, in his dashing car. From then on in, he stayed close to Bambi. In 1952, they were married and, as far as I know, lived happily ever after.

1949 WENDI

In January, 1949, one day after I enrolled as a student at the Sorbonne, I bought a used bicycle. It was a racer which had all of three forward gears—a luxury then. A friend of mine who had the means from home had bought it new when he arrived in Paris. Now that he had finished his studies and was preparing to go home to upstate New York, he put it up for sale. At that time, I certainly did not have the money. But I told him that I'd buy it later.

"That's alright with me. Just pay me when you can," he said, "I can't take it with me anyway and I am leaving in two days."

My landlady, Philippine, stored it for me in her tiny basement. I did not want to use it until it was mine.

When I went to see my parents at Easter recess that year, my mother secretly gave me some money. "For some rainy day," she said. "But don't say anything to your father about it."

"No, I won't, I promise. And thanks, Mom."

I splurged all of it on the bike. I sent a money order for what I owed my friend stateside and retrieved it out of Philippine's basement. It was made by Peugeot, silver grey. I kept it in my room, tight and cluttered as it was and carried it up five steep floors every time I used it. I loved my bicycle!

Now that I had wheels, I checked around with my friends to see who would want to go on a biking trip with me. School would soon end for the year. We had a week to go until summer recess. I suggested a trip to Orleans or the Bretagne, before everyone scattered away for the summer. I myself had planned a hitchhiking trip to southern France and Spain. But it didn't matter when I left, because I had no reservations of any kind. I was hanging loose and free as a bird.

I rounded up four of them. We settled on a journey to the Loire river. We packed our gear, what little we had, and left the next morning at ten. It was a bright, sunny, warm early summer day in June.

On the way down Boulevard St. Germain to the river Seine, we passed Gare d'Orsay where those sleek comfortable passenger trains departed, carrying tourists to such favored destinations as "les Chateaux de la Loire."

We headed there, too, except that it took us over two days to arrive at the first of the famous castles along the Loire.

We were a strange bunch of pedaling touring pals. First, there was Wendi, whom I had met shortly after I arrived in Paris. She became a good friend. I was not much worried about her participating in this venture, but the others had reservations about her.

"But she is a girl?" said one. "Will she be able to endure the hardships?" asked another. "How about sleeping in the same place, will she like that?" inquired the third.

I assured everyone that Wendi was okay, that she would be just like us and become an asset rather than a liability. This was easy for me to say because I knew Wendi was a tomboy; she was boisterous and ready for any new adventure, durable and a lot of fun to have around.

Already on the first evening, everyone loved her. This did not surprise me because everyone she ever met loved her. She was just that type of a person. She just became one of us. I often wondered how she felt about that. After all, we were four active boys, and not bad looking either.

But if she felt anything more than the comradeship which tied us together, she would not show it. She was a great person—someone who would fit into a bunch of wild, pedaling bicyclists, or just as well as into an evening dress attending a charity ball, or into making intellectual conversation with people like Gustave Nobel. Read about him in the next chapter. He was a friend of my father and I introduced her to him one evening when he had invited us for dinner at the Sarinov.

Then there was Dick, from a large ranch outside Bozeman, Montana. His light-blue eyes were used to the far distances. They were eyes of a cowboy riding the prairie, looking way yonder to search what lay out ahead. He was a seasoned outdoor guy. We could always trust him to whip up a delicious meal over a crude campfire.

Jorge, from Goeteborg in Sweden, didn't say much at all. But Jorge smiled a lot, all the time, in fact. It took him several minutes before he would start to speak, often when we had passed that subject already and gone to others. But then, when he realized that he was slow, he wouldn't mind. He would just fall back into smiling again.

Both Dick and Jorge were extremely solid and reliable buddies. They balanced my own quick temperament and Wendi's mercurial bubbliness.

Finally, there was the snail man. His name was Horst. He was from Tuebingen, Germany. He studied snails, or "*Schnecke*" in German. Wendi and I called him the "*Schneckologe*", meaning a scientist studying snails.

But Dick dubbed him the snail man, a word which Jorge must have liked because he smiled even wider when it was used. The snail man was at times difficult to deal with. Because when he would see a snail on the side of the road, he would forget all about biking. He would stop, pull out one of his books, study it, then pick up the animal to dissect it, take it apart to see what made it tick.

All of us would be waiting for him several kilometers ahead. Wendi always felt especially bad when that happened because she recommended that we take him along and was inclined to assume responsibility for him. They had both come to the Sorbonne from the University of Tuebingen, on an exchange program.

We told her not to worry. Except, when Dick asked one evening:

"Snail man, can you start the fire, please, we have steaks ready for broiling soon!"

And the snail man said:

"*Ja!*"

And then nothing happened because the snail man was reading a book on—you guessed it—snails. It was then that even Jorge brought out some vocabulary which we had never ever heard from him before. I didn't even guess that he knew those words:

"Snail man, get your f...... ass over here and start that damn fire, NOW!" he barked out with the brightest of all smiles he could muster up. His whole face lit up like a Christmas tree when he said it!

Jorge was a great guy. We were all a great team.

We slept in hay barns every night except in Ambroise where we checked into the local youth hostel.

But we felt that our chances for successful barn lodging would be greatly enhanced if we sent Wendi in first, alone. We were hiding behind some bushes meanwhile, with our bikes hidden as well, our faces unshaven, our jeans greasy and spotty. With her innocent facial expression, she would ask if it was all right to sleep in the hay barn for a night.

"Bien sur, Mademoiselle,"

"Is it also all right to have a friend with me?" she would continue.

Now that question would normally raise no single eyebrow in France, and if it did with our farmer hosts for the night, it was only that Wendi asked in the first place.

"Certainement."

Wendi would then flash the okay sign and we would push our bikes out into the open and march single file to our shelter for the night. What our farmer friends thought about Wendi's ability to handle so many men all at once, we never asked and never found out.

But the following morning, we would all make sure to say *au revoir* to our hosts who invariably would offer us farmer's bread and fresh milk still warm from the cows, to start out our day.

"Merci, Madame, merci, Monsieur, merci beaucoup," we said

before departing. We wanted to be sure to show our best manners.

We reached the castle country of the Loire in Orleans and pedaled along the river to Ambroise, visiting on the way many of the splendid structures of earlier times. I did not know then that I would be back there again to visit one of the largest—the one Rodin's family owned.

But the most impressive was the last one, the sumptuous Chateau d'Ambroise, looming over its venerable town on the Loire river. Built in large part by Italian artisans, this chateau was for a time the home of Leonardo da Vinci.

After we all left school the following year, I never saw Jorge or the snail man again. But Dick came to see me in New Jersey once several years later. And I returned his visit when I passed through Montana.

And Wendi? After graduation from the University of Tuebingen, she entered the German Foreign Service and was attached to her country's embassy in Washington for a few years. After a stint in Germany's Foreign Office in Bonn, she eventually married a career diplomat of the German Federal Republic, with the rank of ambassador. He became his country's emissary to the United States for six years during the late seventies.

I took Hanna down on one of my frequent business trips to the capital to meet her. We had tea and biscuits on the new Embassy's spacious patio.

1949–1950 GUSTAVE NOBEL

It was deep winter in Paris, January 1950. Some light snow had fallen. The temperature stood at two degrees Celsius. My room was heated only once a day, early in the morning. The rest of the time, I spent in school where steam heat overdid the comfort level. We sat in shirt sleeves, dozed off often because the hot air made us sleepy. When I came home, I put on three sweaters to stay warm.

I had met Mary Anne during the preceding summer, at one of the many parties thrown by wealthy Quakers with whom I had become friends. Mary Anne was from California. Her father owned a large vegetable farm and vineyard there. She was a typical California kid, blond, tall, outdoorsy, with all sorts of crazy ideas and lifestyles that to this day originate in our western-most state and characterize many of its residents.

Mary Anne's job was that of a secretary to the Ambassador. She never discussed her work and I didn't ask her about it either. I went to see her often at her office, to pick her up for a picnic basket lunch at the Tuilleries, just across Place de la Concorde on its opposite side from the gated Embassy of the United States of America.

On the first such occasion, the Ambassador came out of his suite into her office and greeted me cordially, somewhat absent-minded but fatherly. The next time he came out while I was there, he remembered my face but not my name. No small wonder considering how many persons a gentleman of his stature, and rank must remember.

Mary Anne owned a sleek, white Hudson convertible. Driving it with her at my side, my life as a poor student on a scholarship in Paris had blossomed into something much more glamorous. I was suddenly invited to many parties given by other Embassy staff members, where I would meet a lot of boys and girls of the international set. I also attended several of the more formal Embassy receptions, rubbing elbows with some American and foreign dignitaries of the time.

I drove the Hudson out to many picnics in the country, top down more often than not, sometimes with some of Mary Anne's other friends along, and more often, alone with her.

Madame, at my *"pension de famille,"* loved her and admired her ever-changing wardrobe.

"My salutations to Marie Anna," she would say to me one day when I went by her apartment to go to classes. "She is jolie, is she not, Pierre? You love Marie, right? Too bad, Marie not French, French better than American."

I just laughed and left. I knew her by now. This statement of hers, in her vocabulary and mentality, was a big compliment to me, on my taste in elegant women.

One evening when I returned to my room, I found in my mail an envelope addressed to "Pierre," engraved on its reverse side by the purple Coat of Arms of the Nobel family and the sender's address near Bois de Bologne, Paris' most fashionable district. My dad had written, during the preceding summer, that he had a friend living in Paris who, upon hearing of my presence there, told him that I should contact him. His name was Gustave Nobel, of the Swedish family of the same name. I had seen him last when I was eight years old, my dad reminded me in his letter. He also expressed his hope, in closing, that I would mind my manners.

The envelope held the by now-familiar gold-embroidered card inviting me to dine with him at the Sarinov again the following week. "And don't forget to bring Wendi along," read the postscript.

I had received this invitation before when I returned from classes, about six weeks previously. It was close to Christmas, I remembered it well. Madame had told me excitedly when I passed by her apartment that it was hand-delivered by a uniformed chauffeur.

"And he pulled up Rue de Buci in an immense Rolls Royce," she continued with a face glowing from the experience. "It blocked our narrow street for the time it took him to give me the envelope."

From that moment on, I had grown ten feet tall in her mind. Because I had rich friends. I was also sure she had peeked into the envelope. But I was safe, because she spoke no English.

That first invitation, like the second one in my hands now, had invited me to come to the Sarinov, a well known restaurant featuring Russian cuisine, on the right bank, near the Opera, the following Tuesday at nine in the evening.

"And if you have a friend you would like to bring along, do so," the note had ended.

I took the invitation and went over to where my friend Wendi lived. You remember Wendi? You got to know her in a previous chapter. She was the one who went bicycling to the castles of the Loire, with a bunch of wild, unruly boys.

"Of course," said Wendi when she heard what was planned.

Then as now, I took out of my tiny closet uncle Freddy's old suit, my one and only, and hung it out to straighten. Next day, I borrowed a steam iron from Madame and went to work on it. God, it was an ugly color, pale-purple and opaque. Maybe the color was the reason why uncle Freddy did not like it anymore. Whatever reasons he had to dump it on me, I was grateful to have it, because it enabled me to go out and dine in an elegant restaurant where, I was sure, I would not be allowed without proper attire.

Madame had waited in the hall for me when I first went out with Wendi. She had inspected me closely, adjusted my tie, dusted off a bit of fluff from my shoulders with her gentle hand, checking out my shoes which I had shined to an unusual high polish. "*Tres chic*," she had concluded her examination with a nod and smile.

Wendi and I arrived at the Sarinov at nine sharp. We had taken the Metro over to the right bank, then walked two blocks to the restaurant's inconspicuous facade. The weather then was as wet as it was now, grayish, miserable. We opened the door and were in awe over the splendor and rich decor of the establishment's foyer. Deep carpets engulfed our shoes. A gentle hum of many voices came from the dining room two steps down from the entrance. Lights were dimmed to allow the table candles to shine on elegantly dressed women, with their gentlemen properly attired in dark, tailored suits. I felt awkward, clumsy.

"I feel awkward, Wendi. Do you?"

"Not a bit. I love it."

Wendi wore a simple dress which nevertheless revealed her taste for elegance. A piece of heirloom jewelry around her neck enhanced her aristocratic appearance. She looked marvelous.

A busboy had rushed up in the meantime, waiting patiently behind us until we were ready to take our coats off. Mine was an old Loden, stained from many hunting excursions and other outdoor activities. Here again, it was the only one I owned.

When the aloof, tuxedoed maitre d' appeared, to inquire in intellectual sounding French what our intentions regarding dining in this establishment of exquisite cuisine would be, I told him of our host, who was momentarily expected. He looked at us quizzically, with his arrogant face tilted backwards, sizing up our qualifications to be in the company of such an esteemed personality as Monsieur Nobel. Then he pointed to a couple of chairs in the corner and told us to wait there. Turning back to the dining room, he whispered a few words to the bus boy who had retrieved our coats, then pointing in our direction, probably ordering him to keep an eye on these strange *"etudiants."*

When Monsieur Nobel showed up ten minutes later, the maitre d's behavior turned around completely.

"Ah, bon soir, Monsieur Nobel. I have the usual table ready for you in the left corner. You will dine alone ce soir, n'est ce pas, Monsieur?" he said while two waiters hovered over Monsieur's fur-collared topcoat. "Please follow me," he concluded, advancing into the dining room and paying absolutely no attention to us.

But Gustave Nobel did not follow him. He stood and searched around the entrance hall. By this time I dared to disobey the maitre d's orders and got out of my chair. So did Wendi.

Bon soir, Monsieur Nobel, comment allez vouz?"

"Ah, *mon Pierre*, so good to see you," he exclaimed. *"Et ton ami?"*

"This is Wendi."

He tilted his head back a bit, throwing an admiring look at her, then bent down to kiss the back of her outstretched hand ever so gently. A gentleman of the old school, for sure!

Monsieur was old, older than I remembered him, maybe over fifty. He was superbly dressed in an expensive, tailored suit and vest, starched shirt with a high collar, Italian shoes of exquisite craftsmanship and a golden chain strung across the front of his vest to secure his equally golden time-piece in its pocket.

A man of great stature, with his grey hair immaculately combed to the side, he was obviously well-known and highly respected, as I could see from the faces of many other guests who had greeted him formally.

We dined on seven courses. Caviar, borscht, beef cubes in creamy sauces, curry chicken, heavenly desserts—I was so excited then that I forgot the details.

Monsieur had asked me a few polite questions in the beginning and at the end, about my studies and how my parents were doing. The remainder of the most lively conversation for the next three hours was carried on between him and Wendi, who had succumbed to his charm as quickly as he had succumbed to her beauty.

It had given me plenty of time to wolf down great amounts of food which would have to last for at least the following day. Wendi and I left at midnight. Monsieur's Rolls Royce was waiting in front of the Sarinov. Monsieur offered to drive us home. But we politely declined and took the Metro, because we needed time to talk.

But this time around, I couldn't bring Wendi along. She had gone home to Tuebingen for the Christmas season and not returned yet. So I thought of Mary Anne instead. I thought about it long and hard, weighing my chances. If he had made Wendi roll her eyes around in her head, what would ever happen if he met Mary Anne, I wondered.

I slept over that question one night and called her at the embassy the next day between classes, to ask her if she wanted to dine at the Sarinov, at nine in the evening the following Friday.

"Have you robbed a bank? Do you know how expensive that place is?"

"I am invited and can bring a friend along. I thought you might be interested."

"Invited by whom?"

"Gustave Nobel."

"Who is he?"

"A friend of my father's."

"Of the Swedish family?"

"Yes."

"Sounds great. What time?"

"I'll come by your place to pick you up at a quarter to nine."

"I'll be there." Then she hung up.

Her response was typical for her. As long as I knew her, she was curious and wide awake for anything new in life. To her, this promised to be an interesting evening.

Not only was it interesting, but delightful, long and unforgettable. Mary Anne saw to it that I was not shut out of the conversation as during the previous occasion when Monsieur charmed Wendi. This time, I remained a full part of the gathering.

At the same time, she turned Monsieur Nobel's head around so much that he, so dignified and in control at all times, occasionally giggled with pleasure. I could remember that when I brought Wendi, he adored her in an old-fashioned way, related to her because she too, in spite of her tomboy nature, hailed from an aristocratic upbringing. They both communicated on the same wavelength.

Mary Anne approached Monsieur Nobel with an enviable prairie-kid attitude, uncomplicated, at ease at all time, not impressed by his name and stature but very much in awe over his great personality.

When we broke up our dinner shortly before one o'clock in the morning, Monsieur Nobel asked that we repeat the occasion soon again. The next day, he wrote a letter to my father, describing the event in glowing terms and marveling at these "well-mannered kids."

But the next time never materialized. Wendi left the Sorbonne to go home to her Alma Mater in Tuebingen in March. And soon thereafter, Mary Anne was transferred to our Embassy in Lima, Peru.

I myself departed for the United States in the fall and never saw Gustave Nobel again. But I will surely not forget him.

I never saw Mary Anne again either. Back stateside, I married and, although I was in California or Washington on many occasions, I felt I should leave things the way they were. We had a wonderful friendship but perhaps in danger of ruin, if attempted to be renewed by either one of us. Obviously, Mary Anne felt the same. But I will surely never forget her either. She had touched my life.

1950 JACQUELINE

After completing more than a full year of schooling at the Sorbonne in Paris, I met and befriended a number of people who were part of the Society of Friends, or Quakers as they are known in the United States. They maintained an office near the university. Its function was to assist and supervise the vast relief effort the Quakers had undertaken after the war ended in Europe.

The Quakers ran a summer camp for students of all nations in Versoix, on Lake Geneva, in Switzerland. Versoix was fifteen kilometers east of Geneva, a small village then, consisting of large, estate-like homes with spacious gardens and manicured lawns stretching down to the lake shore.

One of these villas had a number of other functionary buildings on the property, such as sleeping quarters for staff, garages, and storage buildings for the boats and the like. The Quakers had rented the property for the summer to house the camp. It featured a large wooden boat dock and as well as anchoring space for several boats.

I had applied for a counselor job in Paris and got it. The Quakers paid my train fare back and forth from Paris and room and board for two months at the camp. Aside from that, I received a very modest amount of Swiss Francs as "pocket money." But since my scholarship at the Sorbonne was quite meager, I had learned to live very well with little money of my own.

My duties consisted of driving the 1948 Buick Station Wagon, with its wooden side panels, which was marketed as ideal for going to the commuter railroad station. I was asked to drive it to the Lausanne or Geneva Terminal, either to discharge departing students or meet those arriving.

And that was how I met Jacqueline. She descended elegant-ly from a first class coach of the Marseille Express, which had stopped in Lyon long enough to pick up those who wanted to travel to Geneva, Switzerland.

Dressed in a sheer, loose and beautifully designed summer dress, her long, chestnut-color hair held up at her slender neck, she strode towards where I waited, holding the sign FRIENDS in my right hand, eagerly reaching for her suitcase.

"Bon jour, tu est Pierre? Oui? Je suis Jacqueline," her mellow, almost seductive voice intoned while fixing her milk-chocolate eyes on my disintegrating composure.

W O W!

But there were other arrivals to attend to and I was busy col-lecting everyone and their bags at the ornate front entrance of the Geneva Railroad Station where I had parked the Buick.

Back in Versoix, the camp's director, a Quaker lawyer from upstate New York, greeted the arrivals and discharged me to store the Buick in the garage, then devote my attention to my daily chores.

Those chores included among others driving the Jeep down to Geneva early in the morning, seven mornings of the week, first to the vegetable halls, and then to a large warehouse-type store, to buy and haul back the daily supply of food and beverages for seventy-six people. For such purposes, I was handed a list of items every morning before I left, detailing the nature of the items and quantities needed. The cook did not wish to leave to chance the procurement of the camp's lifeline, especially if it was in the hands of a student who seemed smart and intelligent but had his mind set on other things.

The cook acted wisely, because for the rest of the day I was given the task of teaching those who wanted it the art of sailing the sloop, using one of two of them available for such lessons. I preferred the larger of the two boats, because it could hold more participants. The boats were owned by the people who rented the property to the Friends Organization.

This severely difficult task would occupy my mind all day. In the cook's eyes, it would divert my attention away from her and the responsibility of feeding students and staff alike, who all were starving from strenuous activities during the day and a busy nightlife to follow. She might have had a point.

Russ, the lifeguard from Harrisburg, Pennsylvania, and I shared a room above the garage. He was big and brawny, and with his suntan, blond locks and well-toned muscles, had no trouble finding admirers among the many girls in camp. He would watch them all day, as was his duty, and boasted about many of them as they supposedly came on to him. He would tell me every detail about the ladies of the day, every night before we went to sleep.

But I got to take them out on the sloop. And I did not tell him much about that. He was terribly jealous and had a lot more muscles than I did.

It lasted two months. It was heaven. It was also to be my last summer as a student, free as a bird, partying and dancing the nights away, as there was no curfew in camp.

The day after she arrived, Jacqueline from Lyon became one of my sailing students. She was lovely.

"I wish to drive *le bateau* with you, Pierre," she whispered into my ear.

"*Certainment, Jacqueline*, but I sail a sloop and not a motor launch."

"*Ah, mon dieu! Mais tu est tres jolie*," she intoned with that radiant convincing smile of hers.

She sailed on my '*bateau*' for three long weeks, all afternoon, every day of her stay at camp.

From time to time, she distracted me from doing what I was supposed to be doing, by just lying on deck wearing one of several mini-bikinis she owned, the smallest, skimpiest I had ever seen. I as willing to bet that such flimsy attire had never been seen in Harrisburg, Pennsylvania, where Russ was from.

But I did not discuss Jacqueline with him, because she was my date. I would allow nothing to interfere with that wonderful situation.

After camp ended, I took her to meet my folks in Lucerne.

I loved my parents and during their long lives, I was always eager to have their approval for what I was about to do.

My Dad met Jacqueline with arms outstretched wide. The two of them related to each other at once.

My Mom didn't say much the entire time of her visit.

PETER IN HIS EARLY 20s, WITH FRIEND KLAUS REESE.
PHOTO BY KLAUS REESE.

Chapter Four:
ANNO SANTO

1950 HIKING BUDDIES

Spring 1950!

My buddy Klaus and I had taken Easter recess and hitchhiked down to Rome, not for religious purposes because we both were Lutheran, but just for the fun of seeing the Eternal City for the first time.

Klaus was six years my junior. I had known him as a kid when I was an adolescent before World War II. My parents were friends with his parents.

During the war we lost contact. But in late May, of 1945, I came out of hiding in the Black Forest and began to search for my parents in the Lowlands. Germany was in defeat and most of it lay in ashes.

Driving north towards the Netherlands, I happened to pass by the stately house I knew Klaus' family was then living in. So I stopped to see how the family had fared during the turbulent war years. Klaus was in his upper teens, had grown taller and now become an adolescent himself. He, his mom and four siblings had lost their home to the British occupation forces and lived with their English grandmother in her spacious house on the Rhine river south of Bonn.

As a US citizen in postwar Germany, I bought a car one day

after Germany's surrender at Reims, France. It was an Opel, prewar model. A farmer had stashed it away in his barn when gasoline ran out in 1940. It was registered in Germany and therefore had German plates. But to better be identified, I also mounted a metal Stars and Stripes emblem to the rear bumper.

Klaus' father, also named Klaus, had been a colonel in the "Wehrmacht," Hitler's army. He was missing in action. But someone living in the Russian-held territory had allegedly seen him there.

His mother Erika in her desperation then asked me:

"Could you try to find him? Because you are the only one I know who has a car and is allowed to travel freely in Europe."

"Sure."

"Do you want my oldest son Klaus to come along?"

"Definitely!"

We crossed into Russian territory without problems. I told the border guards that Klaus was my kid brother. They hardly believed me. No wonder. Because he had bright blue eyes and coal black hair that stood straight up. Mine was red and wavy. I had tons of freckles. But also blue eyes. That worked.

So shortly after the war, Germany had not yet been divided into four occupation zones. The West was territory conquered by the western Allies, the American, English and French troops. The East was held solely by Russians. Berlin was the place where all four powers met, to celebrate V-Day. No one then expected it would be a divided city soon thereafter.

I carried four 5-gallon US Army canisters of gasoline in my trunk, along with five cartons of cigarettes. I had secured them at a PX near Frankfurt. There were no inns, no hotels, no places of lodging at all. Whatever was not bombed out was closed, if for no other reason than lack of guests. There were no restaurants either. We lived on cold food we had taken along.

Occasionally, we would pass a small farm and stop to ask for a hot meal. Even farmers didn't have much to eat then. But potatoes with gravy made solely with flour and nothing else, and some fresh cabbage from the first harvest of the season were almost always available. We paid with a pack of Lucky Strikes. They carried the value of a pound of butter then. Barter was the currency of the time.

More often than not, at night, we slept on wooden benches in beer saloons after they closed at ten. Sometimes, there was only one bench not even two feet wide, which we had to share to get off the dirty floor.

During the nights, Klaus often got up to smoke a cigarette—Lucky Strikes of course—from my supplies.

"You need to move your bones?" I asked.

"Naaa. Just can't sleep." Then he fell silent again.

"You okay, bud?"

"Yeah."

Yet I knew he was deeply troubled. After a while, he would come back and stretch out in our cramped quarters.

Russians in sloppy, drab uniforms were everywhere. It was reported that they used the toilet bowls to wash their hair. German policemen in well-worn but faded, green uniforms regulated traffic that didn't exist. We were eyed with great suspicion by both. The Russians even showed some hate in their faces.

The Cold War had just begun!

We spent nearly two weeks crisscrossing Germany's eastern provinces. We followed every tiny lead on our way. We went door to door, talked to countless people, checked out official records in town halls.

"Have you heard of Colonel Klaus Reese?" his son would ask.

"No. And we don't care where he is. We have enough trouble just to survive, find food, hide from the Russians. So don't bother us. Go away," they would reply.

Indeed, Russian troops were looting, marauding, raping, stealing, killing everywhere, as people had done before to other people and as Serbs would do fifty-five years later to Albanians in Kosovo. History has a tendency to repeat itself.

"We won't find him," Klaus often said, his face shadowed by deep sadness.

"We will," I responded, still hopeful.

"There is so much I still wanted to ask him," he would say.

And to this I did not have an answer, because deep down I knew he was right. I said nothing. But we both knew that silence can express many unspoken emotions.

We shared hopes and defeat, joy and sadness. We relished memories of common childhood when we talked about his dad. I was able to fill in my remembrances of him.

When Klaus senior was drafted into the German army, Klaus was only nine years old. One year later, World War II began. His father was last seen in Russia near Stalingrad where some of the worst and bloodiest battles of the war were fought.

And all this time we spent every minute of our waking hours on our desperate search for him.

Often now, toward the end of our efforts, Klaus was outright depressed. But he always tried to keep his usual upbeat outlook on life. That was one of many of his characteristics which

I could well relate to. I tended to be upbeat also. I still am.

But even I now realized our efforts were in vain and helplessly witnessed our hopes dwindle.

There was not much I could do for Klaus at this point, except to stand near him, be there for him, help him carry a burden so heavy for shoulders so young.

"Come on, bud, I'll buy you a stein of beer," I would tell him then, grabbing his arm. And we drank in silence.

We never found Klaus senior.

But a close friendship was cemented during that sad excursion. It is as close as ever to this day.

On our return trip, the Russians did not want us to leave "worker's paradise." They held us for more than five hours at one of only three checkpoints to the west. From their shabby barracks where we were held, we could see the Union Jack flutter in the wind some twenty yards away. We did not know then that those twenty yards would soon thereafter be widened to seventy-five yards and become a 'no man's land,' a stripe of the earth surface razed of all vegetation to clearly detect those who would dare to leave their paradise. Although officially, it was explained by the Russians that they would better see those capitalists from the West wanting to infiltrate their "ideals" and "welfare."

Almost six hours later, we were waved through without an explanation. I have never been happier in my life to see a Brit.

Five years went by. As on that earlier, first expedition when we shared adventure, hardship and risk, when we depended on each other every minute of the day and night, we had bonded even closer during our subsequent journeys. Now we put our friendship to another test through a strenuous hitchhiking venture to Rome.

ANNO SANTO, the Pope had proclaimed 1950 to be.

Once again, it was early May when we arrived in the Holy City. Italy was already warm. I was a student at the Sorbonne, Klaus had just enrolled in a German university for a Master's degree in architecture.

Money we didn't have, of course.

"I have an aunt living in Rome," I told my buddy. "She is my father's first cousin, but I have always called her aunt."

"Can we hang out there?" he asked.

"I don't know."

"What's her name?"

"Lida Louise."

"Do you know where she lives?"

"Yes, Palazzo Taverna. Via Monte Giordano. Thirty-six is her number."

We got a ride into downtown Rome. We asked the kind man who had taken us along where the Palazzo was. His eyes popped.

"You got rich friends, no?" he said, eyeing us with suspicion. We could read his thoughts: what in the world are these filthy vagabonds doing at the Palazzo?

We found it on our first try—off Rome's main downtown avenue which was still named after Mussolini. The Italians simply hadn't gotten around to renaming it since the war ended five years before. Remember we were in the land of *DOMANI MATINI!*

Palazzo Taverna, it turned out, was built in the 13th century. It used to be a fortress surrounded by a moat. The Popes were housed there centuries ago.

Now it is surrounded by some of Rome's least desirable living quarters. Narrow streets are kept dark by ten-floor apartment houses. They are so close that clothes lines are strung window to window high up across the street. Laundry flaps on them in a gentle city breeze.

But once we stepped through the huge arched gate—its ancient heavy oak doors open but still intact—the quiet surrounded us and we had the distinct feeling of having been transplanted into the middle ages.

The French Embassy occupied one entire side of the inner courtyard. An Italian Government agency had offices on the far portion. The rest was split into town apartments.

Bougainvillea, prickly pear cacti and exotic flowers were in bloom everywhere. Ferraris, Lancias, early postwar Mercedes sedans and Cadillacs were parked unobtrusively in nooks and corners of the spacious inner sanctum.

"I bet the staircase over there leads to Aunt Lida's penthouse," I told Klaus.

As we climbed up, our backpacks hardly fit through the well-worn, tunnel-like staircase leading to the upper floors.

We found her front door and rang the bell. Nothing happened. We rang again. Another pause.

Then the door opened. A housemaid in a black dress and miniature white apron stood there. We noticed the dress was cut as a short skirt, leaving us with an attractive view and grins on our faces. She stared at us in obvious disbelief. She didn't respond to my friendly "*Bon Giorno*" in any way, but rather asked in Italian what we wanted which did not sound altogether friendly.

"Aunt Lida," I said.

She gestured to two chairs in the elegant foyer and disappeared. They looked precious and fragile. We didn't sit down. We were afraid to. We stood instead, with our backpacks hanging off our right shoulders.

The maid reappeared and gestured again to follow her.

Then, there she was.

"Hello, my dear nephew, it is so good to see you. Come here, so I can kiss your forehead. And this might be a friend of yours, might it not, the one you wrote about?"

"Aunt Lida, this is my friend Klaus."

"So good to see you, Klaus. Please do sit down."

Klaus did, but not before he had bent down and kissed her hand ever so gently. Aunt Lida at once swooned over him, took in all his good manners and looks in one brief glance. I felt better. He surely had done his share to soften her up.

The chairs in her living room were equally old and delicate. We sat on their front edge. We didn't dare to be comfortable in them because our jeans were rather filthy.

"How is your dear father?" she asked after we had settled.

"He is fine and sends his very best regards to you."

"I have not seen him now for fifteen years or so," Aunt Lida continued. "You know we grew up together in New York. His mother and my father were siblings."

"I remember him telling me about your childhood," I threw in to keep her on a roll.

I lived on Long Island where I was born, he on Fifth Avenue in Manhattan, in the same house where he was born. In the summer, they often came out to our house. It was not very big, just six bedrooms or so. And in the winter we often went to see them in the city—theater time, you know. Such gracious times those were."

I had no idea what theater time really meant in those trouble-free years in New York's upscale circles.

Then she turned to Klaus: "Where are you staying?"

"We don't know," I said quickly. I didn't want my buddy to be in on this delicate talk. He had already done his share, kissing her hand, showing all his good upbringing.

But Klaus and I of course knew exactly where we wanted to stay, right here!

"Do you want me to make a reservation for you? I know this darling hotel right nearby. You'd love it."

We simply HAD to tell her the truth.

"Aunt Lida," I began, "I am afraid we don't have enough money for a hotel. We had hoped we could sleep here in your apartment. Would that be all right? We would only be here one night."

That of course was a small lie. We had planned to stay at least three nights. But we could negotiate that later once we had the foot in the door a bit.

But Aunt Lida's chin dropped. It took her a moment to grasp this totally new situation. But then her face lit up and she said,"Well, my guestroom is occupied. My daughter Lida and her husband, Prince Radziwill, are here from South Africa. They own some grazing land down there. I bought it for them. Think it is some 60,000 acres or so. I forget."

"Wow," said I.

"Neat," said Klaus.

"Well, Aunt Lida, then we're going to look for a youth hostel. We don't want to bother you anymore," I replied, trying to sound not too convincing.

It must have worked because she said, "Oh no. If you two can manage to sleep together on the couch in my study, then you should really consider staying here with me. It's as wide as an American double bed."

We had no problem considering it. Besides, we were used to sleeping in close quarters on the hard wooden benches of some dilapidated East German beer halls. But to this day, we feel a pang of guilt that, in our desperate need of inexpensive lodging, we had steered her into the direction of offering us her home to spend the night.

"Grrreat!" It slipped out of Klaus whose face was shining with a wide and happy grin.

The next morning we went down to Mussolini Avenue, found a flower stand and bought a HUGE bunch of lilacs for Lida Louise, so big that Klaus who carried them home to the Palazzo couldn't see ahead of it.

We stayed four nights. During the day, we roamed through the city. At night, we came back around six, then sank down into an oversized bathtub in one of Aunt Lida's bathrooms—the one she had assigned to us. The view from the bathtub revealed Rome's red tiled roof tops through French doors and lead to a miniature balcony. It was the one right across the hall from her study, where we slept and which featured etchings of most of the horses she had ridden and owned in her life.

Dinner was at nine in the evening, twice at home, and twice in outdoor sidewalk restaurants.

We liked Aunt Lida's daughter, also named Lida. I had never met her before. She was my cousin, about my age, a fox, with long, slender legs and a finely chiseled face, as her mother, Lida Louise, had been when she was younger. I was sure of that! Both had the charm of the Medlicots, Aunt Lida's grandmother, and my great-grandmother.

But the Prince was rather dull and distant. With him, we had nothing in common.

On the morning of our departure, over croissants with marmalade and black coffee served by the maid, Aunt Lida said, "I shall guide you out of Rome."

"You don't have to do that. We are experienced troopers," I said. "We'll find our way,"

"Nonsense," she answered, in a manner which indicated that she was used to getting what she wanted. "I will drive you to the edge of town."

No use arguing with a feisty lady.

We hopped in her 1949 Plymouth four-door sedan. Then she drove cautiously but expertly through Rome's roaring traffic.

At the outskirts, she stopped the car.

"You boys take your rucksacks and disappear behind those trees, down the embankment. Yes, those," she ordered. "Then I'll have a better chance to flag down a car for you."

Wow! She WAS a neat lady!

No sooner had she positioned herself next to the left rear of her car, her face radiating the innocence of a helpless, middle-aged lady, a black Lancia limousine appeared in the distance. Its chauffeur stopped at once.

Aunt Lida smiled through all her rattling Italian to tell the signor that she had these darling young boys—indeed her nephews, to be truthful—who needed to go towards Genoa and back to Paris to continue their serious studies to become architects and lawyers and…!

Then she waved us back. We reappeared. The chauffeur began to look distressed.

But he opened the trunk for our backpacks, then unlocked the rear doors for us to step in and lounge in the spacious, comfy leather seats for a four hour ride all the way up to La Spezia.

As the driver pulled out onto the highway, we turned around to wave at Aunt Lida once more.

And there she stood, with a couple of tears running down her cheeks, and with an absolutely adorable and mischievous smile on her beautiful face!

Klaus and I returned to Paris eight days later. I took two more days off from classes and roamed the city with him.

He became an architect and now lives with Brigitte on Spain's Mallorca Island in the Mediterranean.

No friendship in my life has lasted longer than his!

CABALLEROS PRIMEROS

Chapter Five:
IN MEXICO

1961 BALLERAS

Balleras is Spanglish for Caja de Bolo. In English, it means ball bearing.

Hanna and I were going north on route 55 out of Taxco, the silver city, on our way home from an expedition to Acapulco, through Toluca and points beyond. It was January, 1962. The settlement was still a small fishing village at that time.

Suddenly, up on the high plateau between the Sierra Madre Occidental and Sierra Madre Oriental, the left rear wheel of our Mercury started to squeal, increasingly louder, until it screeched.

It was noon, the middle of winter, in the mid- to upper-nineties, and bone dry.

I stopped the car, walked around and inspected the left rear wheel. No signs of damage or malfunction were visible, yet the steel rim of the wheel was piping hot.

We were in the middle of nowhere in a foreign country. We did not speak the language. We knew we couldn't go any further.

An hour passed. No car came by. The map indicated we were on a secondary road. To us, it should have been graded much lower than secondary.

Finally, one car approached and stopped. A Jeep-type vehicle.

A uniformed man behind the wheel asked in broken English, after he had seen our American license plate:

"Problem, Senor?"

"Si."

He climbed out of the Jeep and came over. I showed him the wheel. He touched it and said, "OUCH."

Then he walked back to his vehicle and commanded,

"Follow me."

"Yes, sir," I replied, "anything you say. *Gracias*. But go slow, *por favor.*"

He nodded. The markings on the Jeep's door panels and hood showed him to be a soldier of the Mexican Army.

We crawled along the narrow road. The noises from our wheel became ear piercing. I prayed for an end to this soon. Our guide stopped his Jeep and pointed to a thatched roof on four crude wooden poles by the road. He talked to the men seeking shade, gestured to us to drive in there and left before I could thank him for his help.

About a dozen men crouched in the sand under the roof. All of them rose to their feet to see what was making that terrible noise. One of them signaled for me to stop and then talked to me in Spanish. I shrugged. He looked at our plate.

"*Gringo*," I heard him say to the others.

They went to work instantly, cranked up the left rear wheel in the air, loosened the lug nuts, took the wheel off and threw it into the sand. Then the brake drum came off and also landed in the sand. Then, with much gesture and laughing, they pulled half of our rear axle out of its casing, placing the meshed tooth gear portion into the sand as well, to inspect the end of our axle where the wheel and brake drum were located. Then they dismantled everything.

Looking at all my car's parts in the dust, I thought we would never ever get out of here. A terrifying thought for sure.

"*Balleras*," said the man who gave the orders and therefore appeared to be the head honcho. Then he showed me the broken and worn part. Ah, he had meant the ball bearing, using the Spanglish term for it because he probably thought I would understand that.

I hadn't. My knowledge of Spanglish is as limited as that of my Spanish. But now, I saw the part and knew it to be a ball bearing.

Seemingly endless discussions among the twelve followed.

Eventually, the head man got onto his bicycle, and another hopped onto the rear wheel where two extending pins made it possible for him to stand. He carried the entire half of our rear axle on his shoulder, the tooth gear portion of it in his cupped hands, the axle shaft extending over his shoulder like a hunting rifle. Both set out in the direction where we had come from and soon disappeared.

"There is nothing that way," I said to Hanna. "We didn't see a town or even a village in at least fifty kilometers. Where in the world are they going with our axle?"

"I don't know," she replied. Of course, what else could she say.

We were left with the rest of the men. They soon crouched into the sand again. I suggested to Hanna to sit in the shade of a nearby tree. She did.

"I better stick around here, near the car," I added.

"But you have no place to sit, no shade?" she said.

"I can always sit in the sand, like our friends over there do," I answered her, trying to sound cheerful. But I was not cheerful.

I stood by the car, in the hot sun. All of Hanna's jewelry was in there. We had gone to a Philadelphia New Year's Eve Gala affair on the way south. Tuxedo and evening gown were lying on the bottom of the car's trunk. Probably all dusty now. It seemed eons ago that we were there. Will we ever get out of here, back home, to see the kids?

I had lots of time to think. Once in a while, I would walk over to Hanna and bring her something to drink out of our cooler. Then I would return to the car and the hot sun to assume my vigil again.

Meanwhile, a very old woman hobbled in the direction of Hanna. I watched her closely. She was bent over about ninety degrees, obviously suffering from extreme bone deterioration. Her straggly hair hung straight down her face. Her knotty fingers grasped a crude wooden stick, made of cedars growing nearby.

She stopped about a foot in front of Hanna and stared into her face for a long time, as if she thought Hanna was from an unknown other world she had never seen before.

We had not anticipated a stop anywhere during this long day of traveling. So Hanna had put on shorts that morning and prepared a small basket with fruits, cheese and tortillas for a lunch stop somewhere in the mountains. But at that time, shorts on a woman in Catholic Mexico were a taboo. Was that the reason why the woman stared at Hanna?

A witch, Hanna thought. A witch had descended from the Middle Ages into the 20th century. Here, in the middle of nowhere she had come. Hanna was scared beyond belief but tried to fix her eyes on the woman and smile. Eventually, the woman left, hobbling along with her knotty cane to ease the pain of her advanced osteoporosis.

Hours passed. Nothing happened. I was beginning to get very

nervous. After all, there was no settlement anywhere near. We had nothing to eat anymore. Our liquids in the cooler were running low as well. By this time, the temperature had reached into the high nineties.

Finally, after more than three hours, a dot appeared on the horizon. It became larger soon. It revealed some legs pedaling a bicycle. A large, long object stuck out in the air above the bike rider's heads.

Our mechanics were returning!

They both were beaming when they pulled under the thatched roof and got off the bicycle. The one shouldering our axle proudly waved a small box at me, meaning they had the parts needed to get us going. I looked at the box. BALL BEARING, MADE IN JAPAN, it said on its top.

God only knows where they found it in this forgotten part of the world. But they found it.

All twelve men were up on their feet again, to help or simply watch how a few of them were sliding the new bearing onto the axle. It stopped sliding about two inches away from where it was supposed to sit, namely adjacent to the brake drum housing.

The part was too small! It didn't fit our Mercury! NOW WHAT?

Long discussions among the men followed. The someone picked up a crow bar, held it against the edge of the bearing while another man slammed a large hammer onto the bar's opposite end — BANG, BANG, BANG. They finally jammed the bearing into place that way, leaving a lot of scratch marks on our axle.

Never mind that. If it would work, who'd care?

Then someone picked up a garden hose from the deep sand

and wanted to stick it into our gas tank, to suck up some gas for cleaning the axle.

"NO," I shouted, then motioned for him to clean the sand off the hose first.

But by the time the men started to place the axle's gear teeth first into its casing, they had cleaned the hose off alright but had forgotten to use the gasoline they sucked out of my tank to clean the gear teeth with it.

"NO," I shouted again.

After five hours, they had us finally rolling. Everybody smiled. Lots of "amigos" were being said.

I asked for the charges. They drew the figures into the sand, meaning pesos of course. It equated to $4.50 for the ball bearing and $8.00 for labor. $12.50 total for all this work!

Unbelievable!

I gave them $20.00 and refused to accept the change. That brought out twelve smiles. We also had an sealed carton of Lucky Strike cigarettes in the trunk which we had taken for the purpose of giving out a pack here or there for special services rendered. We gave the men the whole carton. That caused another round of twelve smiles.

Then we took off to the north, to drive towards San Juan del Rio as evening descended onto the Mexican high plateau.

Wonderful people they were, —helpful, ingenious, patient and friendly.

Back home, after another 2,600 miles, we went to our Ford Mercury dealer, to have him check out the work the Mexicans did.

"It's okay and wearing well, but the part doesn't quite fit your car, sir," the service manager said when I picked it up, "so I suggest we put a new ball bearing on your left rear wheel."

"Will the Mexican bearing work if I don't change it?" I asked him.

"Sure will."

"Will the scratched axle have any effect on the performance of the wheel?"

"No, it won't," he assured me.

"Then we should leave it in just as it is," I told him.

And that's the way it happened. And for the remainder of the years we owned that car, it worked without a flaw.

The moral of the story: DON'T TOUCH IT, IF IT AIN'T BROKE!

1994 MARIA CORDOBA

One night in Mexico City, Hanna and I had a mediocre dinner at the Intercontinental Hotel's Belvedere Room, surrounded by well-to-do tourists, and businessmen exclusively from foreign countries.

But we felt the urge to see Mexico and her people again. Descending to the lobby, we asked the concierge where we could find a place to have an after dinner drink, an establishment which would be typical for the country. He looked at us in disbelief. His face told us that he thought this to be a highly undignified question. Instead, he suggested a few places, which, by the sound of their names, were probably not what we were looking for.

"Senor," I said. "A place where everyday people would go."

He shrugged. "Don't know any," he replied, which we knew was a lie because we were sure that in his off-time he did what every Mexican seems to do, namely seek the company of his countrymen in local establishments of food and spirits. or in the squares of the city during long evening hours.

We walked outside and hailed a cab. With the few words we knew in Spanish, we explained to the cabby what we were looking for. "A place where you would go—dancing, Tequila, Tecate, fun. Right?" I added in English.

The cabby laughed, looked at us in his rear view mirror, disbelief in his eyes, and said: "Si, senor, El Gallo."

It was a dinky place in a dark side street not far from the Intercontinental. We thanked the cabby. He was kind and helpful. I tipped him well.

We walked inside. Dimly lit, the place was large. Most of the tables were taken, but we found one near the dance floor. Its occupants were just rising to leave.

The waiter came and I ordered Tecate, a well known local beer, for myself and "whiskey" for Hanna, taking a chance as to what type would be served. Most Mexicans throw all types of brands (Canadian, Scotch, and Blended) into this one category: whiskey.

A band of perhaps eight or nine musicians entertained the patrons of the place for the evening. Most of them played the ever present violin and the remainder strummed their guitars or blew their trumpets. But all of them sang the songs they played in the melodic and expressive manner typical for this country.

Many people danced. There was noise all over the establishment: happy noises from music, laughter, clapping hands in rhythm. The place vibrated.

Our drinks came. I used the customary wedge of lime to wipe the mouth of my bottle of Tecate and the edge of my glass. Then I grabbed what looked like a potato chip from a bowl placed at the center of our table. Biting into it heartily, I soon shuddered. It was a piece of pig skin marinated and heavily spiced, burning hot. A Mexican delicacy, but not made for my stomach.

For the following half hour or so, we watched the scene unfold before our eyes. Next to us, five tables had been pushed together, to accommodate a large group of people who clearly knew each other well.

A lot of happy banter took place there, mostly aimed at a couple sitting close and holding hands.

"I'll bet they just got married," I said to Hanna.

As if she had heard it, one of the women from the large table looked over to us, got up and came over to where we were sitting.

"I am Maria Cordoba. You look alone," she said in heavily accented English. "Won't you come over and join us?"

We nodded happily and stood up. She then introduced us to her large group by our names which she had inquired. Pointing to the young couple she said,

"They will be married tomorrow."

People made room for us and pushed two more chairs into their middle. No one spoke English, except Maria Cordoba who had invited us over. We laughed a lot. So did our hosts. They ordered Mexican wine for us. We communicated with our hands, sign language so to speak. It worked splendidly.

Then one of the participants, a woman of about thirty-five with one long braid hanging down her back, got up and gestured to me to dance with her. I did of course, although I did not know any of their dances. However, she showed me through her vibrant movements and rapid steps what to do.

Hanna, meanwhile, was swept away by one of those dashing young Mexicans who twirled her around the dance floor with great speed and élan.

Both of us were out of breath after only one dance, not because it was too exhausting physically but because of the almost 6,000 feet elevation of the city. After all, we were sea rats.

Later, Maria, who had invited us over, came to sit with us and I had a chance to ask her: "Where did you learn your English?"

"In Oklahoma City," she replied.

"Oklahoma? How did you get there?" Hanna exclaimed.

"I was a nurse in a hospital there. Good pay. I sent money home to parents. They were old, could work no more."

"I bet you were a good nurse," I said.

"Did you make any friends there?" Hanna wanted to know.

"Difficult."

"Why?"

"Oklahoma different from Mexico. Here we go to El Gallo with family, or friends. Or we meet friends. I thought Oklahoma was like it. Went to coffee shop there often. But no one ever talked to me, asked me to dance."

Then Maria stopped abruptly. She looked frightened, as if she was afraid she might have hurt us and our feelings for her and her country.

"So sorry," she murmured.

But she surely hadn't hurt us, not at all. What she did, though, was to make us realize what had just happened to us in the way of hospitality. Her gesture made us feel embarrassed and somewhat sad as to how cold her reception in our country must have been.

Soon thereafter, we rose to leave, waving to the gathering and uttering many *"gracias, gracias amigos."* Everyone waved back.

To Maria, the nurse, we only said:

"You opened our eyes to the friendliness of your people. Thank you so much for inviting us over. We will forever remember this evening."

"Good bye," she replied, grabbing our hands and giving each of us a hug. Then, with moist eyes, she added:

"Hope you are not lonely anymore."

Maria Cordoba, you opened our eyes wide to the occasional rudeness of our own people!

1994 THE BRIDGE

Our map listed what looked like a paved road leading from the north-south highway #5 to Coahuila. From there, a thinner line showed that it apparently continued on to El Golfo de Santa Clara, where the great Colorado river empties into the Sea of Cortez.

This 'paved' road, shown in a black, solid line rather than the red color used for major through roads, bore the number four. Railroad tracks were marked parallel to this route.

Hanna and I were traveling back from Cabo San Lucas, on the southernmost tip of Mexico's Baja California, in late March, 1994. Coming up from San Felipe where we had spent the night, we took #4 east about fifty-five miles below the border city of Mexicali. At once, it became narrow, with no shoulders and the broken edges of the asphalt falling off into the muddy soil on both sides.

Although no center line guided the traffic, it appeared passable even if quite limited in width. There was only local traffic anyway, like vintage 1951 Chevrolet four-door sedans, slow moving farm trucks, and tractors moving even slower.

Farmlands on both sides of the road were irrigated with modern rotating sprinkler systems of American origin and bore rich harvests even early in the year. The water for such irrigation came from the Colorado River ahead of us.

When we came to it a while later, we saw the pavement disappear. In front of us instead emerged a large, gaping hole, a distance of nothingness measuring at least one-third of a mile.

Approaching the end of the road, we noticed the remains of a bridge scattered and broken in the Colorado's water. When we asked him later, the Coahuilla policeman said in accented English that it had been out for almost two years.

We stopped to think about what to do. After a few seconds, a short blasting sound behind our car made us jump in our seats and turn our heads. A huge eighteen-wheeler had stopped inches away from our rear bumper. Its driver leaned out and pointed to the left in front of us, indicating for us to move up to what appeared like an earthen dam or ramp.

I put the car in first gear and slowly moved up the rutted, boulder strewn path. The truck followed closely.

On top, at the end of the makeshift ramp, we stopped again. The improvised road had ended. In front of us now were the railroad tracks, which ran parallel to Route #4 ever since we got onto it.

The eighteen-wheeler stopped too, of course. It couldn't go anywhere with us blocking its way. I heard the driver say something in Spanish. So I leaned out of my window to see what he wanted.

With a happy grin on his dark, round face, he pointed ahead, accompanied by sounds of encouragement.

"Onto the railroad tracks?" asked Hanna in disbelief.

"I am sure that is what he means. There is nothing else in front of us."

I inspected the scene. Someone had placed large railroad ties on the inside of the rails, running parallel with them. They were perhaps as much as a foot wide and quite long, obviously meant for cars to drive on.

In between the ties, the bridge substructure was visible about two feet below. Through its openings, we could see the slowly moving greenish waters of the mighty river some hundred feet further down.

"In other words, it seems that's where we are going," I said to Hanna.

I put our small Ford in first gear again, grabbed the steering wheel so tight that my knuckles turned white, holding it as steady as I could. Then we started moving onto the rails.

It soon became clear that the car's wheel width was just a touch more narrow than the width of the rails. It meant that we were sliding and skidding along the slippery iron bands, alternating between one set of our wheels riding on them, the other side wheeling on the supporting beams green and slippery with mildew—or vice versa.

It was also obvious that under no circumstances should I let the Ford's wheels slide off the OUTSIDE rim of the rails. There was no support there in the shape of wooden ties. Our car would tumble down two or three feet to the substructure.

The truck behind us obviously had no such problem as I could see when I occasionally glanced into my rear view mirrors, for no more than a second. It had eighteen beefy tires to guide it along the slippery rails without a hitch.

The distance across the water seemed never ending. Yet it was no more than a third of a mile. Pearls of sweat ran down my face.

Without daring to take my eyes off the tracks or the inside mirror to watch was the truck was doing, I said to Hanna:

"Get the camera."

"Where is it?" she asked with some exasperation in her voice.

"Behind me, on the back seat. Grab it. Quick."

Yet the small sideways motion of our car caused by her turning around made me sweat even more. But she took some excellent shots through our windshield, as smeared with mud as it was.

The big eighteen-wheeler was right behind us. We both slowly approached the other end of my nightmare.

Then somewhere ahead of us, out of nowhere really, appeared the ghost I had been afraid of ever since we entered the railroad bridge. Because, out of nowhere, came a huge diesel locomotive toward us, its powerful, rotating headlight blinking at us like the single eye of the devil in person.

"Oh God, no, please stop," I muttered between my teeth.

The engineer of the train did. He pulled a long line of freight cars. He might not have seen our Ford but surely couldn't miss the monstrous truck behind us.

When we rolled off the railroad bridge onto another makeshift earthen dam leading us back to the highway below, the engineer waved at us and laughed.

By this time, I dared to take one hand off the steering wheel, to wave back, not only to acknowledge his greeting but foremost to indicate my gratitude that we had made it and were now on solid ground again.

The farmhands working the fields nearby and around us had laid down their shovels to watch the unfolding scene on the bridge. Now they too waved at us and we returned their greetings.

"What would have happened, do you think, if the car had fallen between the railroad ties up there?" Hanna asked, "or even down from the rails on the outside?"

"No problem," I replied. "All those hundred-plus guys out there in the field would have come up and lifted us right back onto the rails."

"Yes, I know. They would have. Because this is Mexico," she mused. And indeed, they would have!

1994 ELISA

The town of St. Miguel d'Allende is one of Mexico's true gems. Hanna and I came there one sunny day in early December. We were driving the chase vehicle for Skip's *Pancho Villa Moto Tours*.

Located on the high plateau between the Sierra Madre Oriental and Sierra Madre Occidental, the town lies nestled in a valley with a mountain ridge on its eastern side, high enough to shelter it from the cold plateau winds. It lies at an elevation of 6,100 feet and features a cool, dry and mostly sunny climate year round.

The settlement's history is rich, documented by many Spanish-built churches, palaces and patrician homes. Streets are narrow, with cobblestone pavements that have endured centuries.

St. Miguel's main plaza, shaded by large oak trees, is bordered by arcades on three sides and the stately cathedral on the fourth. It represents the focal point of the town. A wrought iron gazebo serves nightly entertainment. The plaza's size is spacious enough to hold hundreds of the town's citizens and their visitors. It seems everyone converges there for the evening hours, as is customary throughout Mexico.

The town also holds in its boundaries an exquisite art institute, called Instituto Allende, housed in a former hacienda. A small museum attached to the Institute and located in one of its many courtyards, displays current works of resident artists. Up the street lies the Instituto Nacional de Bellas Artes, another famous art school.

The Instituto Allende can also be reached from the Hotel Aristos by walking through its manicured garden, then passing through an arch in a high stone wall, into the first of the Institute's courtyards.

We checked into the Aristos at noon. A wrought iron gate leads into the spacious grounds surrounding the large old building of the hotel. Once inside, wrought iron French doors open from the downstairs guest rooms out onto a small, private patio, which offers a view to the well kept gardens beyond.

All floors are covered by mosaic tile typical of Mexico— colorful, with interesting designs almost always featuring the sun. There are comfortable lounge chairs, a large coffee table, ample lights, solid beds, and a bathroom where all the plumbing works.

The dining room is huge, almost cavernous, but sunlit. The service is magnificent. As a matter of fact, the entire hotel is staffed with an abundance of help which include waiters, bus boys, room attendants, clerks, gardeners and bell boys everywhere, unobtrusively waiting in the deep shadows of the building's corners and courtyards for a chance to serve and please the guests.

Then there also is an Olympic sized swimming pool, encircled by a large sun deck which loses itself in tropical flower beds, exuberantly blossoming shrubbery, cacti and oleander.

Walking out of the central lobby in my swim trunks, a hotel room bath towel wrapped around my neck, a newspaper and a book under my arm, I saw the pool unoccupied and serene. Only when I passed one of the deck chairs did I hear a soft voice say,

"Hello, there."

I turned, noticed a casually but elegantly dressed woman wearing some sort of pantsuit. I had never seen one like it, but then I had never been very good in recognizing or even identifying female wardrobe. Her head was covered by a sombrero which shaded most of her face. She seemed to be in her mid to late thirties. So I answered:

"Hi, there, how are you?"

"Very well, thank you. A lovely day, is it not?" Her accent was New England, perhaps Vermont.

"It is, and perfect for a good book and a snooze."

Seeking a deck chair at the other end of the pool, I began to realize that the lady had greeted me in English rather than Spanish. A fellow American, I thought, glancing briefly back at her. She was well-dressed indeed, and by her manners, speech and posture could have well been a local jet setter.

"Are you going swimming?" she asked across the water.

"Yes, if it isn't too cold, I will."

"I thought of going swimming myself, but there wasn't anyone around and I don't like to swim alone," she continued.

Hint, hint! Obviously, she hoped I would offer to go swimming with her. After a moment of reflecting, I didn't think I would. So I said:

"Well, I am not ready to swim yet. I'd like to just soak up some rays, have a snooze, read some, you know."

This was supposed to be my best effort to let her know that I really wanted to be alone.

"Too bad, then I will change into my swim gear anyway and hop in alone."

Before I could mutter a reply, she had vanished.

But then panic set in. I would never have the peace I was seeking, if we were to swim together then talk.

In one big leap, I hit the water head first from my lounge chair and plowed furiously through the pool, both because I needed vigorous exercise and wanted to be back in my deck chair by the time she returned.

Wrong. She beat me to it.

In the shortest possible time, she had changed I don't know where and reappeared on the deck in the skimpiest bikini I had ever seen. Not even in St. Tropez had I ever laid eyes on something like that.

She was tanned and statuesque. But her attitude bothered me. I was not ready for this kind of overt approach.

I climbed out of the pool before she had thrown her towel on the deck chair she had occupied before. I gathered mine, on the other side, to dry myself. The warm, yet very dry air made me shiver. I rubbed my body vigorously then plunked down on my lounge chair again. I felt exhilarated, my skin prickled.

She had meanwhile marched to the edge of the pool, tipped her toes into the water while sitting, rather gracefully I thought, on the deck terrazzo floor. Then she cried out:

"Heavens! This is too cold!"

But she remained seated on the floor, with her tanned, well-shaped legs stretched out on the marble ring bordering the pool.

"My name is Elisa, what's yours?"

"Peter."

"Nice to meet you, Peter. Too bad you went swimming already. You are not from here, are you? No? Where from? North Carolina? Isn't that near Memphis? No? Memphis is the place where my husband was from, you know, the man I was married to for a short time. We lived there, somewhere, I believe it was an old, restored section of town, near downtown, as a matter of fact, near the river."

"I know that section, have been there," I managed to squeeze in.

"You do? That's strange. But what's the name of the river again? Can't think of it right now. Anyway, I didn't like him, couldn't stand him. We broke up, a few years ago. No, wait a minute, I guess it was six years ago, yes, that's correct. Have not seen him since." And on and on she went.

Except for the one short sentence, I kept silent during this waterfall of personal information.

She got up and walked over to my side of the pool and, gracefully again, sank into the deck chair next to mine.

"Are you here alone?"

Now, if that wasn't a leading question I wouldn't know what would be one.

"No, I am here with my wife. She is in our room reading. Maybe I should go and ask her to come out, to meet you."

Not at all perturbed with that bit of information, she ignored my suggestion and continued to tell me her life's story.

"You have somewhat of an accent. I am trying to trace it. European?"

"I grew up in Europe but I am a born American citizen."

"Why don't you live in Europe then? It is so much nicer there than in America, so very sophisticated."

I didn't answer immediately. I had seen a lot of places in Europe that weren't sophisticated at all. Poverty in Serbia and Romania, crime in Sicily and the rest of Italy, a public park in rich, bourgeois Switzerland—Zurich to be exact—overrun by drug addicts tolerated by their country and city, and a place the Swiss police try desperately to bar foreigners from visiting.

And more of that sort of thing.

"I want to live in the United States. It is my home country.

In Mexico • 127

I belong there and want to be there." I was trying to be as polite as I could, yet came close to getting up to leave.

"But who in his right mind would want to live in America, really now? No one does," she exclaimed, more excited now.

"Well, I know of some 265 million people who do," I said.

"Yes, but they don't know any better."

This wasn't getting us anywhere. She was one typical representative of an American expatriate. My family has its fair share of them, all living their luxurious lives abroad, over in Europe mostly, but none of them are willing to give up their US passports.

"For tax reasons," she said. They all talk of America when they mean the United States. They never live in Liverpool or Toulouse but rather in Cannes, Rome, Lugano or Paris.

"You obviously live well, here, don't you, Elisa? I suppose the Mexican economy enables you to live your lifestyle?" I knew this was too personal an approach to her privacy, but then she had done it to me, too.

"Heavens, no," she replied with disgust on her pretty face. "I derive my income from my former husband and from other sources in the States."

So much for that. At least, she had said 'States' and not 'America'.

"I live across, up on that hill over there. The natives call it 'Gringo Gulch.' I have an apartment there. I often come here to swim, though. They allow me to do so."

"I see." I didn't know what to say and was afraid she would lead me further into the question of her apartment.

"But you know, the problem I have with the servants is really horrible. I have to tell them every little detail, I mean e v e r y t h i n g! They are so lazy."

We didn't have any help at home. So maybe we were safe from these horrible things.

"Would you like to see my apartment? The view from there is really very pretty."

So that was it. I almost smiled. It was all so predictable.

"Well, I'd like to relax here, thank you. Maybe I'll take a little snooze." It was a desperate attempt to save my hide.

"But you MUST come, to see how we live in this country," she insisted.

I had seen 'Gringo Gulch' that morning. And I had seen the mostly extremely modest housing in the rest of St. Miguel in which the Mexicans lived. There was positively no relationship between the two.

I got out of my chair, determined to flee. Yet she kept talking more aggressively now as she realized that I was slipping away. She had also never acknowledged the fact that I was here with my wife.

"We could have cocktails here later, then go to dinner. I know of this divine little restaurant. You would like it—candlelight, exquisite food, heavenly wines."

Then suddenly rescue had arrived: "Hi, Elisa," said a voice behind us. I KNEW THAT VOICE! I shot around, facing my buddy Skip.

"Oh, hello Skip. it is so good to see you," Elisa bubbled. "What brings you here? Why are you not going swimming with me? So get your trunks. Are you staying here? Like Peter? Oh, you know Peter? Let's go in the water. No, it isn't that cold, it is heavenly. You want to have a drink with me? No? Maybe later. Maybe we could have dinner tonight, you and I, because I know of this divine little restaurant, you would like it, candlelight, exquisite…"

I had turned around when Skip came, had silently picked up my towel, sun glasses and book, sliding away into the shadows. I did not hear the rest of her sentence but knew what it was.

TODD PUTS A LID ON THINGS

Chapter Six:
A TRUE SOULMATE

1962 TODD

It was fall in the Midwest—rainy, damp, cold. A Friday, noon.

I was returning from an extensive, weeklong business trip to a number of off-the-beaten-track places in Ohio and Indiana. To reach these, I often took the car rather than flying. This gave me plenty of undisturbed time to think without telephones ringing. Besides, it always felt good to get away from my high-pressure job in New York's Rockefeller Center, where my employer maintained its headquarters.

It also gave me a chance to take my toy out, for a long run: a 1956 Thunderbird, two-seater, grey outside, red leather inside, with a thundering V8 under the hood. Mind-boggling!

I had stopped for gas at the Indiana Toll Road's first rest area east of Gary. While there, I had bought a sandwich and coffee from the take-out counter and was planning to eat it on the way east, to make better time and come home by Saturday noon the latest.

As I stepped on the T-bird's gas pedal and let her roar off, I noticed two parka-clad figures near the exit of the rest area. They did not wave or thumb a ride. They just stood there.

I stopped, rolled down my right window and asked where they wanted to go.

"East," one of them said. "Are you going by chance to the vicinity of Cleveland?"

I hesitated for a moment and paused, to take a good hard look at these fellows.

Then I said,

"Hop in."

I pulled on the latch next to my seat to open the trunk so they could throw their bags into its tight spaces. Then they slid into the narrow passenger seat—the two of them. The guy next to me introduced himself:

"I am Todd. And this is my roommate Shane."

"You guys go to college?"

"Yes, Oberlin, in Ohio."

"Going back then, aren't you?"

"Yes, sir."

They only talked when I asked them questions. Other than that, they were quiet. They never talked between themselves either. They knew the rules. I knew those rules also, from miles and miles of hitchhiking myself. I made it easier for them by asking a lot of questions.

Shane didn't say much over there by his window. As a matter of fact, he fell asleep soon after they boarded. But Todd next to me was alive and alert.

I liked the kid. Dark-blond hair, cut in crewcut style, brown eyes, an open face, free in handling himself, obviously resting on solid ground. He had the neck of a football player and his hands were square. He appeared like someone who loved the outdoors.

So I asked him:

"Are you active in sports?"

"A little," he replied. "But not necessarily team sports."

"Which then?"

"Mountain climbing."

"Great," I said, "That's my most favorite too."

By the time I dropped them a few hours later at the entrance of Oberlin College, Todd and I had laid the foundation for a friendship.

During the winter, letters went back and forth. In the spring, I came by Oberlin with Hanna on the way to Chicago. We had lunch with Todd and his friend Angela.

During the following summer, Todd and I formulated plans to climb our first mountain together. It was slated to be Mount Elbert—Colorado's highest peak, 14,433 feet above sea level.

From my home in suburban New Jersey, I drove the Thunderbird out in mid- August. It bore all the gear we needed. We met at Denver's Stapleton Airport where Todd had flown in from Cleveland. The next two days, we stayed in the foothills, training in the lower altitude of 5,600 ft. Then we drove to Twin Lakes, at the mountain's base, at an elevation of 9,100 feet. The Twin Lakes Lodge had a simple room with two bunks and a stall shower. We trained some more for three days.

On the fourth, we awoke at 4:00 a.m. Twenty minutes later, we drove the T-bird one-half mile up a dirt road to the trail head. By a quarter to five—still dark but with light beginning to shimmer at the eastern edge of the Front Range—we were climbing up. Steady, step by step, in even movements, not too fast, not too slow, things we both knew were necessary for conserving strength.

Then Todd asked, "What's wrong with your leg, Peter?"

"Oh, I thought you knew. I have a fused knee from several accidents."

"Will it hamper your climbing?"

"I don't think so. It happened when I was a child. I am surely used to it by now," I assured him.

Three-and-a-half hours into our climb, the trail steepened considerably. We hit a few spots where we needed our rope. Todd started to breathe heavily. I thought it was because we were now at about 11,600 feet. Another five hundred feet up, and he was breathing even harder. He had to stop and rest for a moment.

Then I asked, "What's wrong with your lungs, Todd?"

"Oh, I thought you knew. I have a slight case of asthma."

"Will it hamper your climbing?"

"I don't think so. Have had it since I was a child. I am surely used to it by now," he assured me, grinning now because he had used the same words I had.

The last 1,000 feet were extremely steep, sometimes almost vertical. We climbed slowly, carefully seeking our best positions and footsteps. The rope was in heavy use then.

We reached the summit at noon. It was August 30, 1962. The temperature stood at 32 degrees Fahrenheit—seven hours and thirty minutes up, almost non-stop!

We sat, retrieved woolen sweaters and parkas from our backpacks and rested for almost two hours. We munched our sandwiches and a power bar and forced ourselves to drink Gatorade. Although we didn't noticed any sweating on the way up, we were sure we had. Our faces, forearms, and hands were caked with a heavy layer of goose fat to block out the deadly sun rays.

And here were two nomads who had climbed a steep mountain and each of them had a handicap! We talked about that up there, kidding each other with the fact that one hadn't known of the other's shortcoming. And we laughed and were happy. We had helped each other out and were there for each other.

At two, we climbed down again, first slowly using the rope on the 1,000 ft. drop, then almost leaping down the steep trail. We were back in our lodge at six, in time for a long, hot shower and a huge dinner. Then it was bed at eight, for an un-interrupted eleven hours of sleep.

We spent the weekend following our climb at a horse ranch near Granby. It was owned by a business acquaintance of mine. A number of other guests were there. One of them asked over dinner, "Why did you guys climb up there?"

"The view is magnificent," I told him. "It is exhilarating to have conquered a mountain that steep and high, to sit up there, on top of the world so to speak, no one there, no sounds except the howling winds."

"Hell, I can have that in less than fifteen minutes out of Denver Stapleton Airport in a jet. And the wind wouldn't even blow my hair apart, either."

Silence! Nobody said a word. Everybody appeared shocked, anxiously waiting for our reaction. But Todd and I had nothing to add to that. We were millions of miles apart from that kind of outlook on life. We felt we didn't belong there.

So, we told our host we'd be leaving in the morning—and yes, thanks a lot for your hospitality.

We left without breakfast at dawn and headed east, back home. I dropped Todd off in Wisconsin at his mother's house, then went on to New Jersey and pulled into our driveway two minutes before midnight on September 6, our tenth wedding anniversary, in the nick of time to give Hanna a huge hug!

It had taken the T-bird seventeen hours at eighty miles an hour to run the 900 miles from Madison, Wisconsin to my home. So I had lots of time to think about Todd and our expedition, our relationship. I felt that we both had realized we were kindred souls, had both felt we shared thoughts and interests.

Much of this was fairly commonplace with all good friendships between men.

If no friendship would have existed before this happened, it sure did now after we had achieved the strenuous climb.

If I could still pursue such bonding experiences, I would certainly have offered Todd this chance. He would have qualified with flying colors.

He married Angela the following summer, at Palo Alto's Stanford University where he had accepted a position as lecturer. He asked me to be his best man. But I was out of the country on a business trip. I could not be there for him at that important event in his life.

A year later, he climbed Mt. Popocatepetl in Altiplano, Mexico's highest at 17,883 feet. He had counted on my coming along, but because of my job, I couldn't get away. Again I was not there; again I failed him.

Angela never brought it upon herself to forgive me. Because as I couldn't make the climb with him, he climbed alone.

He never returned.

Mexican authorities said he must have fallen more than 6,000 feet to a ridge at the 11,000 foot level.

He was not even thirty years old; his body was never found.

PETER HILGER, TRAVELING WEST IN 1982, ALONG WITH LAUNDRY DRYING IN THE BREEZE. *PHOTO BY KLAUS HILGER.*

Chapter Seven:
OUT WEST

1980 AMERICAN TRUCK DRIVERS

At home in North Carolina one day in early March, my family doctor advised that the lump under my right ear should be removed. It had been there for quite a few years and did not bother me except for its appearance. But since I was scheduled to go out to my employer's plant near Denver, Colorado, I made arrangements to have the surgery in St. John's Hospital in Denver. There, our company doctors knew the right surgeons and I could be chauffeured to and from my residence in a nearby hotel.

I left home in my Ford Pinto late in March and went northwest by way of Iowa City.

Heading west on March 30, in the afternoon, the weather was wintry, cold, but clear. The following morning, after an overnight stop in western Iowa, I woke up to a grey sky. I left the motel at eight.

Crossing the high river bridge spanning the Missouri in Omaha, I arrived in the State of Nebraska. Interstate 80 had widened to four lanes in each direction. The first milepost hurrying by on my right indicated the number 454, the distance to the western end of the great road at the Wyoming line.

Seven hours, I thought, give or take a few minutes. I knew the roadway from many previous trips. I could make Denver in ten if

I kept going at 65 mph and had lunch munchies in the car while driving. I checked the car's clock. It was 9:30 in the morning Central Time, or 8:30 Mountain Time. I would arrive at the Palace Hotel in Denver at 6:30 in the early evening, in time for a shower and dinner at my favorite restaurant. All of this planning sounded like clockwork. That's the way I was accustomed to managing my life.

I would be in Denver at the plant the next morning, April Fools Day, get a few things dictated, attend a meeting. Then my secretary would drive me over to the hospital where they wanted me to check in latest at five pm, in time to prepare me for surgery the following morning at nine. It was the usual clockwork planning, all right.

I left Omaha and its urban clutter behind, finishing all my deliberations while managing the city's morning rush hour. Ten miles west, I knew, was the Welcome Center for Nebraska. I would stop there briefly and get a free cup of coffee on the way out, as well as some skimpy weather info delivered over a crackling loudspeaker in that monotonous voice unique to most weathermen.

"It will be cloudy today in the state's eastern section. In the center, there will be a slight drizzle which could turn into ice rain by afternoon. The western portion should expect some light snow late afternoon, or early evening. Highs will range from the upper 30s east to freezing central and the upper twenties west. Lows are expected to be near freezing in Omaha and the teens at the western state line. Tomorrow, very much colder, with high, gusty winds and ..."

I had heard enough. Light snow, he had said. I knew the western area of Nebraska, like eastern Colorado, was about

5,400 feet elevation. The snow would therefore not be too bad because it would be dry and fluffy. Most of it would blow off the pavement. I could still make Denver, maybe not at 6:30, but closer to seven. Let's go!

I hit the superslab again and put my pedal to the metal. Sixty-five, seventy, seventy-five. That seemed to be a good cruising speed. I locked back into cruise control. Denver it would be, for dinner. I loved the restaurant's "Rocky Mountain Oysters." I might have them tonight.

One hundred twenty-five miles later, at the Grand Island exit, I filled up. It was close to eleven o'clock. When I got out of the car and looked around before inserting the nozzle into the tank fill outlet, I saw that the sky had turned much darker, especially so looking west. That's where the mess was coming from. It was cold, yet there were puddles on the ground. It must have rained. As a matter of fact, I felt a slight, wet spray. And I shivered in my shirtsleeves running inside to pay and pick up some junk food to nibble on and a large container of milk.

"Have you heard the weather report?" I asked the cashier.

"Yeah. Snow's coming. Will be a wet one," he said cheerfully.

Wet one? He had to be wrong. Maybe he listened to another station.

Yet he looked so snug when he said slickly: "Well, at least I don't have to be out there fighting all that mess. I'll be home watching the tube."

I got back into the car and on to the Interstate. Traffic was heavy with eighteen-wheelers. Passenger cars had thinned out. Seventy-five again, my friend, let's get a move on here, my Rocky Mountain Oysters are waiting.

Three hundred seventy-five miles to go. I moved the cruise control to eighty. *I've got to get to Denver, TONIGHT!*

Another twenty miles further west, the road surface became wet.

My wipers came on. The cruise control was set back to seventy-five. Ahead of me, the sky was the darkest blue-black imaginable. The eighteen-wheelers rolled by at eighty miles per hour. I did not dare to go along with them. Besides, their tires kicked up an oily mess streaking up the hood of my car and beyond onto my windshield.

I activated the windshield wiper solvent spray. Nothing. The reservoir was empty. The wipers continued their streaking sounds across, leaving an ever increasing smear of oil and soot. I slowed down to sixty. Damn, I would be late for dinner in Denver.

I slid a tape into the deck—Mozart. Maybe that would cheer me up. Jupiter Symphony. I loved it.

But Mozart must not have written his symphony with the thought of heading into bad weather. He couldn't have possibly been as cheerful as his notes expressed.

The Ford sped along, at fifty-five this time. The wet pavement hissed. Mozart was in his second movement now. I hummed along. I knew this piece so well, I could probably conduct it without music. But my attention strayed back to the road. Never mind, Wolfgang Amadeus, do you know what just happened? The hissing stopped. Wolfgang, you still there? THE HISSING IS GONE. IT'S ICE I AM DRIVING ON!

Get out of cruise control, NOW! I let the car coast and didn't touch the brakes. The Ford waggled its tail a bit but stabilized. The wipers now started their different sounds. The oily smear became icy. The blades scratched across the windshield and left ice streaks behind. Put the defroster on, switch the fan to high, and for heaven's sake SLOW DOWN. Lights on, it's getting darker by the minute. It's pitch dark.

Forty-five, forty, thirty-five.

Traffic became heavier. I could see a lot more taillights. The pavement ahead was a band of grayish slush. Markings on either side, as well as the centerline, had vanished.

Thirty.

Then it started to snow. Lightly at first but that did not last long. Within fifteen minutes, the snow came down in buckets—heavy, moist flakes. And they stuck to the ground.

Twenty-five.

I had to go to the bathroom in a bad way. No time for that now. Keep your eyes up front. Besides, I knew we were in the middle of nowhere, out there in the state's western part, surrounded by prairie as far as the eye could see on a clear day. Now nobody could see anything beyond twenty to thirty yards.

Twenty.

God, this country is so fabulous when it's clear. The North Platte River must be over there to the right. Its willow trees, bordering the waterway, now bare of leaves. Beyond, I knew, were the vast grasslands. They sway in the summer winds like elves dancing their ritual rhythms. On the left, were the endless fields of wheat and barley, stretching way south to Kansas and the Texas Panhandle—the breadbasket of the nation.

Fifteen.

The long ribbon of red lights in front of me had thickened. I was in the right lane. But maybe the left lane would be faster. It normally was. I veered over when there was room. The car in the left lane, which I now followed, started to slide. I stepped on the brakes, forgetting the road conditions for a split second. The Ford spun. I let go at once and eased back into my lane. No room for maneuvers.

Ten.

The falling snow was very dense by now. It built up fast on the pavement. I could only see as far as two to three cars ahead of me. It became darker. I looked at the car clock again. Three fifteen. I studied the map. We couldn't be far from Big Springs where I would branch off onto Interstate 76 to Denver. Some 240 miles to go. Jeepers, I won't make dinner in time, not in this mess. Maybe I should go out in Big Springs to have some grub and let the traffic thin out a bit.

Five.

I HAVE TO GO! The shoulder? Shall I pull over? No, bad idea. There was a snow bank there already, no room for a car. I would never have gotten out of there again. Ignore it, then.

Zero.

We had stopped. Nothing moved, in either lane. It's probably the snowplow up front. We should be moving again soon.

The clock was now three thirty.

We sat, motionless. Within a few minutes, at least an inch of snow had settled on my car's hood. This looks bad, real bad. I slid over to the car's right side, opened the door and let it all go! What a relief. Then I saw others were doing the same thing. Perhaps I had encouraged them. If anyone would have tried to arrest us for indecent exposure, we all would have smacked him one, I was sure.

Four forty-five.

I crawled forward not even a mile, using the last mile post where I got relief. It was dark by now.

Five ten.

We had moved perhaps ten yards. I checked my gas gauge. A quarter full. Yet I had to keep the engine running for warmth. But what if? Don't think of that now. There is not a thing I can do, if I run out of gas.

Five thirty.

I leaned back to see what kind of warm stuff aside from my ski jacket I must have in my duffel. Ah, here it is. Marine wool sweater, a turtle neck—at least something.

Five forty.

We had moved another twenty yards or so. A shadow on the right. What was it? Another five yards forward, I recognized the shadow in the thick, falling snow. A big, green road sign announcing in its large white letters that the exit for Big Springs was two miles ahead. Two miles. We should be there in a few minutes, even given this molasses in January traffic mess. I will get out then, get some gas and food, before heading out to Denver.

Never mind the Rocky Mountain Oysters.

Well, never mind getting to Big Springs anytime soon.

Nine ten.

It had taken three-and-a-half hours to crawl two miles ahead. The snow came down even more during this time. My guess was that we had close to fifteen inches on the ground. Any movement of any car made its wheels spin.

Most drivers stood doggedly in line waiting for traffic to move again. But I knew better. Apart from needing gasoline in a bad way, my needle stood firmly on empty. My stomach was growling.

The right lane started to move forward, very, very slowly indeed. The left lane stood motionless.

A few minutes later, I saw the cause of this motion. A huge snow bank, at least double the height of my Ford, separated the two lanes from the exit into Big Springs. Some cars had managed it, probably sport utility vehicles with four wheel drive. Yet I knew my light, low two-wheel drive Ford would never get through this sheer wall of snow.

But my chance came. The eighteen wheeler two cars in front of me activated his right turn signal and started moving into the exit lane the minute the car ahead of it had offered enough clearance to do so. The big truck plowed through the snow wall like a mighty bulldozer. It had to be heavily loaded because it didn't even swerve once.

The two cars in front of me followed him at once. By the time it was my turn, the snow wall had been rolled down a to manageable height. Nevertheless, after the car ahead had cleared it, I let it move up the ramp a piece and then pressed down on the gas pedal hard even though the wheels started to spin, gaining momentum to carry me through the deep slush.

I hit it hard. The tiny Ford disappeared into the snow. I could see only white out of all windows. But the little car kept churning along. Had there been a vehicle ahead of me, I would have never noticed it. Then I saw red taillights again. I was through. I had made it. The snow bank closed behind me as I looked into my mirror.

I fought my way up the ramp. There were lights. Many of them. And cars scattered around, some stuck in the snow on the ramp, many more parked and left in a huge parking lot to my right. A neon sign appeared out of the drifting snow. It told us weary travelers that we had arrived at the Big Springs Truck Stop. Underneath, in equally large, neon lit letters, it proclaimed:

"EATS" and "GAS."

Two things I needed most. No! Wait! It was close to ten o'clock. Never mind Denver, I was not going any place tonight anymore. So I needed a room. And there it was, a bit further away, a yellow sign familiar to all frequent road travelers—a Best Western Motel.

I wandered around in my car through the vast, snow-covered area, searching for a spot to park my vehicle. Cars were virtually scattered around everywhere. There was no orderly parking pattern anymore because there was too much snow. People had left their cars where they had stopped. I did likewise, but I chose the far edge of the field where my car would not be hit by another vehicle sliding in this mess.

I took my overnighter out and started hiking through the deep, white slush to the Best Western. In no time, I was wet. I only wore regular shoes. My feet started to freeze, my socks were sopping.

"Are you kidding?" said the woman behind the counter when I asked for a room. The small lobby was full of smoke and full of people, lying, standing, leaning, and crouching. "We've been full since two o'clock."

"Any other motel nearby?"

"No way, buster. You are out here in nowhere. You should be glad to have this roof over your head."

"I am. Thank you."

I marched outside again for the few steps over to the truck stop. I should really have some food now. In the mist, I saw a one-story building which turned out to house the gas station cashiers, a convenience store, a small restaurant as well as showers and restrooms. It was even more crowded than the motel lobby.

I found the men's room. I again needed it badly. It was drowning in water on the floor. All toilets were plugged up, a brownish slush slopping on the tile floor. But I had to go. So did all others.

The restaurant was across the hall. I fought my way through with numerous "excuse me" or "coming through." Everybody was polite. I did not see nor hear any nasty characters.

"All we have left is a few pieces of roast beef and some hashed browns," said the woman behind the food counter.

"I'll have it."

"Big order or small?"

"Big, if you can spare it," I replied.

"To drink?"

"Milk."

"No milk."

"Iced tea."

"No iced tea."

"Then what have you got left?"

"Root beer."

I hate root beer.

"I'll take the root beer."

All tables were taken. Most of the room in between the tables was taken. People sat there, crouched there, knelt there. I walked outside the restaurant, into the entrance hall. People everywhere. Then a truck stop employee spotted me and said:

"I see you have some food in your hands. There is a meeting hall in the back. It doesn't have any furniture in it, but we turned the heat up so it's nice and warm there. You will have to make do, though, with sitting on the floor."

"Thanks, bud, no problem with that. When is the snow going to stop, you know?"

"Radio says it's going to taper off by morning."

"You got a lot of visitors in here tonight, don't you?"

"Yeah, you're not kidding. So far over five thousand."

"Man, that's a lot of bodies."

"Yeah, for sure. And there will be more coming during the night. So find yourself a spot on the floor where you can bed down."

"Thanks. And have a good evening. You probably can't go home either, can you?"

"No way. But the same to you," he answered with a bright, shiny face.

I wolfed down my food. I have forgotten how god-awful it tasted. I remember only that the root beer tasted even more god-awful. But it was liquid and that counted.

Eleven thirty.

With food now in my stomach, I began to feel sleepy. The heat had been turned up, all right. I found a place at the far wall and settled down. A few dirty shirts out of my duffel and rolled up into a pillow would serve as my headrest for the night. I also took out my marine woolen sweater to cover myself. But I hardly needed it then. Later during the night it would come in handy.

At least two hundred other people were in the room, some already asleep, others, like me, preparing to go to sleep. More people came in as the night wore on. They, too, settled down on the cement floor. They did this quietly, so as not to disturb others asleep already.

I did not witness midnight anymore. Exhausted sleep had caught up with me as well.

Shortly before three in the morning, we were awakened by a blast of blaring rock 'n roll. I shot up, as if coming out of a bad dream. But it was no dream.

A group of eight college kids had entered the hall—all boys. They wore expensive looking ski outfits and carried equally expensive bags and video cameras. Among them was one, talking—as could be expected—the loudest. His face showed defiance of anyone not like him. He was the Great.

The group settled down in one corner where there was some room left. The noise of dropping their gear, the loud chatter of their banter and above all the howling of the rock 'n roll did not subside. It went on as they all sat down on the cement.

One voice yelled, "Quiet."

To no avail. By this time, well over five hundred people in the room were awake. More voices intoned, "Q u i e t."

Some of the youngster's faces turned briefly; then they continued their talk about the fun they had skiing in Vail for Spring Break.

Next, one of the many truck drivers lifted his heavy body up and out of his sleeping position and stood up. He stretched his wide shoulders backward, stroked his unruly, graying hair out of his face, and started walking towards the group.

Other beefy truck drivers followed suit at once. They wore high-heeled cowboy boots, leather vests over short sleeve shirts and had their wallet on a chain attached to their massive belts. They all looked huge.

Good-natured, they are mostly known to be gentle, polite men. They display great courtesy on the road, mostly observing all the rules of the highway.

But when they get mad, I would not want to be in their way. And mad they were. For good reasons, it was obvious enough.

The kids kept yakking along, switching to another all-night rock station, more distant than the last one, so the radio was cranked up louder. They did not notice the truckers approach their group in a wide circle. At least fifteen truckers they were.

The circle became narrower as the big guys came closer. They stopped about two feet away from the group and encircled it in a tight formation. No escape would have been possible.

Then, finally, the loudmouthed leader of the kids lifted his head and saw the bodies around him. He turned his face halfway, threw back his head in a cocky manner and said:

"What do you want?"

"Shut the radio off. Everyone wants to sleep," said the trucker who had gotten up first.

"We turn the radio off when we are ready," said the kid.

"You turn off that radio NOW," said another brawny trucker.

"I don't take orders from nobody," snapped the kid.

"Dammit, turn the f...... radio off N O W."

"Hey, man, that's an insult. I'll get you for that," shouted the leader.

He started to rise, to get on his feet. He was big, all right, a football player type.

The circle of the truckers drew closer around the group. The arrogant leader stood defiantly in their middle.

"Last time," said the burly trucker again, in a dangerously soft voice, "NOW."

Nothing happened. The seven other guys sat on the floor in disbelief. They looked as if they were not so sure of their leader anymore.

The truckers moved their hands out of their jean pockets— big hands, those used to handle big steering wheels of heavy rigs. They formed into huge balls. Their legs were slightly spread apart.

There was a moment of silence. Then the kid broke down.

"Larry, shut it off," he called out to the group below his feet. Someone did instantly.

The truckers returned to their sleeping spots. The kids silently stretched out on the cement. Quietness finally returned.

But before everybody started snoring again, there was to be heard a female voice from one corner of the hall, saying one word only, loud and clear:

"Bravo."

I awoke at seven, got up immediately and stretched my stiff limbs. The bathrooms were now in more of a mess than ever before. They were practically flooding over. Because of it, the toilets had been shut off. Because of it, there was no coffee either, since the water was shut off altogether. Food was sold out as well. And the staff from the night before, on duty now for almost twenty-four hours, had rolled up on the floor too, to catch some well deserved sleep.

But fortunately, truck stops have large gas pump areas. Ours had twenty-six pumps in six rows. So it would not take long to fill up a car in spite of everyone wanting to leave.

Then the sun came up in the east and rose into a pale blue, cloudless sky. The thermometer at the gas pumps indicated two below zero. There was a howling wind from the northwest; straight out of the Yukon it seemed.

I started the Ford, way out there on the icy parking field, by seven thirty. It cranked to life at once. Before I was out on the road, I filled up 14.5 gallons of gas. The tank capacity was listed in the car's manual as 14.9 gallons. Close call!

Then I rolled out, across the clumpy, icy service road to the entrance ramp of the Interstate. The snow wall was still there, except now it had been pressed down by crossing cars and trucks. But by now, it was also no longer soft. It had turned into crystal-clear ice which had to be crossed as a hurdle would, in long distance running. I found some stale cookies in the back seat and left-over, bitter, and cold tea in my thermos. Both served well as some much needed nourishment.

Soon after leaving, I came to the intersection of Interstates 80 and 76, the first continuing west to San Francisco, the latter heading southwest to Denver. Half an hour later, I crossed the state line and entered Colorado. Instantly, the pavement became bare and dry. It had been well-plowed during the night. And the rising sun had nicely dried it out.

The Ford zoomed along again at 75 mph as if nothing had ever happened. Strange, I thought, things like a blizzard we normally see on television in the evening news. We look at it in horror, feel sorry for the folks involved and flick the remote again for our favored evening program. We tend to think such events are somewhere else, they happen to others, not to ME!

But they do. And when they do, they make a person realize real quick how dependent we all are on our little conveniences of the twentieth century.

I did arrive in Denver after lunch, took a long, hot shower in the company gym's locker rooms, dictated a couple of reports and attended a brief meeting.

And yes, I checked into St. John's Hospital shortly before five.

And yes, I welcomed the peace and quiet of my heated room and the softness of my bed.

Even the thought of surgery the next day was a lot more pleasant than the ordeal of the night before.

But from there forward, I developed a special kind of admiration for those burly men in their big rigs. I respect them for what they did at the truck stop. And I show my appreciation by flicking my headlights when they pass me and wish to swing back to the right lane.

Kind as most of them are, they will in return flash their brake lights twice. It means "thank you"!

1980 COUSINS

My maternal grandfather, Carl Luyken, was born in Huize Landfort, Holland, the youngest of ten children. When their parents passed away, his oldest brother Albert inherited the family's country home, which included some 2,000 acres of timberland and a dairy farm. It was customary in those days that primogeniture prevailed, whereby the oldest always inherited the family domicile. Albert, however, was obliged to provide for his siblings, and so my grandfather, Carl, obtained a similar country home called Sonsfeld, not far away. Both straddled the Dutch-German border. Landfort was located in Holland near Gendringen, and Sonsfeld across the border in Germany, near Anholt.

When their father died, his will stipulated that the brothers pay out their sisters. My grandfather, Carl, was strapped for cash and would have been forced to take a mortgage on his property. Stingy fellow that he was, he refused to do so and sold Sonsfeld in order to satisfy his sisters. He bought a villa in Boppard on the Rhine River, where my mother was married to my dad.

When the French occupied Germany after World War I, they seized the Boppard property and made it the stately residence of their commanding general. My grandfather, Carl, told them he was Dutch but they weren't interested. He couldn't stand the French anyway. He retreated back to Holland and settled in a town house near Arnhem.

After the French left, Boppard was ultimately sold. After he left, Carl never set foot in it again. As a matter of fact, in his remaining seventeen years of life, he never even returned to Germany.

My mother was born in Sonsfeld. But her parent's Dutch nationality made her Dutch as well, according to *JUS SANGUINIS*, Latin for blood law, which governed most European Nations.

But Landfort was saved for the family. After all, the country home had already been in the hands of the Luykens for centuries. It started out as a moated castle at the time it was built around 1600. *Landfort is een oud Kasteel met vier toorens van sonderlijk maaksel,* wrote a chronicler about the place, meaning Landfort is an old castle with four towers of an extraordinary appearance.

The house would be passed on to Albert's son, Albert Jr. As the oldest son, he would be next in line to inherit, keep and maintain it. But he and his Danish wife already lived there when I was a teenager. They occupied a small apartment in one of the wings. With some thirty-two rooms, the house was big enough for everyone.

Their twin sons were my age. Pardon, I was older than they were. I would rub that in at any opportune time. Five months and one day older. They were born ten minutes apart. Albert first, then Johann. Nobody called them by those names, though. They were Abbi and Jobbi to everyone. They were my closest buddies at the time.

I spent many summer vacations in Landfort when I was in my early teens. I would be there for at least two months. The

twins and I were an inseparable trio. We were also into everything, probably a pest to Uncle Albert Senior and Uncle Albert
Junior. But old Aunt Bars, Albert Senior's wife of some fifty
years and the undisputed lady of the house, would hug us often,
give us candy and chocolate and call us *shratteboutche*, which
translated to "darling." Since I never knew my maternal grandmother Lientje, Carl's wife, I quickly adopted Aunt Bars as my
substitute. It was not a difficult chore, because I adored her.

As Landfort was built as a water burg in the late 16th century, the moat was still in place and is to this day. The entrance to
the mansion's circular driveway and its stately dual front door
led across an old drawbridge. Opposite the drawbridge were
the horse stables. In their upper floor lived Gerritt and his wife.
He tended the horses and also functioned as the horsehandler/
chauffeur, either with horse-drawn carriages or the first automobiles the family had as early as 1902.

The spacious, park-like forest and meadows surrounding
Landfort, —some twenty acres or so, were our vast playground.
Hide and seek, pony riding, tree climbing and swimming in the
Ijssel, the small river separating Holland and Germany, were
our favorite pastimes day after day after day.

The pigeon tower by the moat was an especially gruesome
and mysterious place for the imagination of growing boys.
With a height of a two story building, the birds would use the
pigeon holes on the tower's outside to slip in and build their
nests. From down below, we couldn't see the animals but could
hear them distinctly gurgle along. Our imaginations would go
wild with thoughts of what all these birds were doing up there.

"But where do they go to the bathroom?" I asked.

"Just take a deep breath," Abbi would say and laugh.

Uncle Albert Senior had also designed a paddle-wheel device which would fit across the heavy, wooden row boat. It was anchored on each side by one heavy leather loop to hold it in place. Gerrit had built it for the twins when they were old enough to be left alone with the raft on the moat. By turning the device, the wheels on both sides would rotate and propel the boat forward. The three of us would spend hours each day circling Landfort on the moat, dreaming of present and future things as all boys do.

We were unusually close. If we had an argument or disagreement, there would be two against one, as is natural in a threesome and also beneficial for any democratic decision. While one might think that I was always the lonely single vote because the twins were twins, it did not always turn out that way. As often as not, one of the twins voted along with me. Which made our being together a delight and cemented us together even more.

In Holland, lunch is a light meal, and dinner, as the main event of the day, is served early, about six in the evening. After sharpening the long carving knife over a grinding stone, Uncle Albert Senior would carve the roast beef. His long-handled knife and fork had a buck's horn as handles. While slicing the meat ever so thin, his tongue would be wedged between his lips and we knew he was not to be disturbed while performing this evening ritual.

The twins flanked him, imitating their grandfather, and I, sitting next to Aunt Bars at the other end of the table, had a heck of a time not to burst out laughing. Aunt Bars, in her great wisdom, probably knew why she had arranged the seating that way, separating the three of us.

After supper, Aunt Bars would invariably entertain their ever-present house guests, by playing chamber music in the music salon. We would be asked to go upstairs, take our baths and get ready for bed.

What Aunt Bars never knew, or pretended not to know, was that we sat for hours on the upper step of the spiral staircase, listening to a concert of Vivaldi or J.S.Bach and to the grownup chatter during intermissions. From our vantage point, we could see her sitting on the extreme forward edge of her stool, in front of her piano or spinet, her Ben Franklin glasses on the tip of her nose, trying desperately to read the notes and never really succeeding because of her extreme nearsightedness.

But she knew those pieces by memory and never once stumbled across a single note. We just adored her and loved her like any grandson should.

All these events occurred when the world lay in her very last throws of a gracious period in which violence was not really known, when Europe had enjoyed the unprecedented period of some twenty years of peace.

My last such summer vacation was spent in Landfort during July and August of 1939. A month later, Europe embarked on a bloody war, which lasted six years and destroyed not only much of her cities but also changed her way of life forever.

Heavy fighting rolled back and forth across Landfort, in the months following the Allied invasion of June 6, 1944. Heavy artillery fire destroyed most of the park-like grounds surrounding the mansion. Many of the centuries-old oak and beech trees fell. The venerable manor house itself was mostly a roofless and room-less shell. Just one of the wings was intact enough for Uncle Albert Junior and his family to inhabit.

Uncle Albert Senior did not live to see the demise of Landfort.

Aunt Bars, in her upper eighties, died shortly after peace finally came in 1945.

Since I was free to roam through Europe again immediately after May 8, 1945, I set out to visit Landfort in the fall of that year. Aunt Bars had just passed away. Uncle Albert Jr. was away on a trip. His Danish wife Musse, the twin's mother, refused to see me. She had stood apart from the family for as long as I knew her.

Abbi lived in Amsterdam. Jobbi felt crowded in the tightness of small Holland. He went to live in Monrovia, Liberia. Gerrit had aged more than the six years since I'd seen him and looked starved and thin. The pigeon tower still stood, so did one half of the mansion. An era had ended, never to return!

Soon thereafter, I went to study in France, then later returned to the United States. But in 1967, on a visit to Europe with my then eleven year old son, Peter, I took him to Landfort. Gerrit had died. Musse again refused to see us.

Uncle Albert Junior had tried to rebuild Landfort, with the limited resources he possessed—to no avail. Yet he at least managed to roof the entire building to prevent further deterioration from the weather. In the end, the huge taxes levied on the property in post-war, socialized Holland drained all his reserves.

So, in the late sixties he gave up. He offered Landfort to the Dutch Government as a historic landmark, under the condition that it be kept as such for centuries to come. In return, the Government gave him living rights in the house which were to be transferred to the oldest Luyken son of each following generation. After his father died, Abbi returned from Amsterdam and lived in the house.

The Dutch Government restored most of the inside rooms, and called it officially "Huize Landfort." But to this day, the rooms are empty, devoid of furniture. Whatever was not destroyed during World War II, Abbi and Jobbi Luyken kept.

Much of what was found behind the artificial walls of the mansion during the rebuilding period—silverware, Delft China, old books, all of that dating back to around 1600—was donated to the Rijks Museum in Amsterdam.

Why artificial walls in a house the size of Landfort? One of my greatgreatgreat grandmothers had them built when the thirty-year war broke out in Europe in 1618, to hide her treasures from the marauding French and Swedes. By the time the war ended in 1648, she had long died and the following generations never knew about those hidden treasures.

The twins and I lost contact. We lived far apart, one in Landfort, one in Monrovia and I in North Carolina.

In the late eighties, about fifty years after my last summer vacation spent with the twins in Landfort, my sister visited with Abbi. She called me afterwards and told me everything she had heard about the twins.

"And Abbi told me that Jobbi's son, John, is going to school in Minneapolis," she said on the transatlantic wire. "I thought that you would want to know because your son, Peter, lives there as well."

I called Peter at once.

"Son, find your cousin, John Luyken. He is studying for his CPA at one of the colleges in the Twin Cities. Maybe you want to meet with him. After all, you are related, cousins once removed," I told him.

"Sure thing, Dad."

He tried. He started with the University of Minnesota, then Macalester, then every other school in town. To no avail. No John Luyken was listed anywhere.

I wrote Jobbi the following day: "Where is John? Give me his address."

Weeks went by. Mail in Liberia was often lost or stayed in some remote corners of the postal service facilities.

Finally a reply came. "He is not in school right now, but rather driving a taxicab. Because of the revolution here in Liberia, I cannot send him any money. So he had to interrupt his studies," wrote Jobbi.

Peter found him on first try. "Come over for dinner, John," he told him on the phone. "Becky and I would like to link up with you."

"When?"

"Next Friday, about six in the evening. Okay?"

"Fine. But I have a friend."

"Bring him along," Peter said.

Friday evening, shortly after six, the door bell rang at Peter and Becky's house in Minneapolis. They both walked to the front door to open it. And then, there they stood, motionless. Their chins dropped! They didn't manage to utter one single word!

A young black man, stood before them, with a ravishingly beautiful black woman at his side.

"Peter, I am your cousin John Luyken and this is my girlfriend Maria. Aren't you going to ask us in?"

"Of course, come in. DO come in, please," said Peter after their initial reaction had subsided.

Jobbi wrote later that he had never married. But his business of importing European machinery into Liberia took him often into the interior of the country. He maintained a big house on the Atlantic Ocean in Monrovia where he housed at all times eight to ten children from the tribes of the interior sections, to afford them a better education in the country's capital. He himself had two children whom he had fathered. Both had different tribal mothers.

Maria's maiden name was Morgan. She is a descendant of one of the earlier slave families to which President Monroe had offered a chance to return to Africa and settle down in Liberia which he created for that purpose. Liberia's first head of state was no other than a Morgan: Maria's great-great-great-grandfather was an American slave who had returned to the country when the new republic's first constitution was voted into law on July 26, 1847. Liberia's currency is still the US Dollar, its official language English.

John and Maria were married in Minneapolis two years later. At their wedding, there were only guests from Liberia, in the US for one reason or another. Peter, six foot four, was the only white guest present. He was undoubtedly not from Africa.

So others asked him, "how did you get invited to John's wedding?"

"I am his cousin."

"You are WHAT?"

Jobbi died a few years ago from liver and kidney complications. Soon thereafter, a second and fiercely bloody revolution in Liberia made it impossible for John and Maria, as descendants of the "ruling elite," to return to their home country. Jobbi did not witness anymore the tearing apart of his country of choice.

But it was rewarding for Jobbi and myself to know that the tradition of cousins lived on, under rather drastically changed circumstances, in a setting totally different from Landfort, in the NEW WORLD!

The two of them are quite a bit more than five months apart in age. And one is six foot four, blond, with a full reddish beard and outspoken Scandinavian features. The other is shorter, with a distinct Dutch face of a milk chocolate color. But other than that they are cousins who do not get into trouble in Landfort during school vacations but rather play basketball together in their free time.

Aunt Bars would have hugged and called them *shratte-boutches*. She would have loved the two of them had she lived long enough to witness this reunion of the next generation.

STUDYING THE MAP FOR POINTS WEST, BIG BIG, 1983

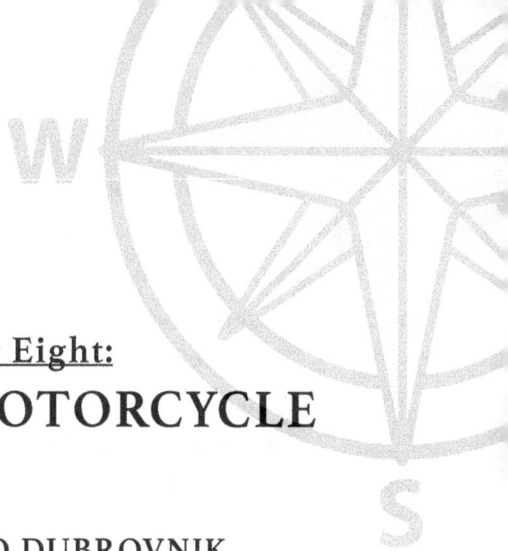

Chapter Eight:
TRAVELS BY MOTORCYCLE

1953 THE ROAD TO DUBROVNIK

In 1953, I traveled into the Yugoslavia of Marshal Tito. I rode my BMW R25 motorcycle and was equipped to camp as often as I wanted, or had to for lack of accommodations.

Crossing the border from Klagenfurt, Austria, south on Loibl Pass, 4,225 ft in elevation, I saw a small hut below the crest. In front of it, a wooden gate blocked my further progress.

I waited, shut off the engine. Nothing happened. Five minutes went by. I knew that impatience would get me nowhere. I waited some more.

Then suddenly, all the might of Tito's dictatorial regime descended on me, in the form and shape of six heavily armed border guards who had obviously eyed me from within the building.

They were in absolutely no hurry to please a traveler from another country by clearing him through expediently.

They surrounded the Beemer. They barked out orders in broken German for me to get off. And when I did not immediately respond, they grabbed my jacket and pulled me out of the saddle, threw me against the station's wall and frisked me from head to toe.

They found nothing. I waved my passport in front of their eyes, which they could not read because they didn't speak English.

Their concern and confusion was augmented by the fact that the BMW had a German license plate and white international sign "D" for Deutschland in the back. But it also displayed an AAA chrome oval emblem on the front fender.

The chief border guard pointed to the front fender.

"What?" he demanded.

"American Automobile Association," I replied.

Silence. Puzzled faces. Discussions in Croatian.

"Auto Club, America." I added.

Silence again. More discussions in Croatian. My heart pounded.

Then a small smile appeared on the guard's face. I never knew why. I did not dare to ask. Nevertheless, he took my passport, driver's license and registration and disappeared into the building, the other five guys trailing him single file.

I fried outside in the hot August sun, leaning against my bike.

An hour passed. Again, nothing happened. No word from the guards. No explanation either. I knew they were inside, the six of them.

I heard them talking and laughing. But I did not think it to be wise to follow them into the hut to see what was going on.

Another hour or so, and the chief guard came out, handed me my papers, smiled for the first time and sent me off with a Prussian style salute, hand flat on his cap's rim, elbow stretched out straight.

During the entire two hour procedure, no one else had crossed the border in either direction.

"Bon voyage," he shouted after me in his guttural tongue.

Danke schoen, I hollered back, waving my left arm.

Welcome to Yugoslavia!

I traveled down through Lubljana where I desperately looked for a gas pump. Finally, the only one I found, on the south side of town, was mounted on the sidewalk and had just enough of the liquid left to get me going again. It was still 127 kilometers, or seventy-nine miles, to Opatija, on the shore of the Adriatic, where I wanted to sleep that night, But in the Yugoslavia of 1953, it took well over four hours to get there because the condition of the road was so bad. I stayed two nights in this Adriatic Spa full of politicos.

Two days later, I went back twenty-six kilometers east to the port city of Rijeka and found a much needed gas pump, by the edge of the sidewalk. Again, I waited. And waited some more. It took the owner fifteen minutes to finally come out and fill my tank, smiling all along through his almost toothless mouth. Nowhere in the country was I ever allowed to do that job myself. And more than once, gasoline spilled all over the tank onto the hot engine.

Then it was back to the highway southeast, now heading straight to Dubrovnik, along the gorgeous coastline of the Adriatic. I rejoiced at its smooth pavement which let me enjoy the vistas out to sea without paying too much attention to the riding. I was whistling and happy to see that this stretch of the 404-mile road was obviously much better than the AAA road service had told me.

Then without any warning, the pavement stopped and the roadway abruptly devolved into the one-foot lower dirt trail. It also narrowed to about half the former width. Its shoulders now became fieldstone walls, its surface loose gravel.

I hit that spot at sixty kilometers per hour. I barely managed to keep the machine level and myself in the saddle. NO WARNING SIGNS ANYWHERE!

That was the last pavement I saw in Yugoslavia. The rest of the 382 miles to Dubrovnik were narrow, rough and unpaved, but beautiful beyond belief.

It took me seven days to travel the distance. The dust was thick, the ruts were deep, stray cattle were everywhere, and goats and sheep considered the roadway their domain. They were not used to motor vehicles of any kind. They never moved even if I honked at them. Only patience and waiting prevailed.

But then, who cares. The scenery was magnificent, the weather hot, the sun bright every day, all day, and definitely no need for a rain suit.

In the small hamlets along the way, I found tiny stores, often located in the kitchens of farmhouses, to buy goats milk, cheese from the sheep and fruit from the abundant orchards inland. And there was always a great, crusty farmer's bread available. I would take these provisions out with me to a meadow somewhere along the dusty road; I could pitch my tent on soft ground, not far from the water and mostly right on the Adria's edge. I lived spartanly and consumed what the country had to offer.

Among those offerings was a local wine, a jug of which I surely wanted with me at all times, dangling from my duffle bag strapped onto the Beemer's back rack. It was much preferable to the traditional Slibowich—which is a grain-made, 40% alcohol schnapps-type spirit most often consumed with a chaser of beer.

Almost always, during those six nights in my tent along the coast, I was able to walk right out of its open flaps into the crystal clear water of the Adria, to cool, or cleanse, or both.

During the noon heat, I would find a Gastonia, as country inns were called, in some village I happened to pass through. People would at once gather around my loaded motorcycle, but here, in contrast to the larger cities, no one would touch it or steal any of my gear. I would eat then what the owners of the establishment served up on a plate, often not knowing what it was that I ate, Neither did they have a menu nor could I have understood.

Just as often, they would invite me to come into the kitchen and see for myself what was boiling in the pots.

Afterwards, I would stretch out on a stonewall under a shade-giving tree and indulge in an hour of siesta.

One night, south of Sibenik, I could not find a spot near the water. So I set up camp on a small meadow where sheep were gazing. They just lazily lifted their heads to see who was causing the commotion, then continued their eating routine. Soon thereafter, they lay down because they knew by instinct that the sun would set at any moment. I heard their scratching all night.

The next morning when I awoke and stuck my head out through the flaps to sleepily see what the new day looked like, I noticed a small parcel in front of my tent, wrapped in a Dalmatian-language newspaper. I crawled out altogether in my briefs, opened the package, and saw a piece of goat cheese with a slice of brown bread in the newsprint.

Puzzled, I looked around searchingly because I knew I was all alone there with the sheep. But there were two farmers, a man and a woman, working in the fields nearby. They looked at me, wearing my scanty outfit, then pretended not to see me while raking their field.

I held up the parcel high and called out, "Hello!"

Then they smiled and bowed their heads. I waved back in gratitude, and then called out,

"Thank you. *Danke schoen!*"

It was a deeply touching gesture of welcome to me as a total stranger in their land, made by people who had hardly enough to eat for themselves.

The following day, I rolled into the ancient city of Split, or Spljet as it was called in Croatian. It was once Spalato when the Italians settled there during the fifteenth century. I whiled away one whole day sightseeing, window shopping, eating, resting. Days like that are needed once in a while on long journeys.

I would have loved to stay overnight in one of the small country inns the town provided. But my tight travel budget did not allow for such extravagances. I had to save my lodging money for the nights in Dubrovnik and some of the spots in Italy, Switzerland and Germany on the return trip where I knew I could not camp.

But then camping had been gorgeous in this country so far. No campgrounds, of course, but Mother Nature provided ample space for pitching a tent. So, after a light evening meal on the patio of a simple eatery by the bay, I mounted the Beemer again and headed out of town on the dusty road south in search of my usual campsite on a meadow. Yet there was nothing but rocks and steep drop offs to the water below. Very picturesque, no doubt, but not what I needed most.

In the small hamlet of Krilo, twenty-five kilometers south of Split, I stopped. It had turned dark. I was tired and my vision was obscured by my sunglasses full of sweat and dust. I got off and knocked on the crude, wooden door of a low hut across the street.

No answer. I knocked again and after another pause, an old man cranked open the screeching door a crack, eyed me with apprehensive suspicion and waited. I gestured with my arms stretched out to indicate my desire to lie down somewhere.

When he looked puzzled, I placed my right hand under my cheek and pretended to snore.

He stared at me for while, searchingly, thinking. Then he called out something in his native Croatian into the depth of the house behind him.

A distant voice answered. Finally he smiled faintly, and then gestured for me to push my bike around the house, through a gate which was not locked, into the courtyard where the man emerged from the back door of his house. He pointed to a small outbuilding on the opposite side of the court, opened its door, smiled, bowed, and retreated back into his abode.

I placed the Beemer on her center stand, making sure it would not tip over on the soft ground of the man's yard. Then I took my flashlight out of the duffel as there was no electricity, walked through the door too low for my height and explored the place of my night's lodging. Inside the outbuilding, my flashlight's beam bounced off a large number of bright spots—round, multicolored buttons. In reality, I had descended upon a peaceful herd of goats that had all been awakened by the noise and now opened their eyes to see the cause. But they were too sleepy to get onto their feet and stayed where they were resting.

"Okay, guys, move over, here I come," I told my companions for the night.

But this time I did not unpack my shaving gear and fresh underwear as I normally do. I also left the sleeping bag in the duffel, for fear that it would smell like goat dung for the rest of the trip if I used it. I just rolled up my white ski jacket into a bedroll and stretched out on the floor. I did not need a blanket. The goats took care of heating the place albeit in some sort of smelly way.

About five thirty the next morning, the farmer came in to guide his flock of goats out to pasture. They would have trampled all over me had I not hurriedly gotten up. This time, I was ready to roll out of there in as long a time as it took me to string my ski jacket back on the bike.

But a stout woman, presumably the farmer's wife, gestured me into her very simple kitchen. There stood a glass of cool goat milk she had poured from a pitcher which was stored all night in the crawl space under her house where it was cool. With it came a piece of dry corn bread.

I offered to pay her for food and lodging, but she shook her head vehemently. Obviously this did not work, so instead I stretched out my hand as a gesture of friendship and appreciation, but she did not grab and shake it. According to local custom, I found out later, women were not allowed to talk to men or touch them, except their own family. Finally then, I bowed my head which she accepted gratefully with a faint smile.

Ah, those wonderful people who inhabit Yugoslavia! How different they were from the armed border guards and the politicos buzzing around in big Zis limousines, in the resort of Opatija.

I was out on the road at six and did not regret it. Early mornings are beautiful in that part of Europe,—cool, crisp, and full of life and promise. It was another 202 kilometers, or seven hours ride, to Dubrovnik—my final destination in the country. The town is a small port on the Dalmatian coast and the most picturesque spot of all places I had seen along the Adria. There were splendid houses dotting the hills, surrounded by lush gardens and well-paved palm-lined streets leading to them. But Zis limousines were everywhere again, attesting to the presence of a privileged few.

Ordinary citizens were not even allowed to enter.

By five in the afternoon, I found a garage with a mechanic who spoke German. He changed the Beemer's oil, long overdue, and it dripped into the pan the color of coal. "How does Bimvee run on Yugoslav petroleum?" the bearded man asked.

"Poorly. Why?"

"Yugoslav petroleum only 76 octane," he said laughingly. No wonder the engine had pinged since Lubljana.

I checked into a small hotel in the center of town for $5.50 a night. It even featured a bathroom down the hall. I stayed two nights in this enticing city and enjoyed its beauty, which was largely destroyed during Yugoslavia's civil war of the 1990s.

On the third morning at seven, the sun rising over Albania to the southeast, I boarded the ferry for an all-day journey across the emerald waters of the Adriatic Sea to Bari, Italy. As Dubrovnik disappeared in its unbroken, beautiful glory when the big ship pulled out of its port with my Beemer in its hold, I leaned on the railing and looked back, wondering if I would ever see this poor but charming country again.

I have never returned.

1981 BRIAN

On a motorcycle journey through the southwest, one summer day in 1981, I ventured into Mexico for the first time and visited Puerto Penasco, on the coast of the Sea of Cortez.

Filling up with a first load of Mexican gasoline from Petromex, the stateowned Mexican oil company, I soon experienced some sputtering in the bike's engine, making it unwise to continue my travels in Mexico without proper service. But such service was not available in that small fishing town. I decided to return briefly to Arizona to have it done and then come back into Mexico at Nogales.

I traveled on my Kawasaki 750cc two cylinder motorcycle. Its name was Willy. It was no longer new. I had covered thousands of miles in the United States and Canada with it. Although I frequently serviced the bike myself, the engine had run rough already on the way west, sputtering a lot. Before going into Puerto Penasco, I had a dealer in Tucson look at it, and it checked out fine.

Now, however, I was hoping to get home before more serious problems occurred. The engine just did not sound right. But the dealer in Tucson checked it out again and said it was running okay.

Alright then, back to Mexico. On the way down, I saw a sign along the Interstate leading to the border. It pointed out the old Tumacacori Mission. Since I was in no hurry, I thought I'd better stop and see what it was all about.

Entering the Mission through its massive, carved wooden portal, I found the National Park Service office to my right and checked my helmet with the ranger on duty.

"Sure, will do that. Mind if I keep an eye on your bike? Not that people do any harm around here, but you never know," he said.

"Would appreciate it, thank you."

Then I was on my way through this marvelous example of early Spanish development in the Arizona valley stretching from Nogales to Tucson. I strolled around at ease and enjoyed the new policy of the National Park Service to now only partially reconstruct and restore ruins of worth. This eliminates human error and leaves the original shape up to the viewer's imagination.

I had noticed a family before, strolling leisurely through the museum and courtyard. Grandparents, parents and four very blonde kids were a delight to watch. They were also in the auditorium when I came in to see a slide show explaining the Mission's history. I found a seat apart from the others. I became deeply engrossed in the history of this first Catholic outpost of the Spaniards and fascinated by its construction and how it withstood decades of desertion.

Then, without noticing anyone near me, a small hand found its way into my big paw. The youngest of the kids had decided to sit near me to ask,

"Can I have a ride on your motorcycle, Brian?"

"Sure thing, but I am not Brian, you know."

He did not quite understand, as he was barely five years old.

"What's your name?" I inquired of my newly gained friend.

"Johnny."

"Okay, Johnny, nice to meet you. My name is Peter. You know, like Peter Pumpkin-eater."

Johnny grinned. He could relate to that.

"But why did you call me Brian?"

"My dad has a brother. He has a motorcycle. He is Brian."

"Okay, Johnny, now I understand."

From then on, for the rest of my tour through the Mission, Johnny did not move from my side. I seemed to have become his hero, his role model.

When we encountered his parents and grandparents who looked puzzled and somewhat worried about Johnny's new company, he introduced me to them:

"This is Brian, no, Pumpkin-eater. Naa, his name is Peter."

We all laughed and shook hands. Then the parents and also

the grandparents told Johnny to call me Mister. Johnny piped up,

"But he did not tell me his last name."

I told Johnny and the older folks that it was all right for him to call me by my first name.

A little later, out in front of the Mission, they all waited for me because I had told Johnny earlier that I'd give him a ride around the parking lot. He was waiting and ready.

Afterwards, as could be expected, his brothers and sister wanted rides too, and I asked Grandma if she wanted one also.

"Heavens, no," was her horrified reply.

Johnny got his ride, but when it was his sister's turn, Willy quit. And I mean quit! Nothing would do to start the motor again.

Mr. and Mrs. Whitmire, the grandparents, suggested that I have lunch with them across the street. We all walked over and entered the small place which was tastefully decorated in a lot of different colors, reminding us of the proximity to our southern neighbor Mexico. I did not want to impose myself onto the family but upon their insistence, had a cup of soup and many crackers with it.

The kids fought over who was next to tell me something or ask a question. By now, everybody called me Peter Pumpkin-eater. After lunch, we went outside, hoping Willy would start. No way. Willy did not budge. The kid's faces dropped, because I had promised the other three youngsters that ride around the parking lot after lunch. I was sure Willy would start then.

But Willy did not give a sound, except "whufff," and I became a bit frantic. After all, the Mission was in the middle of nowhere.

Grandfather Whitmire and his son-in-law, Robert, got down into the sand with me to find out what was wrong. We couldn't find anything wrong. I then walked over to the phone booth, consulted the yellow pages but did not detect a listing for an accredited motorcycle dealer in Nogales, the next town right at the border. Except there was a Kawasaki dealer listed in Tucson which was sixty miles to the north. Of course I knew him; I had been there twice.

But then there was a listing "Pedro and Pablo Motorcycles" in Nogales. I dialed Pedro's number.

"I am over here at the Mission and my 750 does not start," I told Pedro on the phone.

"I have got the same bike you do, so now do this, then that, and then try this."

I went back to the bike and tried. Nothing.

Back to the phone to talk to Pedro again. He gave me some more hints. Again nothing. By this time, even Willy's "whufff" had ceased—not a sound out of him.

"Let's hot wire it," Robert finally said.

I knew that was a risky move, meaning a straight connection from the battery to the spark plugs, eliminating all fuses.

"Let's," I said.

Fortunately, I had a piece of wire in my junk box where I keep odds and ends for exactly such occasions. It was barely long enough to stretch from the condenser to the battery.

But Willy sprang to life at once! It was beautiful music coming out of his exhaust pipes. And I did not shut the engine off anymore and in the commotion of my impending departure shook hands all around and mounted the bike.

"No, kids, you can't have a ride anymore, Peter Pumpkineater has got to go," said grandfather Whitmire, wiping his face with hands oily from trying to fix my bike. I put Willy in first gear, flipped down my face shield, gave the thumbs up sign to little Johnny and roared off.

On the way down to Pedro, I all of a sudden remembered that I had forgotten to ask for the Whitmire's address. I turned around, went back to the Mission and looked for them. But they had already left. How could I now thank them once more by writing a note?

But Grandfather Whitmire had said earlier:

"You would have helped us too if we had been in a bind, wouldn't you?"

Yes, sir, you bet I would. Thanks, folks, wherever you are.

1981 PEDRO AND THE
MEXICAN WHOREHOUSE

Willy, my Kawasaki 750cc motorcycle I was traveling with, still sputtered at high speeds going back again on Interstate 17 in Arizona, down towards Mexico. I had visited Tumacacori Mission not far from Nogales and was now speeding back to town in order to have Willy looked at by Pedro and Pablo Motorcycles, a name I had found in the yellow pages at the Mission.

But they were already closed for the day. I rolled back into town from their place at the outskirts and checked into the Mission Motel where the room rate was $12.00 per night. It was okay as twelve dollar rooms go but not a place to linger any longer than necessary.

I showered, mounted Willy again and crossed the border to Nogales, in Mexico's State of Sonora, to eat dinner.

Piles of tourists! Tingle tangle left and right! A border town! Not the Mexico the way I know it. I felt lonely and I was worried about Willy and his sputtering. But Pedro should know how to fix it. He had said on the phone that he owned the same bike.

"So Peter, don't worry, be happy," I heard myself say.

I found a place to have some dinner and wolfed down my food without really knowing what I ate. Then I mounted Willy again to return to the Mission Motel over in Nogales, Arizona.

Normally, day trip border traffic is waved through at the US border when it is crowded. Except when people return with a lot of packages, they might be asked what's in them.

But that night turned out to be different. When I rolled up to the booth of the US Immigration and Custom Service, the agent stepped out but did not say a word. Instead he looked at me intensely, then at Willy and its license number. Then he barked out his command:

"Get over there under that roof."

I did, bewildered, because I had crossed borders many times and never seen such an unfriendly agent.

The next guy waited for me outside the door of his building, under the roof, as if summoned by an invisible device. He, too, barked out his commands:

"Get off that bike."

"Yes, sir."

"Open your saddle, flip it up, no, all the way, UP I said."

I did.

"Take your tool kit out."

I did.

"Unpack it."

"Yes," I said under my breath.

"Let me see your duffel. No, ALL of it. Empty the contents.

No, not on the bike—on the ground with it."

"Yes, sir." Anger swelled up in me. Why had I left the duffel strapped on the bike when I checked in? I guessed I was just too tired and hungry to move it inside my room.

"What you got in those saddle bags? Dirty laundry? Yeah, I've heard that before from you guys. Empty them, all of them, on the ground."

No more yes, no more sir, no more yes, sir.

He poked through all my belongings on the asphalt with a stick. He emptied my salt and pepper shakers out of my food bag. He sniffed with suspicion at a plastic box containing my last three aspirin. He poked my shirts and underwear apart with his darned stick.

"Hey, you are ruining my shirts," I finally blurted out.

No answer to that. But after a short while, he continued his interrogation:

"Is that radio hooked up to a network I should know about?"

"WHAT?" I didn't even know what he was talking about. It was just my battery powered AM/FM pocket radio he was inspecting.

"Never mind," he said.

Then he looked me over, from top to bottom. I could sense that he would have loved to make me take off all my clothing, right there on the parking lot. It would not have surprised me, because I felt stripped naked already, a suspected criminal, his dignity shred to pieces. Hate stood in his eyes, spite was written all over his face.

Then, finally, I was told, "You can go."

I couldn't help but ask him coldly: "So, what were you looking for, then?"

"You know darn' well what we are looking for, especially when we see motorcycles with North Carolina plates come back from Mexico."

Of course, I had known all along what he was looking for. I just pretended to him that I didn't. Tensions between the United States and Mexico were running high because of controversial drug enforcement policies. Some of our agents in Mexico had received some rough treatment. One was even killed not long before. Understandably, that placed the customs people on high alert.

I forgave him as I rolled into Nogales. He was just doing what he was told to. Maybe the guy ahead of me had given him a rough time. I went back to my room and had more bourbon than I should have.

Pedro, whom I told the story the next day, wondered why the guy had not checked my bum leg to see if it was artificial.

"You could have carried $2 million worth of cocaine in there," he added.

It took him and his Mexican mechanic until almost 5:30 p.m. to fix Willy. The carbs were cleaned, the mixture screws drilled open and adjusted, new plugs with a different temperature rating installed into the bike. Finally, Pedro took Willy out for a test ride and came back smiling for the first time all day. I was greatly relieved.

Then he suggested that I ride Willy up the road myself to see how it worked. I did. Revving the engine up to 7,000 rpm without any problems, the bike all of a sudden cut out completely and I mean totally!

I quickly found out the problem, though. The day's work on the engine, its many test rides and again removing the carbs for cleaning had successfully drained even the last drop of gasoline out of the tank! And here I was, about two miles away from Pedro's shop, out of gas!

But my luck had it that the road was slightly downhill going back. I could roll, ever so slowly, back down. Pedro and his partner Jerry were already on their bikes, though, coming up the highway, trying to locate me.

In contrast to Pedro who was narrow, short and slender as many Mexicans tend to be, Jerry was a big, brawny fellow. I had not met him in the morning because he was in Tucson. I talked to Jerry off and on all afternoon when he was not busy. He wore a gun in his belt, yet he appeared, and actually was, the friendliest soul around. He had handed me his card when we met, showing the shop's address and phone number. On its back was written Pedro's and Jerry's motto:

"You have just met a biker. When we do right, no one remembers, when we do wrong, no one forgets."

I had no problem with either of these guys. They were friendly, helpful and, naturally, belonged to the large group of motorcyclists among whom the bond is almost instant. When both suggested we go over to Mexico for dinner that night, I wholeheartedly agreed.

I went back to the Mission Motel for another $12.00 night in the same room, to freshen up and this time take all my gear off Willy.

By 6:30 p.m., they came by on their bikes to take me along.

"Peter, you follow Pedro closely, about a bike's length away, and I will be right behind you. That is the way we cross the border," Jerry had said before we left the motel.

In a few minutes, we arrived at the Mexican side. All agents saluted when we did. They waved us right through. They knew both of these men well. Jerry had told me earlier that Pedro teaches karate to the Mexican border guards and police.

We went to a place they both favored. I forgot the name of it. The steaks were enormous, the vegetables hot and spicy, the beer stronger than in the US. When the young ladies paraded by on the sidewalk outside and saw the three bikes parked in an angle, they glanced into the restaurant in a way only they can, with a shy smile, but eyes that said: you are okay.

I picked up the tab, the guys had been good to me, and I wanted to have my chance to reciprocate—steak and beer for three for $15.50!

After dinner, Jerry sat on his BMW facing backwards, his long legs dangling loosely over his saddle bags, talking to the two of us leaning on our bikes. I sensed somehow that they both wanted to say something but did not know quite how. Finally Jerry spoke up:

"We've been wondering. You want to come along now to meet some of Pedro's friends?"

"Sure thing," I said, not really knowing what they had in mind.

But I trusted them.

And so we mounted again and, under the roar of three powerful engines, headed out of town south, into the Sonora desert, dark by now. Our high beams bounced back from menacing looking saguaros in the shape of ghosts. We went riding off far into the hills. The pavement had long ago ceased to exist at the edge of Nogales. The road was deep and powdery dust.

After what appeared to be many miles, we eventually arrived in front of a small, modest looking adobe house. Its only visible attraction was a fairly large balcony on the second floor, its ornamental posts carved from aged saguaro.

"This is a place of entertainment," said Jerry with a twinkle in his eye.

"I see," I answered. But I began to feel somewhat unsure of myself.

Yellow light bulbs were stranded over an arched doorway leading into the building's courtyard. I sensed people behind deeply curtained windows, even heard muffled voices talking rapidly in Spanish which of course I did not understand. Sweet smells mixing with the fresh night air of the desert hung over the entire scene.

My youthful readings of Jack Kerouac's *On the Road* had always left me curious about the interiors of a Mexican whorehouse. I had seen enough of Paul Gauguin's paintings and had consumed the writings of such greats as Steinbeck and Hemingway with intense passion to have a wondering fascination with the ladies of the night. But I had never before set foot into their establishments.

I don't do that.

"Come on, Peter, what are you waiting for?" said Jerry, with that mischievous grin I had come to know and like.

The "hostesses" up on the balcony heard him and giggled over my obvious timidity. Then they descended into the courtyard and led us into the dimly lit bar and dancing area.

The petite brunette who had taken me by my arm spoke little English. She escorted me to the bar while Pedro secured a table for all of us. I bought her a tequila. The bartender gave me a voucher for it which I passed on to her. She in turn stashed the ticket for the drink in her bra instead of having using it. She would later cash it in, along with the many others that were in her bosom, already donated by men she had met before me. She certainly had a matter of fact outlook on life, going about her occupation in a very casual way.

She spoke four words of English versus my three words of Spanish. We smiled a lot at each other rather than talking. Finally, she shrugged, gave me that flash of glittering white teeth set in a dark brown face, and walked away to seek other customers.

I walked over to Pedro's table where a large group of his friends—men and women, lively, laughing, many speaking English—were assembled.

Everyone knew Pedro, it seemed, including many of the customers in the place. One black man from Philadelphia who had been living in Mexico for years, came up and talked to us, suggesting to Pedro the need for money. He left happily after Pedro slipped him a bill.

Shortly thereafter, a tall Swede strode into the bar, deeply blond, lanky, and towering over the Mexicans except Jerry and me. His name was Olaf and he was a young-looking thirty-five, as it was too dark to see him clearly. Pedro knew him too. He also had a bill slipped into his ready hand.

I began to feel uncomfortable. I didn't belong here. So I said to Pedro:

"I think I will check on the bikes outside, so I will just walk over to the balcony and see if they are okay."

Everyone roared with laughter, as they all knew that the balcony was the place where those "hostesses" were lounging; those who were not engaged with customers for the moment.

They were still out there. They were actually nice and very friendly. And lonely. Some knew English quite well and I talked to them mostly, aimlessly, about this or that. They soon figured out that I was really not a prospect. But I was Senor Pedro's friend, someone they knew and honored. I bought cigarettes for everyone. They were laughing then, obviously grateful for my gesture of acknowledgement.

One of them, her name was Felicia, spoke English the best. She had lived in California for a while where she held a job in a predominantly Hispanic hospital. While in the United States, she had read Kerouac as well. We talked philosophies of the road until a new group of men arrived. She kissed my cheek gently and was gliding away into the dimness of the interior, before I could respond.

I followed her inside shortly after midnight, to let the entire scene of the place soak in. By this time, the crowds had peaked, the smoke of cigarettes blended with the sweet smell of cheap perfume which hung heavy in the air. The small band performed enthusiastically, moving their violins and guitars with the rhythms of the songs they played and sang.

I found Felicia sitting at a large table with a number of men and some of the other ladies I had met before. She waved me over and introduced me all around. Whatever she said about me to the group, I only understood "Pedro" and "Gringo." I waved back to all of them.

One of the men pulled up a chair; another ordered a drink for me. We talked in sign language. And with a lot of smiles. Mostly we did not understand each other, but when we did, we all laughed out loud.

Later, Felicia sat down on a chair next to mine, moving from her previous location close to an older Mexican with a Kaiser Wilhelm mustache. A twenty-three year old from the State of Chihuahua, she was a stunning beauty, yet had a warmth about her which I could not quite comprehend, given the profession she was in, or so I thought. I then marveled to her about everyone's hospitality, inviting a total stranger into their midst.

"This is our way of doing it," she replied. "We are close to our family and our friends. That's our way of life as you would say in US, no?"

"When you were in my country, did you make a lot of friends there?"

"Yes and no. Among my countrymen, yes, but with Americans I had little contact, except at work. I guess you are not used to foreigners. But that's alright, I understand."

"Why did you come home again?"

"I was homesick for Mexico. So I came back. I work as a nurse in Nogales. Is good job. And when Americans come here not many find us out here, you know. They are much nicer to me than they were in their home country."

How true it was!

By this time, I had gotten to know her well enough to overcome my inhibitions dating back to a guarded, conservative childhood.

"Would you like to dance with me?" I asked her timidly.

As if she had waited for the question, she threw her head back and gave me the huge smile which Hispanics are so good at, with all her snow-white teeth glistening in the dim light. Then she moved through the crowds to the dance floor ahead of me. I watched her closely as she threaded her way through the steaming, dancing bodies like a jungle cat.

I was much taller and stood more than a head over her. Watching her movements match the Spanish rhythms, feeling her slender, panther-like body mold around my large frame, I felt clumsy towering over her. My nostrils caught her mellow scents which even extended to her long, black hair, combed straight and flowing down her narrow back. When she looked up talking to me, her head would tilt back to reveal an almost Slavic face, with wide cheek bones and black eyes set in a slight angle. Then she would smile at me in an extraordinary submissive way before leaning her head in a somewhat humble manner against my chest again.

No one had ever written about or told me of someone like Felicia!

The band stopped. The music faded away into the human chatter. We both stood motionless, in our dancing position, for a few seconds, as if we both wished the moment to continue forever.

Then suddenly she stepped out of my arms holding her, and before I could say anything, bowing my head to let her know that I was pleased with her company, she thanked me for the dance instead.

Then she was gone, sliding away into the mingling crowds.

I remained standing in the midst of the dance floor, in a daze, reminiscing, sensing the faint fragrance of her perfume clinging to my shirt.

It was shortly before one o'clock.

Jerry, who had waited for me by the edge of the dancing area, came up to where I stood and touched my arm. Over the noise in the place he said into my ear,

"I've got to go back. My date is waiting on the other side. If I stay any longer, she might think I have developed something over here."

"Okay, let's go," I nodded.

I knew Jerry's marriage had broken up and I knew he was trying to build a new relationship and a new life. I did not want to hold him up returning home. And I also needed him as my pilot, because without him I would have never found my way back to the border. Besides, it was fun while it lasted, but this was not my place anyway.

I found Pedro still at his table surrounded by several of the ladies who giggled a lot while he was talking to Olaf.

"See you, Pedro; I am heading back with Jerry. Thanks a bunch."

I felt his slender hand in my big paw and I could detect in his face that he was wondering whether or not he should get up and slap me on the shoulder, in that altogether friendly gesture men often use to express their bonding. But he didn't. Instead he said,

"No problem. I want to wait here for the young lady I've been seeing for a while. See you around. Good luck, and ride safe!"

Jerry and I made our way out to our bikes past all the "hostesses" who bade us good night, expressing their hope that we had a good time. Our mounts were, of course, still out there in the dust, parked in an angle, the three of them. Nobody had touched them. Nobody would. These were Senor Pedro and his friends' bikes.

We mounted, started the engines which came to life with a roar, and then rode slowly through the darkness back into town. We rode from the parts of the desert that tourists rarely visit, into the hustle of people and intense trading still going on at that late hour.

I was following Jerry very closely as he had instructed me to do. At the US border, he talked briefly to the immigration agent, gestured toward me and roared off. The agent waved me right through. What a difference from the first crossing the night before. Jerry's and probably Pedro's stature and influence had helped.

At the Mission Motel, its lights switched off long ago, Jerry got off his BMW, looked me straight into the face and did not say a word. Then suddenly, he gave me one huge bear hug which made me cringe in view of the size of his biceps. But it also made me feel good. He just mumbled "be good" and before I could reply, he was gone.

I left fairly early the next morning after breakfast, although I was groggy from lack of sleep. But I felt the need to get out again, back into the wild open spaces. That is where I felt I now belonged.

On the road to Patagonia, I saw Jerry come up on his white Beemer and we both gave each other the thumbs up once more in passing.

1981 EMMA

And then there was Emma—Señora Emma Torrez. One evening, we dined at El Meson de Santa Eulalia, way up a dusty road into the hills around Chihuahua, Mexico. The restaurant was located in what could have easily been a large patrician home in earlier times. It featured a beautiful spacious inner courtyard. We had dinner there, under the starry and warm evening sky.

In the courtyard's center, Emma and her five friends occupied a large, round table. They had already eaten when we arrived and now, over coffee, were enjoying the music of a ten-member Mexican band that surrounded their large table in a scattered circle.

Emma, in her autumn years and obviously well-to-do, had hired the musicians for the evening, to entertain her and her friends. The occasion was her birthday. My companion Francisco had asked our waiter and he had informed us so.

The band—violins, trumpets and guitars mostly—and its singers played marvelous, melodic Mexican folk songs which so often sound melancholy but always end happily. Once in a while, the band leader would ask Emma to dance with him as there were no men in her group. Then Emma glowed.

Francisco and I had taken a table directly across and next to hers when it was vacated by other guests. We sat down on chairs facing Emma directly, a table length away.

Emma glanced at us briefly, sizing up the new situation and absorbing it with her quick mind. Then she devoted her attention again to her friends, observing our table from time to time from the corner of her eyes.

With my height and complexion obviously an *Americano Norte* and recognized as such, I stared at the whole scene in total fascination. Emma must have noticed it, because every time the band started a new piece, she would throw her head back, displaying all her white, glittering teeth with that Pavarotti smile so typical of Latins and Hispanics—then look intensely at me again.

That made me nervous—quite nervous indeed. As the rhythms got into my blood, the happiness of the songs and softness of the starry sky above me made me want to try some crazy things, like asking her to dance with me, and to perhaps introduce her to some good North Carolina clogging, for which the tunes were perfect. But in the end, I didn't, because I was not familiar with Mexico's habits and customs. Certainly did I not want to offend anyone.

When we finally left a while later, I rose from my chair, stood erect and glanced over to Emma, who had noticed our impending departure. For the briefest seconds, our eyes met. Then, remembering my formal upbringing of another era, I bowed my head slightly towards her. Before I turned around, Emma smiled, tilting her head just as slightly as I had nodded mine.

Nothing more needed to be said.

1991 SKIP

Skip Mascorro owns and operates Pancho Villa Moto Tours from his home base in Bulverde, Texas. He conducts motorcycle journeys into Mexico, and jointly with another person, into Costa Rica, Panama and Argentina. His wife Nancy helps him with administrative matters.

Pancho Villa Moto Tours prides itself on its efficiency. Rightfully so, because it is extremely well-organized and tightly run. It addresses its efforts towards the touring motorcycle enthusiast who appreciates the independence of riding and enjoys the thrill of experiencing new places and meeting new people.

Its excursions are designed accordingly.

During my journeys with Skip, he guided us skillfully and led us through a fascinating country which was still foreign to most of the group participants. Of Spanish and Virginian lineage, Skip was fluent in Spanish and English. A vivid admirer of Pancho Villa, the Mexican revolutionary of the early 20th century, he had a good word and smile for everyone. Like Pancho, he was a true friend of the common man.

During our journeys, Skip became my friend as well. Since we both traveled solo, we shared a room on overnight stays. We got to know each other well.

Skip was always eager to please, thriving on exceeding limitations, an experienced formation leader, and a safety-oriented motorcycle rider. I have respect for him as a man who believes in discipline, family ties and established values, and last but not least, for being a father who adores his young son Eric.

I rode several motorcycle journeys with him into Mexico. Admired in Mexico, motorcycles are the personification of the macho image. It is where its riders are treated with reverence, where local men encircle the bike when parked, admiring but not ever touching. It is where kids are reminded in hushed tones never to touch, just look and dream. Women are allowed only at a distance from the scene.

Flying down the highway at ninety miles an hour is the biker's norm. Police cruisers coming up the opposite lane flash their headlights at these macho friends on two wheels. Not to slow them to the speed limit of sixty-two miles per hour, but to greet them and signal their bonding

I also operated a chase vehicle for him on one other such excursion, driving a car following behind the group, carrying supplies and luggage.

I felt comfortable with Skip and value his friendship.

1987 NONAKA

I first met Nonaka ten years ago in western Colorado, right below the Grand Mesa, on US 50 near Delta. I had stopped there in a parking area along the road, to take a photo of the magnificent table mountain to the east. But I also noticed a small figure sitting at the picnic table under a roof that gave shade against the merciless sun. A motorcycle, loaded with gear, stood nearby, leaning on its side kickstand. I raised my arm in greeting. He waved right back.

He looked like a guy, yet he was too small. As I came closer, I noticed that he was Japanese. He told me then in his halting

English that he was on an assignment given to him by a leading Japanese magazine to photograph the United States and her people and places.

"Flew to Los Angeles. Late March. Bought stuff as you say. Outfitting for trip, right?"

"Did you bring your Kawasaki motorcycle from Japan?" I asked.

"No, bought it in Los Angeles. Is 454 cc, small, yes? You have bigger, no?"

"Yes, I do, a Suzuki GS850. But why so small? Distances in our country are great, a bigger bike would have been better."

"Yes, yes. But my legs, see, are short, no? I can reach ground on Kawasaki, because it is lower than yours."

Good point. I hadn't thought of that. Then I asked, "how about your camping gear and your saddle bags?"

"No, bought all in Los Angeles after I step off airplane."

He then told me that the only thing he brought from Japan was an elaborate knapsack which he carried on his back at all times, even while riding his bike. It had been especially designed and made for him in Japan. It held all his many cameras and lenses as well as numerous rolls of film which he carried with him as a professional photographer.

"I did not know country too well. So I sat down, studied USA on maps, in books, in hotel in Los Angeles."

"When did you leave on your trip?"

"Took about a week in Los Angeles. Mapped a course through USA. Wanted to see all parts of country."

"And now you are on your first leg of your trip?"

"Yes, going on across north to east, then south and back to LA next spring."

"Are you traveling on the Interstate? They are marvelous in our country, you know, get you from place to place in a hurry."

"Me not in hurry. Go second roads."

"You mean secondary, right?"

"Yes, yes." Nonaka said.

I left soon thereafter, on my way north to Montana, Canada and then Alaska. It would be more than two months before I would be home in North Carolina.

In Grand Teton's campground a few days later, I picked a campsite as far away from the motor homes as possible. When I was done, I signed the register, then looked around to check the area, to see where the washrooms were and how much the campsite cost.

And here, lo and behold, right across the way, sat a small figure writing in what looked like a journal, a Kawasaki parked near his tent.

"Nonaka?" I called out.

He jumped up and came over immediately, bowing as he approached and smiling all the way. I then suggested that while we were both here, we could spend some time together. He took that as a happy sign and sat down at once at my table, continuing to smile and not say much. This is going to be difficult, I thought. So I said:

"I didn't mean now. I meant later and perhaps tomorrow. Now I need to sit down and write my thoughts of the day into my journal."

"Hai, hai," he said and ran back to his tent. I started to write. But I could sense he was sitting over there eyeing me all the time. It made me somewhat nervous. What had I gotten myself into now? I just couldn't concentrate. So, after a short while, I closed my journal and waved at him. At once, he came running over and sat down again.

I asked him if he wanted some bourbon and he nodded with a smile.

"Bourbon, strong, yes?"

"You will see."

He took the bottle, put it to his mouth and started drinking. And he drank and drank.

"Stop. You had enough," I finally said laughing.

I told Nonaka that I was on my way to Alaska and would not spend too much time here.

"But I will be glad to ride with you the next couple of days and show you the Tetons and Yellowstone."

He agreed at once.

He did everything at once. I think he was just happy to have found a compatible companion who knew his way around and could point things out to him. He was extremely agreeable.

We camped together again the next two nights. He cooked dinner every evening on his and my backpacker stoves—Japanese style of course. It was fabulously delicious.

He also finished my bottle of bourbon. I had to buy another one, and he finished that too.

We parted in Livingston, Montana, north of Yellowstone. He headed east; I went northwest.

After returning home more than two months later, I found a letter from him. He asked that if I'd write anything about the trip with him, would I please send it to his address in Tokyo.

I did send him a copy of my series of Alaska articles, which I had published in *ROAD RIDER*, a motorcycle magazine.

The following spring, I received a large envelope from Japan.

It was Nonaka who had sent it. It contained a long letter in English and a copy of the Japanese issue of *FIELD AND STREAM.*

At first I had trouble reading it, because it starts from the back and goes to the front. You read it columns down, from right to left, last page to first page. Somewhere in there was my article about Yellowstone with pictures of Nonaka and myself next to our bikes.

To this day, I have not found out what the article said, because I cannot read, or understand Japanese. I can only assume it was what I wrote.

But I trust Nonaka.

1987: THE SALTY DAWG

The M/V Bartlett's loudspeaker awoke me from my thoughts, requesting all passengers to go to their vehicles for landing in Whittier. I had reached the end of my crossing of Prince William Sound from Valdez, Alaska. It had taken seven hours. Now the captain readied the ship to slip into its loading bay. It was three p.m. It rained—heavily. Not exactly ideal weather for motorcycling.

I put on my yellow rain suit, untied the bike, started the engine with a roar and rolled out as the first vehicle off the ship. An employee guided me into the direction of a long train waiting nearby, consisting of two diesel units up front and about thirty to forty flatbed gondolas. I was directed onto the first gondola, by way of an unpaved ramp.

"All the way through, son," hollered the bearded guide of the Alaska Railroad from under the hood of his heavy parka, pointing to the long, even string of gondola flatbeds. "Ride carefully now across those slippery wooden planks. Go all the way to the last gondola, park your scooter on the center stand and go inside the caboose next to it. We don't allow passengers to be outside, during the trip."

"Is it warm in there?" I asked with a laugh on my wet face.

"Sure is, son. Toasty! Tie your bike up, though."

"With what?"

"Don't you have any rope with you?"

"Nope."

"Should have brought some. But wait with that. I'll come by later and give you some."

He did, and in my excitement about tying my machine down for the bumpy ride, I had not noticed the sounding of the engine's horn. When I was done, the train was already moving at a fairly good clip:

"Dee...Ding, Dee...Ding, Dee...Ding..."

The gondolas rocked back and forth. I knew then why I was required to sit inside the caboose. Anyhow, it was indeed warm in there. I peeled off my rain suit. The elevated seat was the best in the house anyway. Built for the brakemen of earlier times, its two seats in the raised portion of the carriage allowed a splendid view in all directions.

The ride through the tunnel to Portage took thirty-five minutes. Twenty minutes were spent in the pitch dark tunnel confines where only the diesel's rotating headlights reflecting on the tunnel walls gave a glimpse of light.

When the train emerged on the western end and I looked around and backwards, I witnessed the gigantic masses of Portage Glacier, the underside of which we had just crossed in the tunnel. All car drivers were not as fortunate. They never saw this sight, sitting in their vehicles facing forward, with all windows closed.

After four pm in Portage's train unloading facility, I rolled off again as the first in line, but not without a handshake expressing my gratitude to the bearded, helpful guide in the parka.

"Ride safe, stay upright," he said. I knew that to be motorcycle lingo.

"Thanks, I will. You riding too?"

"Yes, Harley," he replied. I waved and sped off. It was warm all of a sudden. The rain had stopped. It had not been able to cross the mountain crest which we had passed deep underneath. Soon thereafter the sun came out. My spirits soared.

I had arrived on the Kenai Peninsula, my ultimate goal.

I pitched my tent that evening after six-thirty p.m., on the banks of the Kenai River which bisects the peninsula. The campsite was an ideal spot because it was for tents only and all of them were separated by a wide margin of land.

While I prepared my dinner in my mess kit, I had a bourbon and watched my neighbors, who lounged lazily on the river bank across the water from my tent—the OTHER side of the river, that is.

Those big twelve-hundred pound grizzlies teaching their younguns' how to catch the salmon jumping upstream, left me alone. Their bellies were so stuffed with the abundance of salmon that even the smells of my sautéed beef with broccoli didn't stir any feelings in them. They didn't even glance at me.

Nevertheless, I decided not to take my evening cleansing swim in the river. No use tempting my newly gained friends across the water which was THEIR territory anyway.

I slept like a log for more than ten hours, waking only once to hear the sniffing sounds of mama grizzly near my tent. I lay very still and did not even dare to move my eyelids.

The following morning early, after breaking camp, I looked

for my four legged friends, but they were gone, probably snooz-ing somewhere under a tree like all good persons should do after a plentiful meal.

I rode into Soldotna a few miles down the road and found a roadside cafe where they served a breakfast cooked for lum-berjacks.

Fortified, I left town an hour later to head down the last ninety-two miles along the coastal road to my final destination, Homer, the Kenai's Land's End.

While Attu Island, the very end of the Aleutian Chain, may be the geographical end of Alaska, in reality it is Homer which best qualifies for this description. Attu has as its only significant landmark a large complex of United States Service facilities, primarily Air Force bases, because of its strategic location and proximity to Russia. Other than that, it is bare of people and vegetation.

In contrast, the picturesque and mountainous Kenai is sur-prisingly busy and commercial considering its sparse population. A large refinery on the western shore adds to this impression. Any visitor to the area may find this astonishing, having traveled there through vast empty spaces. Nearby, Soldotna serves as a service center for the peninsula.

The town of Seward, on the south shore, is so small that it takes less than three minutes to cross it. It is the end of the Alas-ka Railroad Line and serves as one of two Pacific ports, along with Valdez.

But Homer is different. Its geographic location is truly that of a Land's End. The small settlement and its commercial cen-ter, "downtown" so to speak, sits on the edge of water forming a large fjord or bay. Across from town, snow-capped peaks tower over the majestic scene, rising from sea level to the height of Storm Mountain, 3790 ft in altitude.

What makes Homer, on the south side of the Kenai Peninsula, so special is the long, thin, narrow tongue of land stretching out into the bay. It is called the Spit. At its very end, where the road merges with the edge of the bay's water, Alaska's state route number one terminates. There is no more road to go any place, anywhere.

When the Suzuki and I arrived in Homer in midmorning, it was not surprising for me to discover that these last three miles, from the center of the village of Homer to the end of the Spit, are truly a Land's End.

This is where the action is: hundreds of motor homes, campers, tents, gift shops, restaurants, snack shacks, marinas, and shops that cater to fishing and boating pack the narrow land. There is a clutter as well of low-key, simple establishments serving an assortment of needs the average traveler would have. All this fills the slender strip of sand and rock called the Spit.

The Spit is Homer's lifeline. People wander, stroll, bike, run or loaf. They eat, shop, browse, drink and swim. Fishermen abound. Some guys go horseback riding on the beach. Tents are often set up right by the water's edge. There seems to be no distinct or visible restriction in what people can do or will do.

In May, some bring up their campers or motor homes from the lower 48, park them on the sand, feel comfortable and cozy being surrounded by other campers and those who own the larger motor homes. All of them stay the entire summer.

At the end of August, when the nights become colder, they depart, trekking back the same road they came up, the one and only road connecting Homer to the rest of the country and the world, the Alaska Highway.

Homer is at times compared to Key West. Both are Land's End locations. Probably as a result, both are somewhat peculiar and highly independent in the lifestyle of their respective residents. Homer basks in the relatively warm breezes of the Pacific's Japan current, which brings up warm waters from the ocean's center in a counter clockwise fashion. In stark contrast to the barren mountain world further north, these breezes cause abundant vegetation along the shores of the southern peninsula. Key West, in contrast, is flat, charming and almost grown over with year-round vegetation of tropical origins, spurred on by the lush Caribbean winds.

Like residents of Key West, those of Homer do "their thing". Artists, derelicts, loners, naturalists, drug addicts, elderly, very young and middle-aged, rich and poor, high society or working class, they all seem to blend into each other and exist in peaceful harmony. Most of them came to seek individuality, or a new identity, shedding values of their past in the lower 48.

I stopped the bike at the end of the Spit, in front of a wooden shack with a bulldog face painted on a rough piece of board. I got off and stretched. The sky was azure, the sun shone brightly. Yet, in these parts of the world, I had already noticed that the sun doesn't behave as it does at home. She did not rise in the east, or ascend the sky in a straight line to reach the zenith, then follow the same line down to the west. Here, she circled the edge of the sky. On June 21st, in Inuvik, Northwest Territories, some 350 miles north of the Arctic Circle, she never set all night. Her sweep of the sky and track around the globe was even wider and lower on the horizon.

But in the bright sunshine, my Suzuki looked rather dirty. Only the top part of the tank indicated that it was painted black. The engine was a mixture of silver and brown, whereas the wheels, headlight, rear shaft housing, and all my gear strapped onto the bike looked filthy from the northern mud.

A considerate biker, once arrived in Alaska, shuns showing off that he has "*made it to Alaska by conquering the Alaska Highway,*" as some bumper stickers on motor homes proclaim. He would clean his bike and gear without delay once he found a facility to do so. But in Homer, there was no spray gun car wash. So the cleansing of the gear would have to wait until reaching Anchorage.

My jeans and leather boots did not look much different. Yet my face must have displayed a happy smile, because the fellows parking their well-used rigs in my vicinity, extended a friendly greeting with a wide grin.

"Coming in for a brew?" they asked.

"Come a long way, haven't you?" added another.

"Yeah," I replied, and then asked, "this a good place for grub?"

"Ehhhh, not really, but come in and have a beer with us."

The place was called the Salty Dawg Saloon. Its name really says it all. It is anchored firm at this very end of the Spit, at the bottom of the Peninsula. Unless you had the enviable excuse of stomping the neighborhood for the world's biggest salmon, it's doubtful that you would just drop in for a drink.

But then, if you are just thirsty enough, you might take the drive to the very end where the sea begins. Apart from my curiosity, I WAS thirsty. I followed the fellows from the rig into the dark cavernous bar.

For a fisherman, the Salty Dawg means that this is the first bar in America, a sort of a decompression chamber between the vastness of the Pacific and the warm humanity of home.

The saloon is constructed from several log cabins which over time have merged into one. The string of structures is topped by a lighthouse tower which conceals the water tank and warns navigators of nearby rocks. The main building used to be Homer's first general store, then post office and schoolhouse, or in a similar order and sequence, and then some other general purposes for the last century, because that is how long the white man has been there.

On the inside, every bare wooden surface is carved with initials, curses, amorous and/or lustful intentions. There are also thousands of business cards pinned to the timbers. On a summer weekend, at about three in the morning, I was told a drinker might take a card at random and weave a tale about its original owner, his fantasy fueled by dozens of brews.

Over the years, the place has withstood threats of fire, flood, earthquakes and volcano eruptions. As one drinker near where I sat put it:

"It's as if the Puritans had called out a whole heavenly arsenal against this hellhole, only to find Christ inside drinking with the regulars."

No shirt, no shoes, no problem. But for anyone wanting to blend in with the locals, the dress code is strict: baseball cap with a fish processor's logo, a sweat shirt with its sleeves cut off anywhere between the elbow and shoulder and some extra tough boots, heavy rubber mostly, folded over on the top.

The fellow sitting on the next stool wore them. He had a full, blond beard and bushy eyebrows, under which shone clear blue eyes.

"Crack opened up at the bay," he was saying, describing a recent earthquake, "just sucked in the ocean. That crack ran between Joshua's legs but he hopped up and out of the way. His brother fell in..."

He probably made more money fishing with his trawler during the last two to three months than I will in the next three years.

"Soon I am going over to my villa in Hawaii where I don't have to wear any clothes if I don't want to," he concluded.

The Salty Dawg offers plenty to drink but nothing to eat—mostly beer and whiskey. Of the latter, mostly Jim Beam bourbon. On the shelves behind the bar, there were a few items which could be construed as food products.

"Don't be fooled," said the bearded fellow on the next stool again as he witnessed the direction of my vision. "These jars holding them unnamed meat products up there yonder, they are not to be disturbed. Don't even know the names of what's in there. Some meat, I guess, immersed in gelatin or somethin' like that."

After a pause, he continued: "these there are just props. And anyhow, when you are pulling back into port after a volcano across the bay blows off, what you need is a stiff drink and nothing else in the way."

Some of the string of log cabins were burned not long ago, but the Saloon was saved. It opens at eleven a.m. and does not have a proclaimed closing hour. If you want to call ahead, the pay phone on the Saloon's wall will ring and you have to talk to whoever sits near it and picks up the receiver.

The barmaid on duty is too busy to do that. Her name is Birdie.

And unless you are known to her by the name of your boat, you'd better bring cash.

Ah, the wonderful world of Land's End Homer.

1988 CHARLIE

One misty, gloomy summer day, in 1989, I was cruising down Interstate 5 in Oregon on my Suzuki GS850 motorcycle. I had visited western Canada extensively and was now heading for California and the desert country of Arizona.

This morning, I left the state of Washington where it had poured rain continuously the day before and even during the night in my camp. Although I frequently applied my usual style on this journey, namely to pitch my tent in some attractive non-commercial campground, tonight I would succumb to the weather and live it up by taking a motel room.

I found it in a quaint little inn at Cottage Grove, Oregon, south of Eugene. The place was charming, with a wide overhang in front of the rooms where I parked the Suk for the night. A gas stove inside provided sufficient heat not only for the room but also to dry my tent, sleeping bag, shirts, socks and bandana which I had hung all over the tiny space. It smelled musty when I went to bed later, but then it cost only $12.00 a night and my stuff was DRY!

The sun shone bright and beautiful the next morning when I awoke. It would be a gorgeous day for riding down State Route #1, the Pacific Coast Road, in California. The Suzuki started at once and its deep rumble turned me on. I wanted to get out of there, hit the road, and go places. Forgotten was the rainy misery of yesterday and the day before. This was another day, a beautiful one.

I wolfed down a Danish and some coffee the innkeeper provided in his tiny lobby, then mounted the Suk and headed for the Interstate. About half an hour later, I pulled into a rest area along the superslab for my morning constitutional. As I did, another biker was just readying himself to pull out. When he saw me approach in his mirror, he sat motionless until I pulled up next to him. This is a procedure known to and practiced by almost all bikers. It means: hey, I want to know who you are, I don't mind talking and even riding with you if I find you okay.

I flipped up my face shield and told him I'd be just a minute, if he wanted to ride with me down the Interstate. He nodded and shut his engine off but remained seated in his saddle.

A few minutes later, we both took off, testing each other's style to see if we were compatible. Soon thereafter, we must have both agreed that the other was all right, because from then on, we rode side by side—something I do only with experienced motorcycle riders.

About ninety miles down the road, he slowed down and tried to catch my attention. When he did, he pointed with his left, gloved hand to his tank several times, meaning in biker's language "I have to fill up." I nodded.

We took the next exit and found a Texaco station. He rode up to one side of the pumps, I to the other. I was still in the saddle when he took his helmet off. I knew he was young and had seen the end of his blond locks wiggle in the wind at the back of his helmet. But he was actually much younger than I thought. I gave him twenty max—a kid!

Then my time came to take off my helmet. As I did, my companion of the highway looked at me, his chin dropped, his eyes almost popped and the gas nozzle slipped out of his hand. Then he blurted out,

"I knew you'd be older than I but I didn't know you'd be THAT old!" Kids say the darnedest things!

We both laughed. But it didn't matter how old we were.

Because we spent the next three days riding the coastal road to San Francisco together. The bonding had worked again.

His name was Charlie and his address I did not lose!

1989 GLADYS AND NORMA

When I arrived at Cape North, a small crossroad place where the Cabot Trail swings south again, I stopped the bike to study my road maps. A singular, narrow track turned north there, reaching the end of the Cape, after thirty-nine kilometers or roughly twenty-four miles. That was it! That was the road I wanted. I eased the bike left for the final stretch.

It soon became apparent that I had entered the most deserted, but also the most pristine section of Cape Breton. Shortly after gliding along Aspy Bay and bypassing a spur road into the village of Bay St. Lawrence, I reached the end of the pavement in Capstick. It consisted of exactly two clapboard houses painted bright red. I rode through the hamlet in less than five seconds.

Five miles later, at Meat Cove, smaller than Capstick, I arrived at Point Blackrock, the northernmost tip of the Cape and the Province of Nova Scotia. The road ended.

No one was there. I was very much alone in this world, the unbelievable beauty and splendor of nature basking in bright afternoon sunlight, the dark blue waters of the Gulf crashing against the black rocks which had fallen from the cliffs surrounding me.

I was at the destination that I had traveled over two thousand miles to reach.

But as a nomad who has wandered around a lot in his life, I also knew that the time of the day had come to seek shelter. Although it was only July, it would be cold tonight. And I had not seen a spot anywhere where I could pitch my tent.

Reluctantly, I broke loose from this scene and rode my bike ever so slowly back on the dirt road, to the point where the spur led into the village of Bay St. Lawrence. I hung a left there, hoping there would be lodging of some kind available.

The village consisted of eleven houses and three churches. I did not see any motel or inn, or even a sign pointing to a bed and breakfast. Now I became concerned, being where I was at the end of the world with no roof over my head. It was shortly before five, high time to find shelter and some food.

The tiny building to my right turned out to be the village's post office. It was so small that I had overlooked it when I counted the hamlet's houses. Now I recognized its nature and purpose by its red paint and the maple leaf flag fluttering on its pole nearby.

I parked my filthy bike on its center stand, looked at my muddy boots and grayish jeans and decided that the post office clerk would understand.

I walked inside.

"Hello," said a cheery voice from somewhere behind the counter. I did not see the owner of that voice because my eyes had not adjusted to the dark inside as yet. But the voice sounded friendly—a woman's voice.

"My name is Gladys. I saw you riding up. My oh my, what a beautiful machine out there. What kind is it? Do you call it a scooter, or a motorbike? Where are you from?"

"I am from North Carolina."

"Oh yes, I have been to your home state. Drove through it when I went to Florida several years ago. You know, vacationed there. Do you have a name?"

I introduced myself.

"Nice to see you, Peter. How do you like it up here? I love your country. But you have an accent. Where are you from? Not from North Carolina, are you? Do you like Canada? Yes? Wonderful. And I LOVE FLORIDA! Wouldn't you, if you lived up here?"

"Yes, I would, Gladys." And I was going to add that I would even love it without living up here. But with this friendly waterfall of a conversation, conducted almost entirely by Gladys who rarely sees anybody from outside of Bay St. Lawrence, I decided to keep quiet because my stomach started to growl. Besides, sitting on a motorcycle for many days and riding alone, a person isn't given to talking much anyway. So, I, too, enjoyed seeing someone who really talked.

But I eventually managed to get a word in. "Gladys, I need to look for a place to stay tonight. Are there any motels in town? And maybe a place to eat some good dinner, a spot that serves good, fresh fish—maybe the day's catch?"

"My oh my, Peter, we do not have a single motel in town. No restaurant either. But I bet Norma could put you up for the night. See the docks down there? Yes? Okay, that little, red wooden house there, that's Norma's. I'll ask her. I'll take you there. Got to lock up anyway now. It's after five. So let me do that here real quick."

"No problem, Gladys. And thank you."

"Oh my, you are so polite. It's nice to see polite men. And so verbal also. I'll be right done. Give me a minute."

Then she disappeared in the back room. I walked outside, put my helmet on and started the Suzuki's engine, waiting for her to emerge. I watched her close all the doors and windows tight, but she did not turn the key to lock the door.

"You forgot to lock the door," I said from under my helmet.

"We never do. We don't even have a working key. Don't know where it went. Lost it some years back."

Locking doors and such other things that city folk would do were obviously not needed up here.

Then she boarded her vintage, 1962 Dodge and, before closing the door, said:

"It's been to Florida with me already."

Having said this, she pointed up the hill to a new looking building.

"That's the new school. We are very proud of it. It's much larger than this," and she gestured toward the post office hut we had just exited. "You will see it when you ride up the hill tomorrow morning."

I saw it all right from where I was, no problem. It looked smaller than my house. And I don't live in a big house. Everything is relative in life.

In three minutes, we were down by the dock to see Norma.

"Sure," said she, "I will hurry to put some clean sheets on the bed in the guest room."

Norma was a short, plump woman in her forties.

Gladys bade her farewell then but did not leave before I could give her a big hug, which she gratefully acknowledged with a soft, "Oh heavens."

"I will cook him a good dinner," Norma hollered as Gladys closed her car door.

And an excellent dinner it was indeed. Norma talked even faster and more incessantly than Gladys. I had all the time in the world to enjoy her delicious food. Once in a while, and only rarely, I would have to say yes, or perhaps no. In the meantime,

I feasted on clam chowder, fresh cod, smothered and sautéed in garlic and olive oil sauce, scalloped potatoes, peas and carrots, and a rich-looking and calorie-loaded concoction of sweet custard which I could never quite analyze as to its true contents.

Norma even produced a bottle of Molson's Dry from her husband's stock. He was out for the week in his fishing trawler.

My room was sparkling clean. Nevertheless, it was cluttered with furniture but foremost with trinkets: porcelain puppets were an arranged in a circle on the commode as if they were dancing. Ceramic frogs sat in all corners of the room on the hand-woven throw rug. Plastic flowers were arranged in every conceivable container. A stern looking couple dressed in 19th century garb gazed at me with concern out of their gold plated frame, or was it suspicion? Likely some ancestors banished into the guest room where they could do no harm.

I felt clumsy in my boots, bringing in some of my gear from the motorcycle.

"You can leave your stuff on the motorbike. Put it in the shed. No one will steal anything here," Norma had said. So I only brought in the tank bag holding my overnight things. Even so, I barely found room for it among the trinkets.

But a comfortable, wide bed with starched bed sheets it was.

Before I slipped into bed, I went outside, told Norma I'd be back soon, got on the Suzuki and rode out once more to Blackrock Point. Now it was looking starker, with the cliff rocks black and the Gulf water a blue-ish grey adorned with small pearls of crested wavelets shining in the sunlight's afterglow.

I was all alone again!

I could see the world around me falling silent. I could see the world around me in an almost two hundred degree radius.

Once in a while, a fish would jump, but nature had gone to sleep, and this world around me would soon follow.

The moment had arrived which was the one I had traveled so far to witness: Day's End at Land's End.

1990: SVEN—ANOTHER SOULMATE

On the way to the Arctic one morning in 1990, I boarded the MS TAKU, of the Alaska Marine Highway fleet, at its dock in Prince Rupert, British Columbia. I did not need a reservation, though it was almost the middle of the summer travel season.

Motorcycles generally enjoy priority because of their easy storage in nooks and crannies of the ship's belly where no car could ever be parked. Riders are therefore asked to go to the head, of the waiting line.

At boarding time, I was directed to a space next to a BMW R100, heavily loaded down, with a Swedish license plate featuring the international symbol "S" underneath.

Ships which travel through rough ocean waters, even for the shortest time, provide heavy sisal ropes hanging from the loading deck's ceiling. They are meant to tie down motorcycles, to prevent their tipping over in heavy seas. While I strapped my bike tight, I noticed the Swede had not done so properly. So I tied his firmly as well.

We cruised the inside passage for the next three days. The TAKU featured two or four bunk cabins, as well as private staterooms with full bathroom facilities. But like all other bikers, hikers and cyclists, I preferred to camp out on deck, in the ship's open solarium, under starlit skies.

Food was served in a dining room and also, somewhat cheaper, in a cafeteria-style facility. Showers were available free of charge.

The second day, I literally bumped into a blond, tall fellow, as both of us rounded the same corner on our morning hike around the promenade deck. I had seen him on the ship before. I apologized, so did he. Then he said:

"My name is Sven and I am from Sweden. Don't you ride a motorbike?"

"Suzuki, a rice burner! Then you're the BMW guy, right?"

"Yes, I am. Then you are a friend to tie up my bike with rope?" his accents sang along.

"Yes, I am."

His English was mostly Oxford, accompanied by a delightful Scandinavian singsong accent. He looked and was very young, twenty-two maybe. We soon became inseparable. He followed me everywhere I went on board and even stayed at my side when I talked to other passengers. He appeared to be a playful puppy dog. But he also asked many serious questions, about the U.S.A. and Canada and especially about the North Country where we were both heading.

When I excused myself because I needed to be alone for a while, he would go to the ship's stern and look forlorn and terribly lonesome. I felt sorry for him then, and returned to take him back in tow.

I liked Sven. He reminded me a lot of my wife who is also Scandinavian. But he threw me for a loop when we docked in Skagway, Alaska, the ship's terminal and its northernmost point, asking very shyly,"mind if I tag along on your way north?"

In all my years of motorcycle travel, I mostly rode alone. Occasionally, I would encounter someone I liked and would ride together with him for a day or two. But the road ahead of us to Inuvik in the Northwest Territories, on the shores of the Arctic

Sea, was one thousand miles one way. No motels and no restaurants were along the stretch. It meant camping all the way, up and down, with this guy, who was not even from our country? Camping? Being together all day? That would definitely be something new for me. Before I could finish deliberating, I heard myself say,

"Sure, Sven, I'd be glad to have you come along."

It took us three days to ride the 542 miles to near Dawson, in Canada's Yukon Territory. All pavement had stopped north of Whitehorse. Mud faced us from there on in. It had rained all day, every day, but it stopped each evening when we set up camp. The mosquitoes were fierce, but DEET took care of them. They would swirl around our faces an inch away.

This was now the point where the Klondike Highway coming up from Whitehorse intersected with the Dempster Highway—the road to the Arctic.

We and our bikes were filthy, muddy, but we felt elated. We had reached the halfway mark between Skagway and the Beaufort Sea.

The Dempster Highway has existed only since 1979. Over 455 miles long, the road travels due north from where we were, thirteen miles east of Dawson. It crosses the Arctic Circle and the boundary between the Yukon and the Northwest Territories, ending north of Inuvik at the Beaufort Sea—a part of the Arctic Ocean. The Dempster and the Dalton, the former Alaska Pipeline road from Fairbanks to Prudhoe Bay, form the only vehicular access roads to the Beaufort Sea.

Sven and I sat on our bikes at that point, rethinking probably for the tenth time, whether or not to do the final stretch. Then we looked at each other, and Sven burst out, "LET'S GO!"

Like the Klondike we had ridden on from Whitehorse, the Dempster was unpaved all the way. It was bumpy, yet OK when dry. But it had rained a lot. It was slippery. We were riding mostly through a gooey mess, twenty miles an hour, often with our legs stretched out to catch ourselves when the bikes started to fish-tail. We smiled through it all the way. We spent two marvelous camping nights along the Dempster, in what the Yukon called "Government campsites." We set up only one of the two tents we had with us. Now in late June, there was little if any tourist traffic going up and down. We were most often alone in these campsites. Maybe an occasional motor home would park further away.

The first night, in Tombstone Creek Park, we hiked down to the river after setting up our camp, to strip and take a cleansing swim. The creek cascaded over huge rocks, its water clear and ice cold. Sven didn't mind. He was obviously used to it. For my thinner blood, it was at the extreme edge of my tolerance level.

"We swim naked all the time in Sweden. Do you here, too?"
"I do. But not everybody does. It's a church thing in our country.

People have hang-ups about it. But the bears don't mind," I said.

"Hang-ups?"

"It's slang. It means they are uptight."

"Uptight?"

"Another slang word. It means they are not free about the subject, have reservations about it, that sort of thing."

"Ahhh, so," said Sven. And we laughed romping around in the water.

We cooked our evening meals in our mess kits, mostly preceded by Aquavit, that devilish Swedish brew distilled from grain and flavored with caraway.

On the third day, we reached the Eagle Plains Hotel, the location of the one and only gas station on the Dempster. We were now 270 miles north of the Dawson intersection with the Klondike. We filled our tanks to the top with gas. It ran to $3.40 per gallon of unleaded. On this drab day, with the clouds hanging low enough to touch the roof of the building, we went inside to eat some lunch. A meager portion of roast beef, some microwaved potatoes and a few deep-frozen veggies cost $28.00—too much for so little food.

As we emerged from the hotel, we noticed a camper on the muddy parking lot. It bore the emblem of the Royal Mounted Police. A tall, blond officer stepped out. He had his shirt sleeves rolled up and wore no jacket. We said hello and exchanged the customary greetings. Then Sven asked him in his Nordic accent:

"Are you patrol for road?"

"Yes, I am." he answered, looking somewhat bewildered upon hearing Sven's singsong English.

"Do you live in trailer?" Sven continued.

"Yes, I do. I am actually from Inuvik. But in the summer, we rotate coming here, midway between Dawson and Inuvik, just to be available for tourist information."

"How many of you guys patrol the highway then?" I wanted to know.

"Just me," smiled the Mountie.

It was hard for us to imagine only one policeman patrolling a 470 mile stretch of highway.

"Amazing," I said. "But aren't you cold?"

"No, sir, this is summer for us."

The hotel's thermometer showed 4 degrees Centigrade,

40 degrees Fahrenheit, on June 17th, almost the year's longest day—amazing again!

Something else impressed us greatly: the road widened to triple the normal width in regular intervals. Road signs warned of no parking the next mile, because of the roadway also being used as an airstrip for small, single engine aircraft.

That night we camped near the Arctic Circle and headed up into the Richardson Mountain Range and Wright Pass the next morning. We were now 320 miles north on the Dempster and stopped for a midday pause. It was windy and cold on the pass which was only 2,780 ft in elevation, the sun often hidden by clouds racing across the pale blue sky. We left our leather jackets zippered up to our woolen neck warmers, but had taken our helmets off to let the wind tussle our short cropped hair.

The summit constitutes the boundary between the Yukon and Northwest Territories. Simultaneously, it was the Continental Divide, separating the watersheds of eastern and western America. From this point, rivers flow east and north to the Arctic Ocean, and west to the Pacific.

Then Sven climbed up to a dolphin-shaped, big boulder and called down to me below:

"Look, I found an inscription on this stone. Want to hear it?"

Then he read it out loud:

"NORTHWEST TERRITORIES
You are welcome here, traveler.
Enjoy this land,
with the understanding
that it has been left briefly in your trust
for the benefit
of future generations."

On the fifth day on the Dempster, we reached Inuvik and set up our camp, in Chuk Park, three miles out of the small settlement. The rear of our tent faced north. It was the spot where my sleeping bag was rolled out during the night. I woke up every twenty minutes or so to peek through the screen at the sun. She never set, all night. She kept moving along the horizon, as far above Mother Earth as she would above the mountain ridge, at my home in North Carolina one hour before sunset. It fascinated me. Sven slept through it all. From his native land, he was used to the Midsummer Night, the longest day in the year.

In December, Inuvik's sunlight is zero. Darkness lasts for six weeks. In June and part of July, the sun never sets. Average temperature, in Inuvik during winter, is 18 degrees below zero, in summer 43 degrees above zero. No heat wave there!

Whatever Inuvik's charm, most of its housing was unbelievably ugly, despite the various pastel colors of its newer dwellings built by the Canadian Government, for its exclusively Eskimo population. The architecture could be that of Moscow.

We rode up the road towards the Arctic Ocean the next day, along the huge spread out delta formed by the Mackenzie River. But soon after, the Dempster ended unceremoniously at the edge of the river. We got off our bikes, placed them on their center stands in the soft, muddy earth and took our helmets off.

"Is that it?" Sven sang out. When he was excited, he would fall back even more into his Scandinavian accent, and he surely was excited now!

"That's it. We've done it, Sven," I said and gave him five, a gesture he had already learned in school in Sweden.

"It is wonderful, sort of friendship sign, no?" he had said

when I asked him earlier if he knew what it meant, but now I wanted him to know:

"In the summer, the road ends here. In the winter, it will continue on the packed ice towards Richards Island and the settlement of Tuktoyaktuk. Like Inuvik, it's located in the Reindeer Grazing Preserve, which covers almost as much space as all of your home country."

"Wow," said Sven. Then he fell silent in awe over our accomplishment, our being here, at the end of the world.

"Yeah, buddy, we've come a long way, you and I."

"Yes, we have," said Sven, "And *takks* for letting me go along with you."

I knew from Hanna what *takks* meant. It was Scandinavian for thank you, so I said to him, "I am glad you asked me if you could come along."

On our return trip the next day, a Territory-owned ferry crossed the Mackenzie River some one hundred miles south of Inuit. The crossing is free of charge for vehicles and people. The ferries run during the short summer only, from mid-June to the end of August. For the rest of the year, areas north of the river are isolated from the rest of the world.

The crossing takes place where the Mackenzie merges with the Arctic Red River. On the point formed by the two mighty streams lies the Eskimo settlement of Arctic Red River. We had intended to go there on the way north, but were unaware that we needed to tell the captain to detour there instead of his straight run across the Mackenzie. Now, however, we asked him to drop us off and pick us up again the following morning, although we did not know if there was room to camp or stay in the village.

Arctic Red River was actually a lot nicer than Inuvik, though much smaller. A handful of Inuits lived there now, earning their keep by trapping and producing dried fish and meat staples. One of the older residents told us:

"I would just love to travel like you. But the last and only trip I ever took was to Edmonton some thirty or forty years ago, I don't quite remember the exact year."

"But Edmonton is far away, yes?" Sven said.

"Very far. It took three weeks to get there." Indeed! I knew the city was some 2,000 miles to the southeast. There were no roads then. Those who traveled did so by river.

Above the brightly painted houses sat the parish church. From the crude, muddy ferry ramp, we rode our bikes up there, to pay a visit to this small, wooden structure. It was painted bright red. And just as we pulled to its side, a nun descended its steep stairs. She'd probably seen us approach.

"Hello," she said to us, in her cheerful, soft voice, as if we were long lost friends, "what brings you here?"

"Hello to you, Sister, we wanted to see your church. It is very picturesque the way it was erected on this hill. Who built it?"

"It was built by French Jesuits of the Oblate Order in 1868. But the Jesuit priests have long since left. We are Franciscans and run the parish now," she replied in her pleasant voice. One could not help but like this devoted woman. Sven felt likewise, I could tell, because he asked her:

"I hear some children voices, yes?"

"Oh yes, we have three pupils here. We run the local school and all the children who wish to learn can come up here to do so."

"Are you still having church in the church?" continued Sven. The nun looked puzzled, so I helped her:

"My friend Sven here means whether you still celebrate mass in the church?"

"No, we don't, unfortunately. The church needs a lot of repair. We have no money. We use the kitchen table as an altar for Sunday services."

"But the church looks in good repair," I said.

"Yes, from the outside. It got a new paint job. Some brave people in town volunteered to do that."

Then the kids came running. But when they saw Sven, they started hiding behind the nun's wide habit, to seek security from this huge, tall man she was talking to. Sven laughed, talked to them some, and then produced a few sticks of chewing gum which the kids shyly accepted, with a faint smile on their brown faces. Then the nun shepherded them inside. "Come on, kids, time to go back to school."

"But we don't want to," they said.

"I'll give you some cookies." That worked, as it always seems to.

Before we bade our farewell, we asked where a donation could be offered. The nun pointed to a tin can, which had once held lard.

"For the church building fund," we said while dropping our modest offerings into the depth of the metal container.

"God bless you both," she answered while starting to climb up the steep stairs again. But then, she stopped, turning back to us and said,

"See you at the village square tonight. We are celebrating. It's midsummer night, time for a bonfire."

Then we remembered, it was June 21st! Of course we went. The town folks took us in as if they had known us for years. Word of our presence had obviously spread the settlement in a hurry. It was Midsummer Night all right. Rain or shine. We had both of it. There was a lot of celebrating among the residents. To enhance the occasion, a substance of indefinable nature and origin was passed around in large, homemade ceramic pitchers. Sven and I had a taste of it; after all, we felt obliged to show our hosts all the courtesies due them. We bravely swallowed. After that, we could, according to etiquette, decline with a smile.

"You want something else to drink?" asked Sven nudging my arm.

"Sure, but we don't have anything else, do we?"

"Yes, we do," he said with the widest grin I'd ever seen on his ever so Nordic face. Then he slipped the Aquavit bottle quietly into my hand, for a sip to lift our already high spirits, although they really didn't need any more boosting.

We woke up the next morning in a tiny cottage, in our sleeping bags, stretched out on the floor. "How we got here?" Sven was the first to speak. It turned out that kind Inuits had offered the shelter to us the rainy midsummer night before. Our fogged minds did not clearly remember any of that. Soon thereafter, we heard the ship's horn. The captain was approaching to pick us up.

Three days later, we camped together for the last time, at Tombstone Creek. And again we went down to the river to swim and cleanse. After eating dinner in our mess kit, Sven started to clean his engine by trying to wipe off the mud caked on its housing by the motor's heat. It did not work.

"Sven, you need this." I had searched for my small wire brush and gave it to him. "Otherwise you'll never get the caked mud out from between your engine's cooling fins. It's as hard as rock."

"Thanks, hadn't thought of that. How come you know so much?" he said with that puppy dog face of his all smiles.

"Because I have been around a bit longer than you have."

Then we sat by the river, near our tent, and told stories of our lives until twilight set in at two in the morning.

"We will separate tomorrow?" Sven said with a sad face before we went to sleep in our shelter.

"Yes, we will." And my heart is heavy too, I was tempted to tell him. But I guessed he knew that, as I knew his was.

"Good night, bud. Thanks for coming along," I said instead.

We parted at the intersection of the Dempster and Klondike the next day at noon. Sven went east to Sweden, I west to Alaska. But before we did, Sven climbed from his BMW and silently gave me a hug.

Friends in those passing winds!

HANG'IN OUT AT HAWK'S CAY

Chapter Nine:
THE CRAZY RUSSIAN

1968 TATJANA

The following episode transpired many years ago, when the Soviet Union still existed, when the Cold War still raged and much before Eastern European countries, including Germany, began their movements for freedom.

Romania, governed by the most dictatorial regime of these East Bloc countries, turned out to be the last to commence her drive for liberation from Communist rule.

It was Friday, early afternoon.

My week in New York City had been exhausting—day-long meetings chased by late night dinners and early breakfasts.

I felt drained as I waited for my plane to take me home to Miami, from New York's Kennedy airport. I longed for the tranquility of my seashore home on Key Biscayne and looked forward to the serenity of the island's beaches and some well deserved sleep.

Skimming through the morning's New York Times, I learned that the Soviets had sent dissident Andrei Sakarov into exile in Gorky, 260 miles east of Moscow. Confined, he would not rock the Communist boat. He would be safely locked away. When will people be finally free in the eastern hemisphere? Reign through terror and suppression simply did not subside; on the contrary, it accelerated. Was there a chance for it to end?

The terminal was very busy indeed. Weekend travelers gathered to head into all four directions for relaxation, fun or just to go home as I was. The crowds did not bother me, though. I learned long ago, from traveling thousands of miles in any given year, to shut my mind to noises and commotion around me.

First class travel was one of the few perks my employer afforded me. It compensated for endless hours, days and weeks spent on the road.

Soon after settling into my comfortable, wide window seat, a glass of champagne thrust into my hand by a charming flight attendant, I plugged my ears with headphones and swiftly got lost in the sounds of Vivaldi. Unaware of the world around me and the long waiting line of planes at the runway's head, I barely noticed takeoff.

A casual glimpse had verified the presence of the passenger in the seat next to mine—a tall woman who, as I could clearly see without lifting my eyes, had immense features. But I was not in the mood for conversation. Turning back to the window to look out would, I knew, discourage talkative fellow travelers. I needed my own space, peace to reflect on past events and time to frame my mind for relaxation ahead.

Until we were well airborne, that is, and the smiling flight attendant asked what I desired in the way of a cocktail.

The earphones out of my ears and having ordered a gin and tonic, I at once noticed the great difficulty my neighbor had with communicating her wishes to the stewardess.

"Fottka," she said. The flight attendant looked blank.

"She means Vodka straight up, no ice, no water," I interjected. No smile, no thank you, no acknowledgement that she even heard me. Okay then, have it your way, I thought to myself as I picked up the earphones again.

She was big. Not obese, not overweight, just big in all her features, all her body configurations. She had tremendous thighs as I could observe while pretending to listen to Vivaldi again.

When my gin and tonic was served, I turned my head long enough to notice her facial features to include a nose deriving from Romans and Turks, now predominant in Balkan countries. It was slightly curved in a gentle line. Her cheekbones were widely set, though, and suggested a Slavic origin.

But then I took a look at her dress. And I knew immediately that she was from abroad. The design of the fabric was different—an inexpensive, printed, checkered conglomeration of flowers and birds. Even I who had not much notion of what exactly women would wear, could see that the cut of the dress she was wearing was …well, unusual, maybe even sloppy.

And just as I finally stole a look at her tremendously big and clumsy shoes, I felt a harsh slap on my right wrist, while a powerful voice in tones between male and female ranges hit my ears with: "How to yu to," in a manner of gutteral utterances common to all people living east of Vienna.

Tatjana!

After a few, preliminary exchanges of pleasantries, as much as she was able to deliver them in a language obviously foreign to her, my curiosity was aroused to the point of genuine interest. I simply could not wait any longer to ask her where she came from.

"Romania."

Ah… I should have known. My exposure to European schools in earlier times should have let me recognize her origins.

We continued exchanging small talk thoughts, you know, the

noncommittal stuff people talk about on planes or ships, nothing earthshaking, nothing of much value at all. Hors d'oeuvres were served. By the time the main course arrived—filet mignon medium rare, green asparagus, sautéed potatoes—she had just finished her third straight "Fottka" and was now testing the excellent California Burgundy.

"What is it?" she asked, pointing her knife to the vegetable.

"Asparagus," I said.

"Spargel. But Spargel white at home, no green."

"Spargel is the German word for asparagus, and in Germany it is white, but here we like it green."

"Ah …Goot vine, from France, yes?"

Her English had substantially improved, with the assistance of the airline's vodka.

"No, madam, the grapes were grown and the wine bottled in California," I volunteered.

"California is where in France?" she wanted to know.

"It is not in France. It lies 3,000 miles, or about 5,000 kilometers west of here."

"But that iss desert, sant, sun, I learned in school. No vine grow in desert, no?"

And so was born our first argument, one of numerous to follow.

Tatjana came from Bucharest to New York to attend a United Nations Committee meeting on cultural exchanges, held first at the United Nations headquarters in New York, followed by a more relaxed session in the Florida Keys.

Although a native Russian, she now was in charge of all cultural affairs of Romania. Her rank was similar to that of our Cabinet members and she answered directly to the Romanian President, Nicolae Ceausescu.

But in this capacity, she also was a "politico" as she said, a member of the Communist Party which ruled Romania with an iron fist. For reasons unknown to me, she was somewhat apprehensive as well.

I knew we would have totally opposing views on matters of politics, economy and related items. But I had no idea yet how fiercely she wanted to convert me to her beliefs, how rigorously she argued her points of view, not wanting to even recognize any of mine.

"Your President is a dictator. He is rich, a plutocrat. He wants all for himself, nothing for the masses."

Then, a little later, "you must work for your government, you are rich also, yes?"

"No, Madam, I don't and I am not rich."

But I thought I would challenge her a bit. So I said,

"You must be rich, or privileged as you say in your homeland, that you can come to our country, even traveling first class."

She frowned, and then burst out, almost furiously,

"I am traveling here for the good of my people, to improve their lives by enriching it with cultural impressions gained from other people in this world. You no understand, you are barbaric, imperialistic, yes?"

I reflected on that statement for a while, because I did not quite see the connection between vodka, filet mignon, California Burgundy and magnificent desserts, at 37,000 feet over South Carolina, and "the good of the people in Romania." I had never visited her country but I had heard and read that Romania's people were extremely poor and ruled by terror.

But perhaps later when she would be awake again would I ask her more questions on the subject. Because no sooner had she finished her coffee, her head tilted sideways and she was instantly asleep. It gave me a chance to consider in my mind this rather unusual encounter, to rethink some of our arguments and to finally pick up my earphones again and return to the solace of the classical music channel.

We touched down on Miami's International Airport runway 31L exactly ten minutes late. She awoke from the sounds of squealing tires when the landing gear hit the hot asphalt, throwing off little spiffs of smoke.

I had meanwhile decided to offer her a ride to wherever she would be staying in the Miami area. This would not inconvenience me much, as Harry would be waiting with his snow-white Lincoln, to take me home to Key Biscayne. I had used Harry's limousine services off and on during the last two years whenever I did not want to take my own car to the airport while on extended trips abroad.

Right now, the reason for Harry to pick me up was a different one. Because through a "misunderstanding" with a Florida State Trooper regarding the speed I was traveling on Interstate 75, I was temporarily disqualified from driving an automobile. It was a terrible nuisance. I had just before bought a new two-seater grey sports car, a convertible, with soft red leather seats and an enticing rumble of its engine. I often looked at it longingly and lovingly, because right now I could only back it up to the street, to the end of my one hundred-foot driveway.

Customarily, Harry stood at his spot a little ways back from the gate exit, wearing his usual good-natured smile and waving his hand when he recognized me. This time, though, he obviously did not connect me with the towering Tatjana who walked on my right. Before I could finish my introduction: "Hello, Harry.

I want you to meet Mrs …," Tatjana had stretched out her huge paw, pressing Harry's hand vigorously, causing a grimaced face and audible groan, and she said:

"Halloh, comrade," followed by more guttural sounds which neither Harry nor I understood.

Harry was dumbfounded, stupefied. He looked at me for help. But I just shrugged and smiled, easing him and Tatjana to the curb and the waiting Lincoln, talking incessantly to avoid questions from either one.

Once inside the limousine, Harry did the most sensible thing in the world. He rolled up the window dividing the driver area and the splendor of the leathery passenger compartment. He never did that when we were alone. But now, he eyed me closely in his rear view mirror, through the faintly tinted divider.

Tatjana was quite concerned with this development. "Roll down window," she commanded Harry by leaning forward and knocking on the glass.

Harry pretended not to hear. His eyes flickered, like a chased animal. I could see it in his mirror.

"Make him roll down window," she then said to me, "you are evil to let him do that. It shows you are plutocrat. This is class separation, no? Typical imperialistic."

I grabbed the mike of the intercom and asked Harry to please roll down the divider again, trying to soothe his upset mind with incessantly fast English sentences which I knew Tatjana could not understand, explaining her presence and how she latched on to me.

After that, Harry looked happier.

When she kept ranting about "Egalitism," a Romanian version of equality, I told her that Harry needs to keep his eyes and ears on the road, better not to be disturbed. Harry shot a grateful look at me through his mirror, but he continued to be totally confused and stole an occasional glance at Tatjana.

My armpits were wet with perspiration.

Tatjana and I exchanged some more pleasantries at the hotel where I had jumped to the front desk to insure her reservation while she tried to convert Harry to Communism. Then Harry took me home.

Harry needed a lot of calming down, though. When we arrived at my house, he looked sheepishly at my wife Hanna, with his glance expressing deep embarrassment about my going off the deep end when I had such a beautiful mate at home.

Good, old Harry. One day soon, I will have to explain all this to him. Naturally, I told Hanna every bit of my trip experience. She just laughed.

"If she could not convert you, was she at least pretty?" she asked teasingly. She knows me and my ability to strike up some most unusual encounters.

She is a great sport.

During the week following my return from New York, a hectic work schedule made Tatjana move into the recesses of my mind. I had other things to worry about, among them preparations for a weekend seminar in which I was participating at a business conference. Its schedule required that I address the group on two occasions. It was supposed to last three days and to be held at the Hawk's Cay Resort on Duck Key.

Harry took me down the hundred miles or so on the Overseas Highway on Friday night. Shaded by the deeply tinted windows, I used the comfort of his Lincoln for more preparatory work, which after checking in, I continued over dinner ordered up to my spacious suite.

Occasionally, I would look up from my papers and glance out through the wide, sliding glass doors, pushed back to the wall to let the gentle, salty Atlantic Ocean breezes in. I rejoiced at the prospect of spending a long weekend here. My work schedule would be light enough to allow for plenty of swimming, loafing,snoozing. I might even try to charter a Compact eighteen-foot day sailer for a few hours if the winds were right.

These were the perks of my job I cherished most.

My first seminar was scheduled for ten the next morning. I wore an open, short sleeve shirt and baggy pants along with leather boat shoes, no socks. Formal attire was not required here.

On the way to the suite reserved for the conference's seminar, crossing the straw thatched outdoor lobby to reach it, I suddenly saw a large figure approach the patio extending out from the reception desk. I stopped in my tracks, as dumbfounded as Harry was at the airport in Miami.

"Halloh, comrade."

No, please, not here!

"Are you here on working besenes, yes?"

"Yes, ma'am."

"But you are wrong dressed, no?"

"No, ma'am."

"I see you drive up with Harry, last night."

Oh Lord, now she might know my suite where I am staying.

"Tatjana, I have to work now, I will see you later."

"When?"

"Later. Perhaps in the afternoon. I will buy you a vodka."

"Ah, Fottka, yes, I wait."

The participants of my seminar, perhaps ten or eleven, were

well-dressed and well-educated middle management business-men, with scrubbed faces and smiling, mischievous eyes, eager to learn and equally eager to play. I tried to concentrate on matters at hand, to relay some of my knowledge to these fellows, but I felt I did a lousy job. My mind kept wandering off to Tatjana.

What in the world am I going to do with her? I knew she would be wanting to spend practically all her free time as well as mine trying to convert me to her political beliefs. But that was not what I had planned for the weekend hours in this sub-tropical paradise when I was free.

Yet, of course we had cocktails later that day, relaxing under umbrellas in the shade of some magnificent sea grape and jaca-randa trees. Tatjana loved the vegetation in the lower Keys. And I have always felt spiritually elated and physically fit in the trop-ical, abundant, overflowing splendor of trees, plants and flowers which are the natural result of soft, warm and moist sea breezes engulfing the thousands of small Keys.

Beyond the sandy beach, the Atlantic Ocean stretched as great acres of blue, green and white reflections, its water the color of aquamarine and darker shades of blue. Its temperature was such that a person could float in the crystal clear sea for hours, tiny blue fish nibbling at their toes.

Heaven! Why do I have to put up with Tatjana?

"Why did you come to Duck Key? I thought you were attend-ing a conference in Miami Beach and then on Key Largo?" I asked her.

"Conference is over. I want to see how plutocrats live, so I go here. Man in Miami said this would be plutocrat place."

"But you seem to enjoy the life of plutocrats, don't you?" I challenged her.

She almost said yes, but then reflected on my question a bit more. Finally, she came up with this stunning answer:

"Only Government people here, very rich, like you. Poor people not allowed on Key in plutocrat, imperialistic America."

"Sure, they are."

"Nyet."

What struck me as peculiar in this short dialogue was that in her country, poor people would certainly not be admitted to a luxury resort like this. I had seen those resorts in Yugoslavia. For party officials only.

But her president would be admitted, rich as he surely must be. And as a high ranking official, she of course would be welcome as well.

I should really take the time out to show her around a bit, to see how "poor" people live on the Keys.

Her third vodka finished, she made no move to bid farewell. Her tone and manner had again become much more aggressive, as I remembered from the plane ride down to Miami. America, the President, capitalism, democracy, business, free speech, the whole rotten Western system—all of it was under her attack.

"General Motors makes cars, yes? Is owned by rich Government people. Probably your President, too, yes?"

"General Motors is privately owned and has a million plus shareholders. You could buy shares also," I tried, mustering up the remnants of my waning patience.

She glanced at me disdainfully, then she replied, "That is propaganda of your President, he is telling you so, but is not true."

Yet, for the first time, her behavior was not as vehement; she did not make mincemeat out of me. Alas, progress was made, in small measures.

In true European fashion, she just could not admit that she was ever wrong, as it would have been regarded as unacceptable defeat. But I began to notice small changes, such as more reflective replies to my questions, more pauses between sentences, less dogmatic reactions. I took these as signs of her understanding a bit more the West, democracy, our economic system.

She certainly enjoyed all the trimmings of what she called "plutocrat life." That first evening, which started at five with cocktails, ended shortly before midnight, after a sumptuous dinner of five courses, with "California" Chablis, and coffee and French brandy to top it off.

She purported to look out at the starlit Gulf of Mexico when the check came.

Since my workload was light the next morning, a Sunday, and I was free at noon, I thought I should show her a bit more of America. The resort had a twenty-one foot Compact for charter which I had reserved for the afternoon. I would take her out and sail to a few of the scattered, small uninhabited Keys covered with dense mangroves, impenetrable and serene with ospreys nesting in their tree tops.

Tatjana wore an ill-fitting, beige pantsuit which made her look even bigger than she actually was, also socks and slippers and a necklace. She was impeccable.

I wore cut off shorts and a tank top, no shoes. I was grungy.

Two worlds going sailing together.

She had simmered down considerably by now. No more harsh attacks on me, my country and all we stand for. As a matter of fact, she asked a lot of questions now.

"Why do not people live on islands? Grow corn and tomatoes."

"These islands are not inhabitable. There is only sand, shoals and muck. Only mangroves grow here. But they provide feeding grounds for a lot of fish."

"What happens in hurricanes, you call winds, no?"

"Not much, not to these islands anyway. The ocean sweeps over them and that's it."

"What is Junktiques?"

I was baffled. We had just passed under one of the many bridges carrying the Overseas Highway to Key West. There was a billboard on the shore nearby, which she had spotted.

"This is a place where people bring their discarded stuff out of their attic. We call that junk. Then other people come, buy it and put it in their attic. When they start calling it junk, they bring it back to junktiques for sale."

"We have no junk in Romania," she said reflectively. Very likely, she was right on that one.

"Why is water so warm here?"

"Because the Gulf of Mexico is shallow, the water warms up while it circulates; it flows out to the Atlantic, then up the coast and across to Europe. It even keeps your home country's only arctic port, Murmansk, ice-free in winter."

I was amazed at her knowledge of America, though. Their school system must be excellent.

She looked attractive, and almost western, in her dress when we had cocktails again before dinner at the palm leaf-covered bar by the hotel's beach. I told her so.

"I saw it at the hotel store, how do you say, boootik?" she said sheepishly.

Then I suggested that we should go out to a local fish eatery, the Pelican Roost, for oysters, crabs and fresh grouper. I had been there before. It was a noisy place with great atmosphere, with scrubbed wooden tables and lots of everyday people milling about, drinking, eating, laughing, and swapping tall fishing tales. A place Hemingway would have loved.

We also polished off two pitchers of Coors beer. The ceiling fans, through their wide swirling circles, kept the slight Gulf breezes moving through the establishment.

Tatjana looked around intensely. But she had become very quiet.

"Did I do, or say, something wrong?" I asked carefully.

"No, not you."

But she also said she wanted to go back after we finished our meal. No more was spoken then, and during the short cab ride to the hotel. She simply said good night and left for her room.

It bothered me, this unusual silence of hers. I wished she would tear into me again with some fierce political argument. I would have felt comfortable then, more at ease with her, more like I used to know her, even enjoying it.

In fact, it bothered me enough to sit down, up in my suite, to write her a note, asking if she would be free for lunch by the pool the next day. This would be our last chance, I wrote, to meet and talk since I had to return home later that afternoon.

She sent word back through a bellboy the next morning who knocked on the door of the conference room, interrupting my seminar, my flow of thoughts, telling me that she would be delighted. It came at a most inopportune time.

We met at the pool shortly after noon. I was speechless. Seeing her for the first time in a bathing suit I realized that she was much bigger than she appeared wearing all these bulky clothes of hers. There was no unnecessary fat, no rings, just awesomely big features.

I had never seen a woman like that.

Her swim suit was awful, though, like something from the fifties and early sixties, with a garish, flowery design which was too loud to be chic. Fashions in Eastern Europe seemed far behind our times. We alternated swimming in the pool with wading into the shallow Atlantic.

We soaked up the sun, stretched out in comfortable deckchairs strewn casually over the pool's patio and scattered around on the surrounding lawn which drifted into a distant wall of huge, twenty foot century cactus, thirty foot philodendron and forty foot Schefflera.

Later, we would taste the sumptuous buffet the hotel had set up at the edge of the pool deck, in the shade of oleander bushes, bougainvillea trees and towering coconut palms. Pelicans rested lazily on the tops of the marina's pilings.

She was bubbly, even sounding happy. And she talked endlessly in her guttural tones in halting English. I just sat there, amused.

"Yes," she said, "last night when you took me to fish place, I came to realize that not all Americans are rich like you and your President. I seen some people there, like me, yes, like our people, only your people are happier, having more fun, and laughing, no? They were fishermen or touristi? Like me? But they were friendly, fun loving, good people. My people are good people, also, no? We could all be like brothers and sisters."

I felt elated.

"Do you still think I am rich?" I asked laughingly.

"Oh yes, you are rich, in dollars. But are you rich in ideals?"

"I think I have ideals," I replied, somewhat unsure of what would come next.

"Two hundred years ago, your forefathers had visions, yes, for freedom of speech, for freedom of spirit and movement. Today you have capitalistic ideals. Money, real estate, yes, yes, but ideological concepts to help your fellow man survive, no, no, no, you have not."

"Do you like our country better now that you've been here a while?" I inquired, perhaps to divert from highly controversial subjects, perhaps to avoid another confrontation now when we had reached a peaceful coexistence.

"Oh, America is good, life is good here, dress is, how do you say, marvelous? Food is plenty and good, people love fun, they are friendly, helpful, but do they possess strong ideals? Aside from money?"

"Some of us do... ," and the rest of my thoughts trailed off into the breezes.

I rose and went to the lobby to settle my account at the front desk. I also asked the concierge to tell my wife whom I expected any moment to pick me up for the trip home that I would be waiting outside on a deck chair by the pool. He whistled for the bellboys to pick up my bags in the room. Then I stepped outside to join Tatjana again.

Hanna arrived a little later as I had my last trivial political discussion with Tatjana by now in that friendly, small way we had established as our mode of communication.

Tatjana gave her a long, rather cool appraising look as her sleek figure strode towards us, clad in a ravishly elegant beach outfit, her Scandinavian face smiling, her long blonde hair flowing in the wind.

I introduced both to each other.

Tatjana managed to say a brief "Halloh" in her low voice, but afterwards most of her conversational gestures I had become used to stopped quite abruptly.

We left soon thereafter. As the two of us headed back to the lobby and our car, I quickly turned to wave goodbye once more as I had begun to feel a genuine friendship towards her.

But Tatjana had started to walk to the beach. She did not notice me wave anymore.

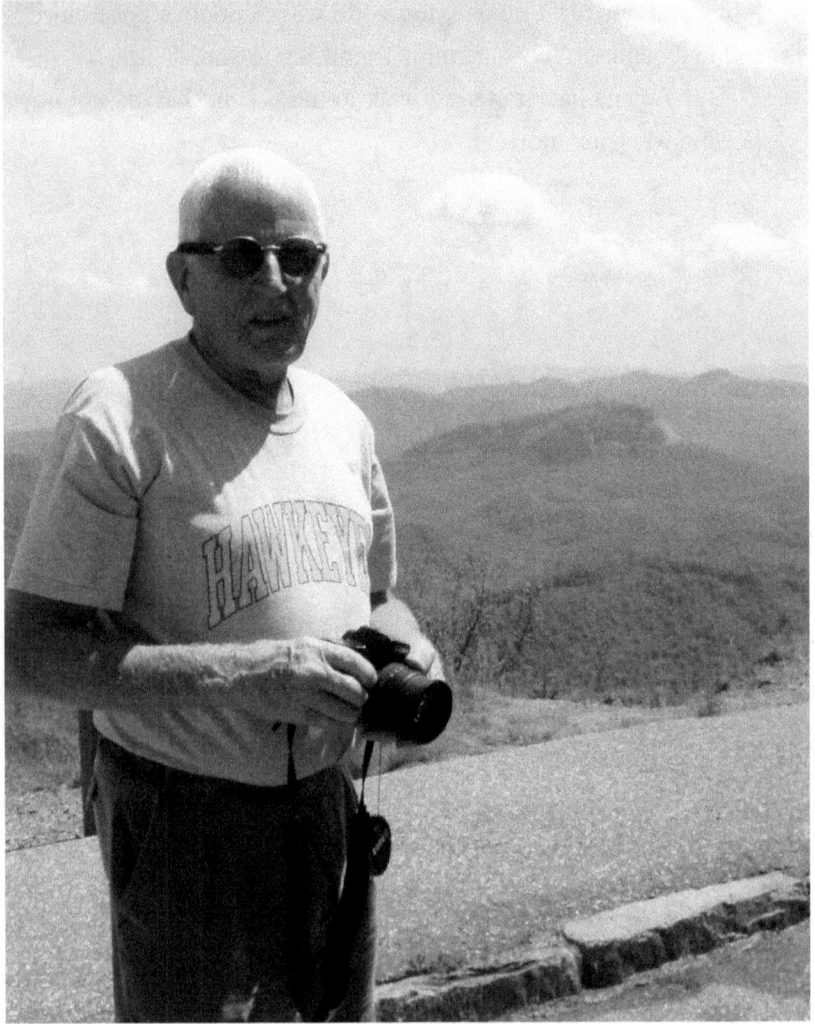

ON THE BLUE RIDGE PARKWAY.

Chapter Ten:
THE NINETIES

1992 NO-NAME STRANGERS

The Delta Airlines Boeing 767 entered the holding pattern of Germany's Frankfurt International Airport on time. The captain had announced when we took off from Atlanta at shortly before six p.m. that we should be over Frankfurt at about eight a.m. European time the following morning.

It was 8:05 in the morning, Good Friday, 1992.

The weather was nothing unusual for this country. Grey mist hung over the countryside below us. Short glimpses through the clouds revealed cars driving with their headlights burning. Traffic was light. Good Friday in Germany is the beginning of a four day Easter weekend.

The flight across the Atlantic had been quiet and smooth. Delta's service was excellent, the sumptuous meal in the evening plentiful and tasty, with spirits served in abundance, the movie adequate. A light breakfast to start the new day appeared about five hours after dinner.

Then we circled for fifty minutes in a holding pattern.

I was in a somber mood now. About to embark on a long European journey, I was apprehensive and restless. I had not been to Europe for years, had heard of the excessive expenses a trip like mine would incur, of unfriendliness, of stealing and petty crime out of control. Probably with all good intentions, people will deliver these tales in great detail to the inquirer, for reasons of their own. They tend to scare those who ask. Although I spent years in Europe during my childhood and adolescence and therefore should know better, they made even me queasy in my stomach.

The intercom's crackling noises rattled me awake. The captain came back on the line to inform us that the delay was caused by an outage of the entire airport radar system.

"But we are now cleared for landing, so please buckle in," he concluded.

We dove into a grey mist that grew darker as we descended. The rumbling of the landing gear indicated the plane's readiness to land west on one of two parallel 12,000 ft. east-west runways.

Seated portside, I witnessed Rhein-Main Air Force Base still occupying the airfield's entire southern portion. K-135's and B-52's in great numbers testified to the American presence. Taxiing back to the terminal, the plane passed the usual clutter of buildings, taxiways, parked aircraft, and numerous additions to the original structures. They were built some thirty years before. But the clutter appeared to be organized at this largest European airport.

The temperature was 4 degrees centigrade, 39 degrees Fahrenheit. I felt lonely and homesick for the 86 degree Atlanta airport and its space which I had left such a short time ago. Nevertheless, Germany, here I was.

Retrieving my large backpack, reactivated from the attic after several years of non-use, I noticed it was brought out to the carousel baggage area in an equally large, airport-owned, plastic container. As far back as I could remember, it had never received such royal treatment. It looked faded and showed its years. But then I love well-worn things. And my backpack housed my memories of exciting, glorious trips.

I found my way through the fairly quiet airport arrival building to the underground railroad station. There, trains operate between the adjacent cities of Mainz and Frankfurt by passing underneath the airport. Air travelers are thus afforded a convenient way of reaching the downtown areas of both cities in their respective main railroad terminals, which in turn offer connecting trains all over Europe.

I did not see any train ticket counter and wandered around, thinking about how I could buy my train fare to Frankfurt's main terminal when I came upon an automatic ticket dispenser. It said in German that to buy the fare, an amount of Deutsche Mark 3.50 in coins would need to be inserted into the slot provided. Yet, I had no German coins on me. I possessed bills which I had brought with me from home, but no coins. And there was no change dispenser from bills to coins around anywhere. Nor were any of the Wechselbuero or exchange agencies open on this one of the most sacred and holy days during any year.

So I stood in front of the dispenser, thinking about how I would manage this unexpected obstacle, when a voice next to me said in fluent, barely accented English, "can I help you?"

"Yeah," I replied, without really looking at the owner of this voice, "I just don't know how to buy my ticket from this machine."

"Just slide DM 3.50 into the slot, sir, and your ticket will come out below."

Now I took a closer look. He was so very polished and smooth. Must be an educated man, I thought.

"Well, I have this problem here. I don't have any coins on me. And I don't see where this machine would take any bills."

"It doesn't," answered the smooth person.

Examining his face once more, I noticed that my friendly stranger was obviously German, well and cleanly dressed. He carried a small overnight bag in his left hand, had an umbrella dangling from his right and wore a Tiroler hat atop his slightly balding head. I had noticed it when in typical German fashion he had tipped his hat. All this gave him away as a Teutonic.

"But here is DM 10.00 in coins," he continued, "you can slide in either four one mark pieces or the one five mark piece and your change will come out below on your left. Then take your ticket below on your right."

What friendliness, I thought! I hadn't really expected that after what people had told me about present-day Germany.

"But I cannot pay you back your ten marks, I only have bills."

"No matter. Just keep the coins."

"Thank you. Thank you very much, you have been very kind, most helpful, indeed."

"You are welcome," he said and walked away.

I did as he had told me and received my ticket through the slot when I noticed my friend and helper had turned around and was walking back towards me.

"I just remembered that perhaps you could do me a favor in return," he said with a brilliant, convincing smile.

"Sure thing, what can I do for you?"

"Well, you see, I am on my way to Atlanta and I just remembered that today is Good Friday. All the banks are closed today. I do not have any US dollars, did not have the time yesterday to change some money. So, do you perhaps have any dollars to spare, like $100? I will give you back double in Deutsche Mark, like DM 200. That's a much better exchange rate than the banks would give you. I really want to compensate you for all the trouble I may cause."

Well, I thought, here is a chance to do something for this friendly soul. I pulled out my money bag from below my flannel shirt where it hung around my neck and ripped open its Velcro cover. I had stashed all my spare dollars into it shortly before we landed. It also contained my traveler's checks and passport.

He looked gingerly at what I was doing.

"No, sorry, can't do it," I told him.

"But you have more than that in your money bag, don't you?"

So he had peeked in there, sizing up the entire contents in a split second.

"Yes, but I need what I have for my return trip home," I replied a touch less friendly now.

"But you have much over $100, that is enough, is it, too much, you say?"

In his excitement, he had begun to lose his smooth English. Influenced by increased suspicions, my willingness to help him began to diminish.

"Okay, I can give you $40, but not more. And that's it!"

"How about $60 that would help me because I am going to be lost in Atlanta. I have to take taxi there, go to hotel, you know, eat some meal. You would help me, would you not?"

"Alright then, $60," and I started pulling three twenty dollar bills out of my money bag while he took out two 50 mark bills and one ten mark bill, as he had given me ten marks already. This made 120 Deutsche Mark for 60 dollars, an exchange rate more than 20% better than any bank would have offered, as he had explained.

He then stuffed his bills in an envelope and suggested we move further over, toward the tile wall of the station, where we would not be seen. I was soon to find out the reason for this maneuver.

"Money exchange like this is illegal in Germany, you know," he stated. Really suspicious now I hollered after him, "why move over there? If you want your dollars, we do the exchange right here." But I did follow him two steps, no more, towards the distant wall, then stood still.

He turned around and came back, handing me the envelope after I had given him three twenty-dollar bills.

"Thank you very much. You Americans are such friendly and helpful people. I really look forward to traveling to your country now. And I hope you will enjoy your visit here in, how do you say, old country?"

Pacified somewhat, I replied: "Thank you, yes, I will, especially since I found such a nice and warmhearted person like you helping a total stranger find his way around. Have a safe flight and say hello to Atlanta for me."

He turned and walked briskly away while the train thundered into the station.

Fifteen minutes later, I arrived at Frankfurt's busy Union Terminal and headed straight for the ticket counter. I did have a Euro-rail-pass for three weeks, but would activate it only the following week when serious traveling would start. Right now, I was heading for a place called Buchen, barely 180 kilometers away, a medieval town with a 700-year-old castle where, on Easter Sunday, a reunion of my family would take place.

I told the agent behind his firmly closed glass windows "Buchen" and he slid out through a slot underneath the window a piece of paper with a number on it, obviously the price of the fare.

Was this measure serving the purpose of explaining to the many non-German speaking tourists what the fare would be? Or was it a safety measure, as in "you show me your money first, then you get your ticket." I don't know and never found out. Instead I reached for the envelope my savior at the airport had given me, opened it to fish out some of the Deutsche Mark bills... and there it was: no money, not one single bill, or even a coin, only shredded paper in there to make it feel like it was stuffed with bills.

Now I knew why he had turned away and had suggested to go to a tile wall. He had swapped my dollars for shreds of waste paper.

I HAD BEEN HAD! GOOD AND HARD!

Welcome to Germany!

I was fuming. I was madder than hell. I felt my confidence had been betrayed, my privacy invaded. I felt lousy. And in my mind, I seriously debated taking the train right back to the airport. I knew the plane I had arrived on was still there being serviced for the return to Atlanta.

I stood there near the center of the spacious entrance hall of the huge terminal, reflecting on the evils of the world, trying to control my intense anger. Busy people were hurrying to and fro, carrying bags and all of them obviously knowing where they were going and what they were doing. I wondered if any of them had ever been cheated out of their wits. I doubted it. They all looked smarter and more street-wise than I.

And I felt lonely again—very lonely and miserable.

I noticed a tall kid enter the station, with a backpack the size of mine on his back, with blond hair cut short in a crew style, with big, blue, shiny eyes. He appeared to be in his mid-twenties. And by his looks, height, complexion, dress and Nikes, he was undoubtedly an American. He paused in the center of the hall, put down a carry-on bag hanging over his right shoulder, not exactly knowing where he would have to go. He was about five yards away from where I stood, his eyes sweeping a wide circle, searching.

Not half a minute later, a short fellow, about the same age, came up to him. He obviously asked him a question which I could not hear. But my backpacker countryman only nodded, with that big, grateful smile which North Americans can easily muster when they have found a helping hand abroad.

The short man grabbed the guy's carry-on bag and started marching briskly, almost running, in the direction of the ticket counters and thus to the exit of the huge railroad station.

Observing all this, I jumped forward, with my backpack on my back, to the side of my fellow traveler and asked him swiftly:

"Are you American?"

To which he replied, "No, I am from Toronto."

"Never mind," I shouted, "this guy is going to skip away with your bag."

I started running in a pace as fast as I could considering the load I had on my back.

"No, he isn't," I heard Toronto call after me.

"YES, HE IS, damm it," I hollered, "come on, let's move."

"But he said … '

I did not hear the rest. I plunged forward faster and now my newly found friend from Toronto was right behind me. Near the ticket counters, I stood, cupped my hands around my mouth, and yelled from the top of my lungs:

"H E Y !"

Then I started running again, now with my pal from Toronto right next to me.

At first, people all around us stopped, then started running themselves, probably scared. Another hold up, maybe?

The man with the carry-on bag under his arm stopped also, turned around, then saw not only one very tall guy with a huge backpack on his shoulders, but two side by side, storming towards him. That made him instantly drop the bag on the floor and run out of the station as fast as his short legs would allow.

"That bag has all my money and my passport in it. Man, am I glad you caught him. But he was so friendly. How did you know?" asked my Canadian friend.

"Because I have been had myself about half an hour ago."

Welcome to Germany, again.

We stood for a while and talked. He wanted to buy breakfast for me, but I declined because my train was soon going to depart. "You know that you made my day?" I told him.

"You made mine for sure. Why do you think I made yours?"

"Because I could prevent you from the ego-deflating experience I went through this morning. I was ready to go back home. I was so furious. Now I feel good because I could help and stop you from feeling as lousy as I did earlier."

We shook hands long and hard and as I turned toward the platform where my train waited, he called out after me,

"Thanks, buddy, thanks so much. Is it alright if I come see you in North Carolina?"

"Sure thing. Do it."

But of course in all the commotion, both of us had failed to exchange contact information.

Happy wanderings, stranger!

1992 THE BAXTERS

During April and May of 1992, I undertook an extensive tour of western Europe. My plan was to recoup some of the impressions I had during my adolescent years, primarily during the time in my life when I attended several European universities.

For the purpose of convenience in traveling, but also recapturing the spirit of other years as well, I took a month-long unlimited rail pass. My attire for the journey consisted of blue jeans, Field and Stream hiking boots, flannel and T-shirts, a ski jacket, wool socks, my journal and my old Northface backpack which I repatriated from the attic where it had rested unused for some years.

Coming in from France to Barcelona to witness the preparations for the summer Olympic Games, I followed up with a visit to Madrid, then headed down to Cordoba.

There was no cab at its clean and modern railroad station when my train arrived in mid-afternoon—no street car or bus either. I asked, in English, where I could find hotels. People smiled and shrugged. No one understood me. I knew then that I was far removed into Spain's provinces, away from the metropolitan centers of her major cities. English was not readily spoken or understood in the south of the country.

I fingered for my notebook in my backpack, tore out a page and wrote "Hotel" on it, including a large question mark underneath the word.

"Si, si, senor, a la Mezquita, tres kilometres," said the first person I showed my sign to. It worked.

"Gracias, senor," I acknowledged his help.

Then I set out to march the three kilometers with my backpack, which I blessed. I knew beforehand that there would be situations like this where no transportation was available. I also knew that I did not ever want to be dependent on wheels of any kind during my travels.

Sweaty from my hike in ninety degree heat, I easily found la Mezquita. It was hard to miss and a first time visitor would stand in awe over its size and uniqueness.

There were a number of small hotels next to its high stone wall enclosing the large courtyard. These linked the various stages of the huge mosque together. Most of them were a stone's throw away from the tall tower which was built around the mosque's original minaret, from which were issued the calls for morning and evening prayers.

I chose the Hotel Marisa, small, elegant, well kept, with tile floors and carved furniture. Its whitewashed walls were adorned by Spanish art in the form of religious carvings or modern oil paintings. A secluded courtyard in the building's rear gave the downstairs its southern accent. It held many loosely arranged, exotic potted plants. They radiated tropical character, along with the water pearling from ornate fountains.

The check-in clerk spoke English, which helped. I felt awkward at first in the splendor of the small foyer, with my shirt soaked from the long hike. But without checking my credit-worthiness by asking for my Visa card or requesting advance payment, he handed me the key to a room upstairs that faced the street. It had French doors, which I opened right away, leading to a small balcony over the narrow street. It also allowed a perfect view of the mosque's brick-like stone wall and the bell tower twenty yards away.

Furnishings were sparse but exquisite. The small but well-planned bathroom off to one side seemed adequate and smelled of lavender soap.

I profess not to be choosy when selecting accommodations for the night and think I have proven that point many times during more Spartan journeys. But I can easily fall for some niceties and luxury, if given a chance to indulge in both.

The Hotel Marisa was a place for such indulgence. I dropped my backpack in the room, then ran out again into the many narrow streets, with hardly enough room even for the smallest of Spanish cars to pass through, to buy some film and sundries. Vendors displayed their wares in open doorways, clothiers hung their colorful dresses and shirts on hooks outside their stores, and leather crafters called out to me in Spanish, to praise their work and entice me to buy. I did, of course. A small wallet found its way into my pocket, to remind me later, at home in the United States, of the splendor and elegance of life in southern Spain.

When I returned to the hotel, I indulged in leisure, taking a long bath and ordering a Campari soda in my room afterwards, watching the sun set over the old minaret, trying to imagine how life must have been in this place almost thirteen hundred years ago.

At a quarter to ten, after my second Campari, I walked three blocks to a place I had spotted during my earlier stroll through town. La Tribunata's had an open courtyard in the same manner and style as my hotel. Tables were small and loosely arranged around a central fountain. Starched white linen tablecloths and napkins marked the elegance of the establishment. When I checked it out with the clerk at the Marisa, he praised its cuisine.

I ordered a four course dinner. I was starving. The last meal was ten hours before, on the TALGO II express train down from Madrid. Antipasta, consomme, then beef cubes marinated with garlic and herbs and boiled to a tender softness, with rice, beets and what looked to me like squash, followed by the all-time favorite, a crema catalana. All of it was accompanied by a bottle of light, red wine from the region near Seville, eighty miles to the west.

There were others dining in the courtyard. I heard French, German, and could make out the often Welch-sounding English of Canadians from Ontario, an accent also found in the Blue Ridge Mountains of Virginia and North Carolina.

Next to my table sat a middle-aged couple from the United States. Following their conversation involuntarily, I knew they were from New Hampshire. They were engrossed in deep conversation about an obviously grave subject and did not pay any attention to me. That suited me fine because I cherished the idea of being alone with my thoughts, to freely observe and soak in the Spanish life around me.

When I came downstairs the next morning after nine to have my breakfast served to me in the hotel's open courtyard, I saw the couple from last night seated nearby. Nobody else was there.

"Good morning," I said, trying to smile as brightly as I can so early in the morning. "How did you like your dinner at La Tribunata's last night?"

They looked up, startled, for a second, then wished me a good morning as well.

"You are from New Hampshire, are you not?"

They looked more startled now.

"Yes, we are, but how… ?"

"I sat next to you last night and could not help overhear your reference to your home state. My name is Peter and I am from North Carolina."

"Good to meet you, Peter. No, we don't mind that you overheard our conversation. There were no secrets. I am Ron Baxter and this is my wife Gladys."

"Good to see you both," I replied.

We exchanged the customary pleasantries and facts relating to our respective lives, professions and current itineraries.

"I just took early retirement from my employer of thirty-four years. My last job was the position of manager of our London office. We lived there for five years," said Ron.

"So the Jaguar parked in front is yours?"

For the third time, they looked startled. Then they laughed and said: "You must be a detective to find out so many details in such a short time."

"Just putting two and two together."

"When we returned to the United States a year ago, we left our car in England with friends," said Gladys, "we thought we would use it for travel in Europe for the next few years. So here we are."

"Great idea."

"Did you rent a car?" Ron wanted to know.

"No, I am traveling on a Eurorail pass for a month. I only carry one piece of luggage. That's why I am dressed the way I am."

"Are you carrying a backpack, then?" Gladys wanted to know. I liked her. She had to be a neat lady to be asking a question like that.

"Yes, ma'am."

"Then we must have passed you yesterday, early afternoon. You were hiking towards la Mezquita. All we could see were your legs and your huge backpack, nothing more," said Ron.

"That's me, sir."

When we rose from our tables, Gladys asked if I had been in Cordoba before, to which I replied that I hadn't.

"But then, wouldn't you want to come along with us to see the mosque? That is alright, is it not, Ron?" continued Gladys. Ron nodded.

"I will be glad to, if you are sure I am not intruding."

"Not in the least."

On the way out, I asked the clerk to have my backpack brought down from my room for safekeeping, until I was ready to depart in the evening.

We walked across the street into the wide courtyard of la Mezquita, through a high, wooden gate carved with religious figures like many in Spain. On the court's other side stretched the mosque's northern wall, the length of two city blocks, immensely impressive.

"Peter, to this day, this largest of all mosques in Europe is a splendid legacy of the Arabs. It is considered the first monument of western Islam. There is none like it in the world," Ron started our extensive tour of the buildings. He was certainly well-versed in the history of this magnificent structure.

"When was it built? In 711 AD?"

"I believe it was started in 780 AD, by the Arab ruler Abderraman," said Gladys.

I stayed with the Baxters all day. Leaving the mosque, we walked across the river Guadalquivir on an old stone bridge built by the Romans nearly two thousand years ago. At its other end stood an oval building, also built by the Romans. Both bridge and building resembled in every detail, if on a smaller scale, its cousins at Ponte San Angelo in Rome, leading to the Castel San Angelo on the opposite side of the river Tevere.

For a late lunch we found a quaint, small restaurant in a side street, called Los Patios. A narrow aisle let to a small, open court which was densely planted with rubber trees, orchid bushes and tall bougainvillea, their red leaves hanging off the walls where they had been tied up for support.

The Baxters insisted on inviting me for lunch. I gratefully accepted without fuss and ordered a clam salad with some baguette-type bread and a bottle of local beer, by the name of Cordoba, of course.

"Where will you go from here, Peter?" asked Gladys.

"Back to Madrid on the evening train, to change at Chamartin Station for the night express to Lisbon. It leaves at midnight."

"We just drove in from three days in the Portuguese capital yesterday. You should really see Belem, Estoril. It's a must. Take a day and drive out to Caba de Roca, and…"

Gladys interrupted the well-meant flow of Ron's suggestions and said: "Peter cannot keep all this in mind. But he has traveled a lot. He knows how to get around and find things he wants to see."

"Well, then let me give you this address of a friend of ours in Lisbon. He works for the same company I did. He is the manager of our Lisbon operations. His name is Fernandoz."

"Thank you, Ron, I appreciate it," I said, folding the scrap of paper onto which he had scribbled the name and address, to place it into my new Cordoba leather wallet.

It was almost four o'clock. I said I would have to leave soon.

"Let's at least stroll over to the Museo des Belles Artes," said Gladys. "After a glimpse into its marvelous halls, we'll let you go," Ron added.

When we emerged from the museum almost an hour later, Ron said: "We will now drive you to the station."

"Thanks, but I am sure I can find a cab."

"That's not the point. We really want to drive you there. It has been a perfect day for us and we fully enjoyed your company," Gladys stated emphatically.

And so it happened, that twenty-six hours after I arrived in Cordoba and marched the long hike to the hotel with my shirt soaked from sweat, I was whisked back, lounging in the deep leather seat of the Jaguar's rear compartment, with the car's license plates and national emblem "GB" leaving no doubt as to where the stately couple exiting the front hailed from.

It was when the rear door opened, a backpack thrown out onto the pavement, and a tall man, looking somewhat unkempt, emerged, that the faces of those observing the scene became puzzled. In their humble opinion, it did not all fit together.

We parted with promises to stay in touch.

"Gracias, muchas gracias, senor y senora," I called after the Jaguar as it slid away. They both waved through the opened windows.

Cordoba, I thought as the TALGO III sped to Madrid through Andalusia, was the jewel of my journey.

1992 LUNCH AT CABA DE ROCA

During a backpacking, rail pass trip to Portugal in the early nineties, I relished this friendly country and her kind, generous people. While in Lisbon for a week, I took a bus out to nearby Caba de Roca, the cape of the rock. It is Europe's westernmost point with a vista from a high cliff down to the roaring Atlantic. The location has a striking resemblance to Cape Spear, Newfoundland, America's easternmost point. Even the sparse vegetation on both coasts is alike.

Hiking back the two miles to the spot where the bus had let me off, I stopped at the Capuchos Monastery, uniquely built in 1532, by Franciscan Petrus Alcantara into a rock wall at the side of a mountain. There is hardly a wall in the complex, except where two natural rock walls connected to form an enclosure.

Monks' quarters were chiseled into the rock, with a small hole to the outside as a window. However, there was no glass to shelter the occupant from the strong winds off the nearby Atlantic. In the mensa, which is Latin for dining hall, the table turned out to be a sizable piece of rock, with smaller ones placed around it as chairs. Although it was a pleasant, warm day, it was so cool inside the cave-like monastery that I started to shiver.

I walked back to the village where the bus had stopped, to catch the next one back to Lisbon. But the crude sign on the wall of a house nearby indicated that I'd have another hour-and-a-half before it would arrive. The settlement was small, perhaps seven or eight farmhouses, typical of Europe. There it is a tradition that farmers live in clustered villages and tend to their fields surrounding them.

I looked around, trying to find a place for some food but didn't see any. So I motioned, imitating the process of eating, to a few fellows standing a short distance away and eyeing this strange man with a huge backpack on his shoulders. They pointed to a modest house, which showed no sign of being an eating establishment.

Knocking on the door, I heard someone call out something I did not understand. The men who were watching smiled now and pointed in a way suggesting that I should just walk in. I timidly opened the door then and stepped into what appeared to be a spartanly furnished living room/kitchen.

A middle-aged woman bowed her head, smiled, pointed to the crude table and pulled a chair for me. Then she must have asked what I wanted, to which I smiled, shrugged and shook my head, because I did not speak her language.

But I had seen the kitchen table when I entered. There was a beautiful looking loaf of bread and a big chunk of cheese placed there. I gestured toward it and we both walked the few steps into the kitchen area.

There I showed her, upon her unspoken question, how much of the cheese I wanted and also pointed to some grapes stored in a handmade straw basket on the sideboard. She nodded to all this in silence, took the cheese and the bread and vanished into the back of the house.

She did not come back for a long time. I had already given up examining the walls of her living room, adorned mostly with religious items including a crucifix in one corner but also one photo, yellow from age, depicting people from another era. I was mostly afraid that I had scared her away. I began to prepare to leave, reaching for my backpack which I had stored in one corner.

Just then she returned, beaming. She carried a large plate where the cheese lay cut into thin slices covering its entire surface, bordered by the bread divided into thick, warm, moist chunks. Grapes and oranges came on a separate, smaller plate.

Instantly, I dug in.

After a minute or so, she came back and placed a tumbler of cool Portuguese country wine next to my plate. Then she smiled, bowed her head again and disappeared.

I thought it was going to be a snack. Instead it turned out to be a full sized lunch.

Feeling great, my hunger subdued, I pushed my chair back. My shy hostess reappeared instantly from nowhere and stood near the kitchen table, waiting, not looking at me. I walked up to her, with my two hands stretched out, one holding a bunch of coins out of my jeans pockets, the other some bills from the money bag around my neck, offering both to her.

She smiled again and picked out what she needed from my holdings.

What she took could not even have amounted to two dollars! Indeed, a gracious hostess!

1993 ARKANSAS LAW

Only one traffic light existed in Russelville, Arkansas, a small sleepy town with its main street only one block long. Considered an exorbitant luxury by some sturdy town folks and calling the device an unnecessary gadget of modern times, it nevertheless fulfilled its purpose by regulating cross traffic between the intersecting highways US 64 and State Route 7.

My light was green when I approached on my Suzuki. So I proceeded slowly through the intersection, then gathered speed, after leaving the main part of town, and soon thereafter resumed my cruising speed of sixty mph.

But hold it right there! A foreign object appeared in my bike's rear view mirrors. By instinct—or is it a guilty conscience?—I eased up on the throttle and looked closer, to inspect and analyze what was behind me. Holy mackerel! Blue lights flashing, that's what it was. Not just one, two, no, several of them mounted on the rooftops of an equal number of police cruisers. My heart skipped a beat or two. My mind raced through what I might have done wrong.

I didn't wait for them to pass and flag me down. I eased the bike over to the shoulder, rolled into the grass and stopped, remaining seated in the saddle. Within seconds, all cruisers—there were three of them—surrounded me, blocking my way, one ahead, and one behind me and one on my right side facing the ditch. The only side open was the left one, fronting the highway, but it was instantly walled off by three monstrous looking cops, standing there with legs spread, hands on their holsters and snarling:

"Get off your bike."

"Yes, sir."

"NOW!" snapped the man who seemed to be in charge. He wore two shoulder bars on his shirt whereas the others did not. I took him to be a captain.

I got off, making painstakingly sure to kick down the center stand and pulling the heavily loaded bike up, rocking it slightly to insure that it was on solid ground. Then they grabbed me, on all sides, the three of them, and threw me on the trunk lid of one cruiser to frisk me. They found nothing.

"Driver's license," I heard through my helmet, muffled by its thick insulation lining.

"Just a minute," I said, took my helmet off and fingered for the wallet in my jean's hip pocket, a movement which brought three hands back to their respective holsters.

I handed my license to the officer in charge who had barked out all those nasty commands.

"What have I done?" I asked him.

"Never mind. You just shut up. We'll get to you later."

Two of them disappeared into one of the police cars while the third diligently inspected my Suzuki.

"Again, what have I done?"

No answer. Silence. A grim look on his face. After about five, or perhaps ten minutes, during which I became increasingly terrified, they came back, the two who had gone into the cruiser, and the captain said,

"You can go now."

No apology, no explanation was offered. Just another command. My anger swelled up dangerously. No wonder, I thought, that Arkansas is called the Bear State.

"Wait a minute. As a tax-paying citizen of this country, I have the right to know why you stopped, frisked and arrested me. I am expecting an answer to my question RIGHT NOW!"

"We didn't arrest you," one of them said. His tone of voice had considerably mellowed.

"You damn well nearly did. So why did you stop and frisk me?"

"We have an APB out for someone we are looking for," said the officer in charge. "He is an escaped prisoner, reddish-bleached hair, about six feet tall. He stole a Suzuki motorcycle from a restaurant's parking lot while the owner had dinner there. Had a North Carolina license plate. Trying to get out of Arkansas, he was, last we heard. You fit the description to the T."

"But I am touring. Look at all my camping gear and stuff strapped to the bike," I said.

"We didn't see that," another one of the three threw in, remarkably more friendly now. "We saw your black and grey Suzuki coming through the intersection in Russelville. So we thought we had our man and gave chase."

"Sorry about that," said the third man who hadn't talked much but was smiling now, "and ride safe."

That small statement gave him away as another motorcycle rider.

HIS hand I shook in parting!

1993 TENNESSEE LAW

I joined Interstate 24 in Monteagle, after cruising US 64 for some 350 miles from Memphis. Now I could finally roll freely. Traffic in both southbound lanes flowed at an even seventy-five mph.

Then Arkansas began to haunt me again. A flashing blue light had appeared in my rear view mirrors. Please, NOT AGAIN!

I slowed, rolled into the grass beside the shoulder and took my helmet off. I always do that, but especially with policemen stopping me on the road. I consider it a courtesy to all persons who approach me, to be able to see my face when we talk.

The Tennessee Highway Trooper stepped out of his cruiser and walked up behind me. He looked stately with his 6'2" height and trapper hat.

"Afternoon, sir." His voice sounded clear, cheerful. No hateful sounds like in Arkansas.

"Howdy," I replied, "what'd I do?"

"Well, you were going a bit fast there a while back."

"The whole traffic was going seventy-five to eighty, sir," I said, knowing darn well that it was the kind of statement almost always used by speed offenders.

"That may be so, but the speed limit is sixty-five mph and you exceeded it by over ten miles."

"Yes, sir." There's no point in arguing with the law.

"Say, that is a real fine motorcycle you are riding there."

"Thank you, sir."

"Used to be a member of the Chattanooga police force. We rode Harleys. What's the cc in yours? Eighty five? That's plenty of power, ain't it? Let's see, do you have a shaft? Yes, I see it. Never rode one with it. Takes some horsepower away, though, don't it? I read about that somewhere. Forget where it was. But you have plenty power, don't you? And shaft is a lot cleaner than chains, isn't it? What with all the oil spilling over the rear wheel and such. Where are you going, buddy? Back home? Been on a trip, I see. Gee, wish I could ride with you. Love the sport."

With all this waterfall-like outburst of motorcycle lingo underlining the man's love for two wheelers, he never heard his two-way radio going:

"SEVEN SIX THREE, COME IN... SEVEN SIX THREE, COME IN, PLEASE!"

"Sir, I think you are being called by your dispatcher," I told him.

His head popped up, listening. Then he said:

"Gee, thanks buddy. Just thought I stop and see what you're riding here. Got to go now. Have a safe trip. Stay upright."

"But . . , ," I started. Yet he was on his way to the cruiser already. He couldn't hear me anymore.

1995 ALICE IN WONDERLAND

"Howdy," I greeted the young ranger, "how are you?" His name tag spelled out Andre. He was on duty inside the ranger station next to the Canyonlands National Park Visitor Center, up on Utah's "Island in the Sky" plateau. Like everything else, the station was simple, no frills, housed in a pre-fab structure. It looked temporary. But then, most of the sparse facilities in the park are makeshift. It had opened to the public only fourteen years earlier.

That suited me fine. As a matter of fact, I liked it that way. The lack of fanciness would keep out the hordes of tourists in tour buses. They already crowd Canyonland's neighbor on the other side of the Colorado, Arches National Park, visible quite clearly twenty-five miles to the northeast.

"Good, thank you, sir," the ranger answered. It was refreshing to see his bright face so early in the morning. Dark brown eyes looked straight forward from under a dense crop of auburn hair. His upper lip was adorned with what might one day develop into a full-sized mustache, yet now only consisted of some light blond peach fuzz. "What can I do for you?"

"I was wondering if I could obtain a permit to run the White Rim Road," I asked.

"Certainly," he said with a smile displaying rows of immaculate front teeth, "have you got a four-wheel-drive vehicle?"

"Yes, I do. My Tracker is outside."

"Great, that's a good SUV for the White Rim. I'll get you some maps. You will need them."

He turned and loped over to the rack where he kept all his pamphlets. He wore khaki shorts and Nike hiking boots. He had a lanky, well-toned body and strong legs. Those of a mountain biker, I thought. He couldn't have been much more than twenty-two.

"Are you alone?" he asked.

"Yes. Why?"

"Well, we don't encourage people traveling alone on the White Rim. You probably know, it's 110 miles long and takes about four days to drive. We patrol it every five days."

"Then what do you suggest I should do?"

"We recommend you hang around until someone else turns up to go the White Rim. Most everyone we ask will team up with another vehicle. For safety, you know."

"Makes sense. Have you driven it?"

"Oh yes, my first time was over ten years ago when I was straight out of college. I had an old Scout, a box on wheels, really. But it had great traction," he replied.

Ten years ago. Out of school. So he must be over thirty! They are younger looking every year.

"I am afraid I don't have the time to hang around that long. Have to head back east. How about the Shafer Canyon Trail? Can I ride it down to Moab?"

"No problem."

He wrote out my permit and handed it to me.

"Here you go, come back to see us. Take more time on your next visit. I know, you'd like the White Rim, if you liked the Alpine Loop in Colorado as you said."

"Thank you. Yes, indeed I did. Got to be going. Take care."

"You too, sir."

All this politeness from a young ranger who looked clean and scrubbed! I did not feel that way at all, almost wanted to tell him to skip the "sir," because I looked so grungy. But it seemed to have been in his blood.

I had spent the last two nights in Willow Flat, the only campground in the vast park. Like its other facilities, it was simple. It had fewer than twenty campsites, far apart from each other, built on the eastern side of a butte, a huge rounded boulder of sandstone rock. So the hefty winds come from the west, I deduced by looking at the site I took, which was right next to the butte.

Outhouses were in two locations on the periphery. I set my tent in the shelter of an 800-year-old Utah pine, the state's oldest and most durable tree, stubby and sturdy, not higher than twenty feet. There was no drinking water anywhere in the park. But I had brought a good supply from Moab in my SUV.

Yesterday, I had hiked some trails and driven others in the Tracker. Today, I had to leave, to go back east because my journey would have to end soon. Besides, I was grubby looking, with a two-day unshaven face.

Moreover, there was a series of fierce thunderstorms during most of the previous night. As a result, flash floods from the sudden downpour cascaded through the campsite, unhindered and forceful. My tent must have been close to one of them, because I awoke with the floor of my small abode sopping wet, my socks dripping and my flashlight out of order. Even my mattress and the sleeping bag were wet, the latter from the outside only. It was a mess.

Yet, stepping out of my tent, I witnessed the sky as blue as can be. It would be a great day to hike or ride some more trails before going home. But there was definitely no time left to go the White Rim Road now.

So I headed for the beginning of Shafer Canyon Trail, one mile northeast from the ranger station. I knew from Andre that it was one of the easier four-wheel-drive roads in the park. It began with well-graded gravel, but no sooner had the trail reached the rim of the mesa, than it became very rocky and started winding down in tight switchback curves. The road was carved out of the sheer, vertical sandstone wall of the "Island in the Sky" plateau, many decades before.

I had the top down, having opened it up this morning before leaving camp. Water cascading down from the rocks splashed into my car. I didn't care. In this desert climate, it would dry instantly.

Sometimes, though, it would splash in the red mud first and then into the Tracker. Now that was quite different. But who cares, the vehicle and I were both filthy anyway. I screamed out loud with joy. And a few seconds later, I heard my scream from the echo in the cavernous canyon. This was living at its best!

In about an hour after leaving the rim, the trail straightened out in the valley almost 2,000 feet below. I could go just a bit faster now, with most of the switchbacks behind me. But the flash flood gullies were still torrents. I slowed to a crawl before entering them because I never knew what these rushing waters might hide or how deep they might be. In no way should the Tracker ever be submerged deeper than the upper rim of its wheels, because water might seep into the fuel injection ports. And that spelled trouble.

Suddenly, unexpectedly, I came around a curve and found myself standing face to face with another vehicle!

I remembered Andre had talked about that possibility. But what's a car doing in this wilderness, was my first thought. Then I looked closer—a passenger car, four-door sedan, late model. It was an Oldsmobile—burgundy color, fairly clean. This boat was designed and soft sprung for smooth boulevards, not this bumpy track.

The sedan had stopped too. I saw two frightened faces behind its windshield. There was no room for the two vehicles to pass. I climbed out of the Tracker and sauntered over to the sedan.

"Hello there," said a sweet voice from the driver's side window which was rolled down. A whiff of air conditioning hit my face. Then a second voice from within the sedan whispered softly another "hello."

"Hi there, how are you both doing, ladies?"

"We are fine. But we were wondering now for a while, is it raining up there where those black clouds are?" asked the driver.

"Probably is. Most likely another thunderstorm; had a lot of those up there last night."

"Oh heavens, then you have been up there? We wondered what it is like. We want to drive up to the rim."

I couldn't believe what I had just heard. The two older ladies, maybe in their late sixties/early seventies, certainly seemed enterprising, but they shouldn't really attempt something like going up the kind of trail that I had just come down.

"Ma'am, is your Oldsmobile equipped with four-wheel-drive?"

"Oh heavens, what is that? We don't know anything about these technical things, you know."

I believed her on that point. Then I explained to them the virtues and necessity of four-wheel-drive. "You need it, going up there."

"Bless your heart, young man. Oh, but wouldn't you know, Bernice, we do have four wheels on the car, don't we?" mused the driver.

"Yes, Alice, we do," Bernice nodded to her companion. I cringed.

Two worlds had met. The ladies were well-dressed, well-bred, sweet, very polite, soft spoken and considerate, no doubt. I stood before them, sweaty, raunchy, in my dusty boots and filthy jeans, with a two-day beard on my face, my short hair matted down from sweating under my BIG DOG cap.

"How far do we still have to go?" asked Alice.

"You have about ten miles ahead of you, 'bout two hours. But be aware! I must tell you, there are several flashflood gullies to cross. The water is cascading through them, quite deep too."

"That is no problem as you would say, wouldn't you? Because we already crossed a few water streams. That was exciting, wasn't it, Bernice?" exclaimed Alice. Bernice nodded dutifully.

"Well, you know, ladies, I can help you turn this thing around, if you would decide to go back down."

Alice looked at Bernice. Bernice looked at Alice. Both had absolutely mischievous expressions on their faces. Then they shook their silvery heads.

"No, thank you," replied Alice. "We think we will go up."

"Just thought I tell you about the risks ahead," I concluded. "Let me back up a bit. Then there is a turnout one hundred-yards up. I'll back my Tracker into it and you can go ahead. Okay?"

I did as I said. The ladies followed me up and then slowly, very slowly passed my vehicle.

"Thank you so much for talking to us, young man. You have been very helpful," Alice chirped out of the open window, her multiples of grandmother bracelets ringing like church bells on Sunday morning.

"You are welcome," I replied, although I wasn't quite sure I knew where I had been helpful. "Be careful," I hollered after the disappearing Oldsmobile. It took the entire width of the trail.

I shook my head in disbelief and drove on. Shortly thereafter, I reached the point where the White Rim Road turns off to the south from the Shafer Trail. I saw it ahead of me, perhaps half a mile away. A white pickup truck approached the intersection from the White Rim, slowed briefly, then came towards me.

I stopped and pulled over as far as I could. I knew the custom on four-wheel roads to slow down and halt for some talk and exchange of information about conditions ahead. The white pickup slowed as well. It had some camping gear in its loading area and a well-used, dusty mountain bike standing upright.

When it came alongside, I witnessed the insignia of the National Park Service on its door.

"How is it going?" I said to the ranger inside. She was young, as young as the ranger this morning. Her long blonde hair, normally loose, was neatly packed into a thick braid, which in turn partly disappeared under her National Park Service cap.

"Good," she said cheerfully, "and how about yourself?"

"Doing great, thank you. But as a biker, I am curious to know why you carry your mountain bike into this gorgeous wonderland?"

"Oh, that? Yeah, we all carry ours along when we patrol the White Rim Road."

"Ah, yes, Andre up at the ranger station told me about that. Do you ever have to use it?"

"Sometimes, when people stray off the road and get injured. The easiest way to reach them is by bike."

"Makes sense," I said. "Did you just do your turn patrolling the road?"

"Yes," she replied, "and I am darned tired. We do it every five days, but we take turns."

"How long does it take for the complete circle?"

"Three days. And I am beat now, look forward to a hot shower and a bed with sheets tonight."

"Yeah, I can surely relate to that," I told her, aware that after two nights in my tent in Willow Flat, I myself was badly in need of a shower.

"Do you guys live up on the rim?"

"No, we live in back of the ranger station in Moab."

"The one on the town's north end?"

"Yes," she replied, "right behind the station are the employee residences."

"Long way to work!"

"Not too bad," she said with a smile, "about twenty-eight miles one way on the paved road."

"Less on this track?" I asked.

"Oh yeah, less than half the mileage."

Hmm. Maybe I could link up with her later in Moab, have dinner together somewhere, and find out about the fate of the ladies.

"That reminds me. You will be seeing another car up the trail."

"Tell me about it!" She suddenly looked strained, drained. 'Leave me alone, I've had enough' her face expressed.

"Two elderly ladies, in an Oldsmobile. They are about a mile ahead of you, toward the rim."

"Oh my God," she exclaimed, "of course no four-wheel-drive?"

"Nope," I replied. "They told me they had done this before. They said for me not to worry."

"What did you tell them?"

"I warned them of a couple of deep, flash flood washouts ahead of them. You know, we had heavy thunderstorms last night. Lots of rain."

"What did they say to that?"

"Nothing," I answered. "So I told them that rushing waters are dangerous and their further progress would be determined right there."

"People do the darndest things," she muttered with scarcely hidden disgust. "But thank you, sir, for telling me. I better get going to see what has happened to them."

She started the engine and moved up the road, waving with her outstretched arm once more before she disappeared. I rode on down the track, thinking about Alice in this Wonderland, but also about the ranger I had just met.

The trail now had an arrow, commonly used as trailblazers, pointing down towards the Colorado River. It became very steep in parts and often I had to find my way across sheer rocks, wet and slippery, without really knowing where the track continued.

An hour later, I reached the river itself and was now directly below the state park of Dead Horse Point. The Colorado was very wide at that stretch. Its green water ran swiftly. By this time, I was less than fifteen miles down the Shafer Trail but had traveled two and a half hours.

Soon thereafter, I crossed the boundary of the National Park and was back on Utah's open cattle range.

And when I rolled into Moab an hour later and passed the ranger station, I thought of her. I was certain then that she had set Alice right.

I also wondered why I hadn't asked her out to dinner, to find out for sure that Alice and her friend were safe.

1995 ALPINE LOOP

Lake City, Colorado, is only a hamlet. It hides at the eastern edge of the San Juan Mountain Range. Its "downtown" section consists of one short block. There, I found the settlement's only bank and the Chamber of Commerce occupying a small room of a residence. Both buildings face a common green. The rest of the village features some small, quaint motels and a number of modest private homes, mostly minute in size and built in the Victorian style which was prominent around the turn of the century.

There was also one grocery store at the edge of town, where I stopped, parked my Tracker in the unpaved space in front of its building, and then walked into its cavernous interior to buy some lunchtime munchies and a gallon of Cran-Apple juice.

Wandering through the aisles in search of both, I peeked into a back room where the clatter of pots and pans and the chatter of human voices could be heard. A person radiating authority was cutting meat, with the help of what I thought to be his family.

Then I found my munchies and juice and walked to the only checkout counter, waiting patiently for someone to take my money.

No one came. Nobody was in sight.

"Anyone there?" I hollered.

No answer came from the back room. Its clatter and chatter continued.

Another customer finally emerged from the shadows of the narrow aisles, took out her purse, counted out $5.56 and placed the amount on the cashier's counter.

"Is that the way I should pay here?" I asked the shopper.

"Sure," she replied, "they are busy back there. We always do it this way."

So did I, too. I didn't think something like that still existed, but happily, it does.

Lake City is tiny, population 223. Eight-thousand three-hundred eighty-five feet above sea level. It seems almost forgotten in its narrow valley, surrounded by "14ers," as 14,000-plus-feet peaks are fondly called here. Dense stands of aspen, glowing yellow in September, adorn the steep slopes. No tourist hordes, no Hollywood refugees here. No skiers from Denver find their way to this spot—at least not yet.

It's the Colorado of decades ago when Lake City was an isolated mining town.

I had come down State Route #149 from Gunnison, in the early morning. And now, I headed a few miles south out of town, to the intersection with the beginning of the Alpine Loop.

The Loop consists of a series of extraordinary, rugged mountain trails through the San Juan Range, forming a triangle of passes between Lake City, Silverton and Ouray. It includes four summits of mountain crossings, all over 12,000 feet in altitude. It is a network of trails labeled "four-wheel-drive only" on all state maps and an assortment of road signs.

The loop is a dream come true!

My Chevrolet Tracker 4WD, took me on this journey in search of some of these mountain trails to be conquered.

But it was past eleven and going on noon. I decided to check into the Old Carson Inn, to while away the afternoon hiking in the foothills or soaking in the Jacuzzi on the hostelry's sundeck, or both. Then I would get an early start for the mountains the next day. I had read about the Inn in a leading outdoor magazine. Not only had they praised the rooms and location but also emphasized the uniqueness of their breakfast offerings—fit for people who are active outdoors. And I can always handle that.

The elderly gentleman at the Chamber of Commerce had advised me that the Inn was ten miles out of town, along the road to the Alpine Loop.

I found it tucked away by a stand of tall aspen, bordering an expansive meadow. Lake San Cristobel, which I had passed shortly before, was only a short hike away. It looked good for my afternoon trek, although swimming would be out of the question. I remembered from past visits to the Rockies that those fresh water lakes in these altitudes stay cold all year.

The Inn's main log cabin lies at the edge of a 700,000-acre alpine wilderness, rugged and remote, which I was about to enter. Its back side, along with an assortment of service structures, was lined with a stand of dense, large ponderosa.

I stepped inside through a door that stood open—no one there. But as in the grocery store, I heard voices from an adjacent room for which I only saw a door.

"Hello!" Nothing moved. "HELLO," I repeated.

"Hi, there," said a bearded man who appeared at that moment. I asked him for a room and I was sure he would have one now, with the season over.

"We are closed today. Sorry," answered the man who introduced himself as the Innkeeper, "It is the only day in the year that we are," he added.

"Too bad," I replied, "any problems?"

"No, but once a year, in the fall, we buy our annual food supplies in bulk. We take two pick-up trucks and a van along for the load."

"In Lake City?"

"No, in Grand Junction. We're members of the Sam's Club there and get additional discounts for large quantities. It is a 145-mile drive, one way. I am sorry we can't put you up. But do come back."

"I surely will. I like what I see. Next time I pass through I will stay with you," I told my friendly future host.

Then I drove on, leaving the Old Carson Inn with its fabulous view of the Continental Divide, from its wide, open sundeck. It looked extremely inviting to stay and relax, after a long day in the mountains.

Further west, the sprawling valley narrowed into a tight strip of road climbing up between two "14er" peaks. There, the wooden sign by the edge of the road repeated the earlier messages:

DANGEROUS ROAD AHEAD—
FOUR-WHEEL-DRIVE RECOMMENDED

Recommended? If it is recommended, it can't be that bad. I was soon to find out differently, because someone told me later that the word "recommended" was used because people in our free society resent being told what to do.

I stopped in the middle of the one-lane trail. Other traffic? Not to worry, there was none for miles. There wouldn't be any for miles up ahead either. Then I climbed out to lock the front wheels for four-wheel-drive. Once back inside, I shifted the short, stubby shifter into 4H, to activate the transfer case into high gear.

The Tracker sauntered up the trail as if nothing had changed, as if this was Interstate 75 in Florida. The passage had meanwhile become as narrow as the vehicle's width. Branches of bordering trees whipped against the headlights, the windshield and side panels.

"For Christ sake," I mumbled under my breath, "why didn't I do what I had planned to do? Put a grill bar and headlight guards up front of my vehicle?" Because I knew that if the grill broke and my radiator bent, I would be in big-time trouble on this lonesome trail.

There were no road signs anymore. Any guidance for the traveler had vanished. But as long as there were ponderosa and aspen, the trail was easy to make out, because the trail markers in the shape of arrows were carved into the tree trunks for trailblazing.

At 10,800 feet, the Tracker and I left the trees behind. The scenery around us opened up to a grand view of snow-covered peaks. The trail first became moist from the snow melting on the bordering slopes in the midday sun. Then water ran down in small, irregular cascades in its center.

From there on, the grade became 18% at first and later increased to 22%. The Carson Innkeeper had warned me of these inclines and inquired whether I had the vehicle for them. I assured him I did.

From there on, the arrow trail-blazers carved in tree trunks vanished as well because there were no more trees.

I stopped to take pictures. I debated whether I should continue or not. After all, I was all alone up there. I hadn't seen another vehicle since I left Lake City.

But one look to my left, down the unguarded edge of the rock road I was standing on, convinced me that a maneuver such as turning the Tracker around, as short and stubby as it was, would have meant possible disaster. There remained only one way to go: UP!

Besides, I loved every bit of it. My adrenalin rush screamed out loud: "GO ON".

I climbed back into my seat and re-started the engine. Soon thereafter, the narrow, trackless roadway disappeared altogether. No arrow pointed anywhere, no tracks left from the last vehicle were visible. Before me lay a sheer, smooth rock, sloping in a 30-degree angle to the left and glistening with melting snow.

I stopped again. I presumed the rockslide had to be crossed to find the continuation of the trail. Right! But where?

I shifted the transfer case into low gear. In conjunction with my transmission's very low, regular first gear, the combination with the four-wheel-drive low made the vehicle roll across the glistening, trackless rock surface as steady as the majestic peaks around me had stood for eons.

I headed straight forward. Hold it there, stop. The rock slid deeply to the left. Not there, for sure. Another 200 feet straight ahead. Hold it again. Now it drooped down ahead of me.

WHERE IS THE TRACK?

There was only one way left: up the rockslide. And there I found it, the tracks in the moist, granite-littered surface of the barren soil.

Then the snow started to stick. The temperature must have fallen to 32 degrees. By now, I was climbing up in an almost straight line to the crest I could see ahead of me. My stubby, sturdy car, in all its lowest gears possible, ascended effortlessly. I hardly had to depress the gas pedal.

Suddenly, without any notion I'd be there, the Tracker leveled off on a frighteningly tiny plateau. On its other side, the trail plummeted down, visible for less than a mile, in the wildest switchbacks I'd ever seen. I estimated the angle to be 35 degrees. Then it vanished at the edge of a sheer drop-off.

There, right on the crest, I stopped, pulled the handbrake as far as it would go and placed the transmission in reverse before switching off the engine.

Opening the left door made me quickly put on my hooded parka. A fierce gale of perhaps sixty miles per hour blew across the sunny crest. A wooden sign proclaimed it as:

CINNAMON PASS, ELEVATION 12,940 FEET

Almost 13,000 feet above sea level! In a Chevy Tracker! It was mind-boggling.

I took my Canon and ran up the barren mountain slope, tumbling and sliding through the ankle-deep snow, to take photos not only of the majestic, snowy scenery around me, but foremost of my trusted vehicle which had faithfully worked to bring me here. Standing forlorn, in an angle, splattered with mud, surrounded by masses of snow and waiting patiently to bring me down again, it looked like an invader from another planet who had found his way into this pristine world so close to heaven.

And I saw no other living soul!

I soon retreated from taking photographs. The short run up there had left me short of breath. After all, a sea-level dweller finds it difficult to breathe at these lofty heights.

Yet, I lingered on inside my warm, comfortable car for a while longer, blessing its shelter, munching my lunchables and drinking vast amounts of the Cran-Apple juice I had bought in Lake City. The light, dry air dehydrates the human body in a hurry. And a case of hypothermia would be the last thing I needed up there, all alone in this remote but inspiring alpine world.

Would I ever get down from here? Of course I would. Naturally I did. I would not be writing this here in my cozy, warm study on a late fall day, if I hadn't.

However, I am willing to admit, that I had my moments of anxiety up there. I was disquieted by all these thoughts which normally do not occupy my mind for too long a time. Besides, it was already time to head down the mountain again. My wristwatch showed it was after two, and to be up there in the dark was not advisable under any circumstances.

When turning the key, the engine sprang to life instantly. That was a new, pleasant surprise for me. Older engines of years past lost a lot of power in high altitudes due to lack of sufficient oxygen. But the Tracker's 16-valve power plant was fuel-injected. Its computer regulated the flow of oxygen and fuel mixture.

I played with the throttle for a moment, pretending to make sure that the engine had warmed enough. But of course, I knew that it was a delaying tactic, anything to draw out the moment when I had to start rolling down this mountain.

I shifted the transmission into first while holding my foot firmly on the brake pedal. For safety, I still had the handbrake set as well. Then I shifted the four-wheel-drive into its low 4L position. I gunned up the engine again, letting her rev a bit more.

And then I ran out of any more excuses.

So, let's go, my friend, you brought me up here like a song; you will do likewise downhill.

Slowly, ever so slowly, I let the clutch pedal out, not touching the throttle. I knew that if I throttled her up now, I would slide into an endless spin from which I might not recover. Again, I made sure that the shift levers were locked firmly in position. They were. Then I let out the clutch all the way.

I ROLLED DOWN THE MOUNTAIN, STEADILY! SOLIDLY! IN A STRAIGHT LINE!

The vehicle hung on its four wheels in low-low gears, doing no more than five miles per hour. A marvel of engineering unfolded. My sweat glands, which had worked overtime in spite of the frigid temperatures up on the pass, were finally taking a rest.

And of the trails I drove from there—down from Cinnamon Pass, up to Engineer Pass, down from Engineer Pass and ultimately across an unnamed pass to Ouray—the last turned out to be the most rugged of them all, especially its descent.

Climbing up this unnamed pass, I soon caught up with a GMC Yukon four-wheel-drive. Its owner pulled aside into one of the turn-outs, open spots provided by the road builders for the passing of vehicles in either direction. It was a gesture I recognized at once. He wanted to offer to me the opportunity to get by him. His was the first vehicle I had encountered all day. And it turned out to be one out of only two I saw on the entire stretch of the loop.

I stopped alongside his Yukon, rolled my right window down and said hello. This is an unwritten rule on the trails. Everyone stops for another rider, to extend greetings and exchange tales of the trails past or ahead. Of course, the other reason no one mentions is to see if the other is okay.

"I stopped here because you might want to go ahead. You're faster than we are," said the Yukon's driver.

"Thanks, but I'm in no hurry. If I pass and you are behind me, I can't stop so often to take as many pictures as I now do," I replied. "So please go on."

"Well, when we saw this turn-out, we thought we should offer you this chance because ahead there are not too many of those around," said the driver's female companion. "But we would really appreciate your riding behind us," added her driver-friend.

"Why is that?"

"Because our GMC has a much longer wheelbase. That's why its turning radius is a lot wider than your Tracker's."

"You've done well so far. So why worry?" I asked.

"Because we know the trail. We've been here before. The switchbacks on the way down to Ouray are fiercely tight. We would have to move back and forth several times to negotiate them."

"Then, probably, I'd be slowed down by them too," I added.

"No, you won't. Because Trackers and Jeeps have a tight enough radius to go around the switchbacks in one turn. So, we'd appreciate if you'd be staying behind us, just in case we run into a serious problem."

"I understand. Sure thing, will do."

I watched the Yukon closely for the rest of the ride down the mountain. Its driver was right. His vehicle was a bit too long for this trail. He had to move back and forth numerous times. Occasionally, his grill hung over the trail's edge. Or his tailgate was inches away from a rock wall going straight up.

But then, unexpectedly, my small but high SUV hit bottom. With the left front wheel, I had crawled up a sizeable rock in the road. What was not visible but I should have detected or anticipated, was the sharp, steep drop-off on the other side. The car dropped its left front wheel down and the heat shield protecting the engine and transfer case underneath went "Boaanng!" And this in spite of the car's high ground clearance. It must have been a sizeable drop.

Now I was worried and wished the Yukon was still behind me. I climbed out, lay on the rocky ground and inspected the underside.

Nothing had happened. Not even a dent or scratch. So, I went on.

But the slow pace gave me plenty of time to watch the trees creep towards us, the sky turn azure and the sun descend the western range.

Down at the bottom where the Alpine Loop terminates, by dead-ending into US 550, the "Million Dollar Highway," numerous cars hurried back and forth missing all the beauty of the mountains' sheer force and fierceness, as well as their solitude.

Down at that point, the driver of the Yukon had stepped out of his vehicle, waiting for me to descend. When I sauntered out of the Tracker to unlock the front wheels, he came over, stretched out his hand, and said a simple,

"Thank you for watching out for us. It's always good to ride with someone else on these roads, don't you think?"

"Yeah, I agree. I didn't quite understand why you asked me up there to stay behind you. But seeing the rough trail, now I know."

"Sure thing. It's wiser. We noticed that you're from North Carolina. We were wondering. We are staying in Ouray and thought perhaps we could take you out to dinner tonight."

"Well, that's mighty nice of you. But thank you, I'd rather settle in somewhere, clean up and take my time. Need to call my wife anyway. She is in Munich, Germany right now. So, thanks a bunch. Maybe we'll see each other again on this path."

It was almost six in the evening when I checked into a hotel in Ouray. I had left Lake City at ten-fifteen in the morning. And I had spent almost eight hours on the Loop, covering its forty-two mile distance.

Later, after a well-deserved hot shower to clean and warm me up, I loped down Ouray's main thoroughfare to dine at my favorite steak house.

A rustic place it was, built with pine logs, the inside hung with memorabilia gathered in the alpine mountains surrounding us, sawdust on the floor, men in high boots the way shepherds wear them, the smoke of pipes and cigars hanging thick in the air, and calling cards and license plates from all over the country adorning the walls. A place that was easy to be a part of, to belong to.

This day had been a day in my kind of a world.

And I was sure everybody would recognize my feelings and know how elated I felt over my journey.

1996 LABRADOR TRUCK DRIVERS

This story plays out in Labrador.

It was published in the "Labradorean," Labrador's only newspaper, circulation 7,000.

Allow me to help you with your geography:

Labrador, a province of Canada, is a big chunk of land covering some 140,000 square miles. Its borders with neighboring Quebec have not all been established or surveyed. They are shown on maps as a straight line, with the term "provisional" written beside them. The Labrador Sea separates it from Greenland.

It lies 2,568 road miles northnortheast from my home in North Carolina.

Its population stands at 27,000 people. Ninety percent of them are Inuit, as Eskimos are now called in Canada. Only one town has more than 1,000 inhabitants—Labrador City, seat of the local Government.

On my way back from Paris, in October 1996, it took Delta more than three hours to fly from Labrador's Goose Bay to Atlanta.

My wife Hanna and I went there by car not long ago. Here is our story:

The Province's Route #500 is all gravel. It is called the Trans Labrador Highway. Recently completed, its 528 kilometer length leads through sweeping, pristine open spaces.

For a nomad wandering from the continent's more populated areas, it's a dream come true.

But it is the people who inhabit this harsh land who make the difference. Let me tell you why.

On the first day of September, we were on the final stretch of the 680 miles of mostly gravel road, which leads from Baie Comeau, Quebec, on the north shore of the St.Lawrence River, to Goose Bay, Labrador.

We had traveled the 181 miles from Churchill Falls to our final destination in close to eleven hours. More than 2,500 miles from home, our trusted GEO Tracker 4WD was now due for some required maintenance. I knew I absolutely needed to change the air filter and oil, for we had swallowed a lot of dust.

Seven kilometers west of Goose Bay, where the Trans Labrador Highway finally straightens out and where the dust was less evident than before, I could relax a bit, releasing the tension created when my eyes had to focus intently on what was ahead. I could finally turn my head sideways when I talked to Hanna.

The roadway had just been graded the day before. I could bring up my speed now as high as thirty miles per hour.

Then, suddenly, W A N G !

The GEO's right front wheel hit a rock the size of five footballs. Instantly, we were airborne from the impact. The upward motion starting at the right front wheel sent us flying across the road to its left, steep embankment where the car somewhat regained its stability on its four wheels.

Then we tumbled down the boulder-built embankment in a forward angle, bouncing and rocking downward until we hit plain ground, beautifully soft from the abundant moss which covered it. There we were: healthy, happy to be alive and unscratched. And there was the GEO, on its four wheels, engine humming, and lights still on, tape deck playing Mozart. At a couple of spots, grass peeked out from some of the car's tighter spaces. Other than that, it looked as it had before: dirty, dusty, happy.

The driver of a pick-up truck behind us had witnessed the whole sequence of events. Due to our dust trail, he had not seen us before, until a blue object came flying out of the yellow brownish trail ahead of him, veering over to the left. He knew something was wrong. He stopped at once to see how we were, hopping down the rocky embankment to check on us.

A little later, he and I again climbed up to the road surface to remove the evil rock from the roadbed.

He offered to tow us out. But I told him that I could do this alone. So one hundred meters down the way, he and his teenage son cleared debris and branches from the sandier embankment. Then they waved us on.

Our car, by now in low four wheel drive and first gear, rolled slowly towards the steep embankment. I kept it at 3 to 4 miles per hour because I did not want to ram the nose of the vehicle into the soft sand. Then we started climbing the 45 degree angle up as if this was something the GEO had long been waiting for.

In the meantime, up on the road, every other motorist traveling the highway also stopped to see if help was needed. Among them was a friendly driver of an eighteen-wheeler bearing the inscription of Glenn Corporation.

He and our friend in the pick-up crawled under our GEO to make sure it was intact and in working order. Then they insisted they escort us into town to the Labrador Inn, to make certain we were all right and safe.

I don't even know their names. But I do know that I would want them to be my friends.

One day soon, we shall return to Labrador. And when we do, can the Transportation Department perhaps tell the graders to remove the rocks they scrape up from the road?

Thanks, guys, it would be much appreciated.

1996 BEN

In the afternoon of a mid-January day not long ago, I drove down the Overseas Highway to attend a seminar in Key West. At the end of Pigeon Key, west of Marathon, the Seven Mile Bridge came into view. Crossing it, the emerald-green shallow Gulf waters stretched north and west while the darker-green Atlantic Ocean bordered the southern rim. At its end, I came upon Big Pine Key, habitat of miniature Key deer.

Since it was late afternoon by then and I was not due in Key West for another day, I checked out the "Big Pine Key Campground and Boatel" as the sign along the highway indicated. A left turn off the busy highway brought me onto a bumpy soft shell road for a short distance. At its end, lay the establishment I was looking for. Its campground appeared to be designed for motor home campers, most of them there to stay for the entire winter season.

But also a marina-type row of docks was available for boats of all sizes. They were tied up in front of a long, low-slung, cinderblock building erected along the entire length of the docks, as a motel would be along a paved parking lot.

This was the "Boatel," where the owners of the yachts and boats checked in for the night—a motel for boaters.

"Are you in a motor home?" asked a youngish man behind the check-in counter under a thatched roof open an all four sides. I took his name from a crude wooden nameplate on the counter top, which listed only "Ben."

"No, Ben," I replied, "I have a GEO Tracker with me."

"Then you probably want a tent campsite?"

"Sure do."

"We have a separate section for tenters. It's not very large. But I set it aside, since it is a choice location right next to the Atlantic."

He showed me where it was on the campground map.

"Only two tenters there right now. You will have some great spots to pitch your tent a few yards away from the ocean. We also have shower houses if you want to rinse off the saltwater after you swim. But you'd have to walk a bit to reach them, they are right here in the center," he went on, pointing to the map.

"No problem. Sounds great. Let me have a site, please."

"But there is one problem," continued Ben, "people clean their fish not far from the tent site. We have installed a hose and tub there for that purpose. Smell sometimes drifts over. Got to be seasoned for that."

"I'll handle it."

"You a fisherman?" Ben asked.

"No. Never held a rod in my life."

For a brief moment, he looked at me, puzzled. He had probably never met anyone who was NOT a fisherman.

"What do you do," he asked after a minute, trying to be casual about it. "I mean, work?"

"I am heading for a seminar in Key West."

Another pause. Another puzzled face.

"You still learning or somethin'?"

"It's a literature seminar I am going to attend."

"A what?"

"Where writers can learn and improve what they are doing, writing that is."

"So you are one of them journalists?"

"Not really, Ben, just trying to make some money and publish what I write about."

That answer seemed to satisfy his curiosity. He could relate to that more realistic explanation of my lifestyle.

"Well, have a good evening, sir," Ben concluded. I had become a 'sir' all of a sudden. Before he'd called me bud, or guy. But then he stopped in his tracks on the way to his water-bound home, a trawler where he lived, turned around and said: "Oh, I forgot, there are no hook-ups in your campsite. That's why it is only $14 a night."

"That's okay; I don't need them anyway because I will go out to eat. Do you know a good place to have some grub around here?"

"Fish Market. Over on Sugarloaf Key. A few miles west of here. Emma owns it. Cooks real good. Tell her I sent you."

"Thanks, Ben. See ya."

I set up camp as Ben said, right by the water, two steps away from it. Then I stripped and went swimming, wading out into the Atlantic, which is like the Gulf, quite shallow around the Keys.

Later, I had a bourbon straight in front of my tent, sitting on a rounded-off rock which God knows for how long had been submerged and shaped by the endless waves of the ocean. The sun began to set on my right, sending gold brown and crimson beams of light across the pale blue sky. What a way to spend a late afternoon at a balmy key on January fourteenth.

Later, I climbed into the GEO and drove through the soft night filled with tangy smells of sea grass and fish. The top was down, all windows too. The breezes kept me cool as I rode to eat at Emma's Fish Market, wearing cutoffs, an ancient faded T-shirt and sandals. Wolfing down my oversized grouper platter with coleslaw and a giant baked potato, with butter and sour cream, I was also handed a bottle of Bud without a glass. It meant to me that Emma considered that I fit right in with the locals.

Next morning, after breaking camp, I passed by the thatched roof "lobby" again and stopped to drop the key to the shower rooms. Just then Ben came out of the shadows of thick vegetation behind the roof and hollered a cheery good morning.

"Hey, Ben, how's it going this morning?" I asked.

"Good. Are you on your way, bud?" Overnight he must have forgotten to call me 'sir'. But that was fine with me.

"Yeah. Here is the key back," I replied, climbing out of the GEO. "But since I'm seeing you again, let me ask you a question. I was wondering what kind of a sailboat that is over there? You know, the one master? Small cabin. Looks like eighteen ft. or so. Who makes a boat like that?"

"Forgot the name of the place that makes it. The boat is a Compac. Sixteen foot. Sleeps two. Somewhat tight inside below deck but workable. You'd have to snuggle up," he said with shiny eyes that twinkled like stars.

"Is it made in this country?"

"Clearwater."

"How much is it?"

"I paid five grand for it new. Got everything you need. No jib, though. Just a main sail. Easy to manage alone."

"Hm. Nice boat. She sail good?" I asked.

"Super," exclaimed Ben.

He started toward the dock where the Compac was tied up, with me at his side, trying to keep up with his loping stride.

It WAS a nice boat, something I could handle alright. Like sailing up and down the entire Gulf coast. Five grand. Let's see. How would I manage that, with an almost brand new GEO and lots of other toys big and small?

"You wanna take her out?" Ben added, as if he had read my thoughts.

"Who? Me?"

"Yeah. Here, I show you where everything is."

"But … " Don't worry, Pedro, she's mine. Take her out. I won't be able to go anyway today."

"MAN … REALLY?" I was stunned and happy he was back to the teasing Pedro name.

"Sure thing. Here … well, you're wearing boat shoes already. Got some sun block? No? Here is some #4. Naaa, here is #15, better take that."

"Great, Ben, you sure you want to do that?"

"Absolutely. Just tell me where you're heading so I can come and rescue you, in case you're not back by evening."

I pointed across the highway, northwest, under the bridge.

"Good choice. No Name Keys out there. 'Bout three or four miles. Got some munchies with you? No? LISA!" he shouted to the woman busying herself on deck of his trawler, "fix Pedro here a sandwich. Ham and cheese on rye with mayo and pickles," then turning to me: "okay?"

I nodded and Lisa shouted, "coming right up."

Then Ben turned back to me: "Better come with me and get the cooler jug. You'll need plenty of water to take with you."

"Thanks, Ben. Here are the GEO keys. It's unlocked. The roof is up but all side windows are rolled down. Can you keep an eye on it while I am gone?"

"Sure. I'll park it right in front of the lobby. Nobody here will touch it."

"Ben, is it alright if I settle my account after I come back?"

"What? You already paid last night for your campsite."

"For the boat, I mean."

"Nonsense," answered Ben, almost angry. "You don't owe me anything. Take her out and just enjoy."

"But … "

"Okay, friendship then, how's that?" and he stretched out his hand for a low five.

And so I sailed off to the No Name Keys.

There was hardly a noticeable stir of air out of the mooring and into the small bay. But when I passed under the highway bridge out into the channel between Big Pine and Sugarloaf Keys, the wind picked up quite a bit.

And then, I crisscrossed the green Gulf waters against the wind.

It was absolutely exhilarating.

I found one of the No Name Keys which had a small, cove-like area of shell-littered, snow white beach tucked in between the dense mangroves. Approaching it, I pulled up the center-board early and let the sailboat coast in. As soon as it scraped the sandy bottom about ten feet from shore, I jumped overboard and pulled her in by hand.

I was all alone. There wasn't a human being around for miles. Far in the distance to the south, I could make out the bridge carrying the highway across Big Pine Channel. And I could detect small, black dots moving on it to and fro. They made no sound. They were cars hurrying from here to there, and I supposed their drivers were anxious to get to nowhere, many of them stressed out by the pressures of living.

And here I was, at this peaceful tropical paradise, all by myself.

I had long taken all my clothes off, consumed great quantities of liquids, written many entries in my journal in between bolting into the warm waters surrounding me, and eaten Lisa's ham and cheese on rye which was a size befitting football players.

I felt like Robinson Crusoe, my childhood hero, and I imagined myself transformed from Defoe's 1719 into the late twentieth century.

I felt like lingering. Like staying forever.

But I knew Ben would soon come in his powerboat and look for me, bringing me back into the hustle of hectic life.

And, of course, I knew I couldn't survive here anyway, as Defoe's sailor did for many years, shipwrecked on his uninhabited island. After all, I am a product of the twentieth century. While geared to the outdoors, I guess I would be lost and soon dead, if left here to tend for myself.

No Name Key! I named mine Crusoe Key which means nothing to anybody else except me. The thought of it makes my spine tingle, makes me look into the far distances wherever I am, to see if perhaps and by great chance I could detect it on the horizon.

Wait until I tell Ben about it. I bet he'll understand!

1996 DINING IN PARIS

Paris and I share what can be called a love affair.

In October of 1996, I traveled to Europe for a week to address some urgent matters. At the end of my stay, I visited the Paris not of 1949/50, but of 1996. However, I am no longer a carrot top, I am not called Bozo the Clown anymore. My hair is white now. I am still full of freckles and stand six feet. But the next generation of Frenchman is taller now, more like I am. I don't stick out anymore.

I stayed four nights at the Hotel L'Academie, on 32 Rue des Saints Peres, opposite Sorbonne's Medical School, two blocks over from 29 Rue de Buci where I lived forty-eight years before. It is a jewel of a place. My room again was on the fifth (top) floor and had a small rooftop balcony with flower pots arranged casually. It could be reached from the room by a couple of French doors. From there, I could see the corner of the Louvre to my left and the 700 year-old Eglise St.Germain on the square to my right.

Neatly arranged in the bathroom were softly perfumed soaps, shampoo and after shave. A pair of white slippers embroidered with the crest of the hotel prevented the tender soles of a guest from touching the cool, sparkling bathroom floor.

Taking a bath under the building's slanted roofline meant bouncing my head into the ceiling every time I left the bathtub. That bathroom was designed for the Napoleon types, those so much smaller than today's folks. But the soft white guest bathrobe made the discomfort more bearable.

It cost a cool $210.00 a night.

I shunned the sumptuous thirty-five dollar breakfast downstairs and went instead every morning to the Cafe de Fleur, or Les Deux Magots for cafe au lait and two croissant, consumed at tables outside on the sidewalks. When the weather turns cooler, the establishments provide stoves in the shapes of lamps.

The two cafes are located on Boulevard St.Germain at Place St.Germain des Pres. Overshadowed by the centuries-old eglise of the same name, they have become a famous spot. Les Deux Magots is the older of the two. It was established in the 1860s, in premises used as a silk lingerie shop. Reportedly, two statues of Chinese mandarins, Les Deux Magots, adorned its entrance for some time, hence the name. When I first came to Paris as a student in 1949, it was the most prestigious place to be and to be seen in.

The Fleur on the other hand had no glamorous historic background. Founded in 1870, it was always a cafe and called Fleur because of a statue of the goddess Flora guarding the entrance.

Between the two cafes, Rue St.Benoit threads through like a narrow ribbon.

On that trip, I rode the Metro, Paris's extensive subway system, for miles on end. I walked the streets and boulevards for even more miles. I crisscrossed the city from the Arc de Triomphe to Notre Dame, to Montmartre, Sacre Coeur and Montparnasse.

On my last evening in town, I went to dine at the Brasserie St. Benoit. Like most French restaurants, it was a small and intimate place, to the point where the tiny single tables were separated only by some five inches. Noisy, with the smell of garlic and spices thick in the air, it was crowded by nine-thirty p.m. when I arrived. The peak French dining hour was approaching.

The patron showed me to my table, pulling it into the center so that I could slide onto the bench, then pushing it back close to where I settled down. On one side was an open passageway for the servers scuttling back and forth. On the other side, sat two young couples, mid-thirties maybe, neatly dressed, smiling a lot and conducting a lively conversation. With so little space between our tables, the unwritten courtesy rule called for keeping to oneself, no eye contact, preserving one's own and others' privacy—that is the motto.

Soon thereafter, while I was indulging in my escargots embedded in their shells and drenched in a sizzling garlic sauce, their cote de filet came, served with baked potatoes in foil wrap. Baked potatoes are by now commonplace all over France, replacing the standard pommes frites,—French fries in our country.

I noted through the corner of my eye how before eating, my neighbors loosened a chunk of potato, then touched it tenderly with the sour cream in its small pitcher.

Then my steak came, along with my baked potato. Inspecting the small sour cream pitcher, I asked my waiter for another one and also some chives on the side. He looked puzzled but obliged.

When these additional ingredients arrived, I went to work, loosening the potato from the baked skin and mixing the sour cream and chives into the potato with my fork.

Silence at the next table! Their conversation had stopped. I could sense four pairs of eyes resting on my plate. After I tasted the first forkful of my creation, I couldn't help glancing over to my neighbors. As I did, I saw these four pairs of eyes on my fork in total disbelief. I just smiled.

Vous etes Americain, Monsieur? asked the man next to me.

"Oui, Monsieur," I said and continued smiling at them.

"Is that the way you eat baked potatoes in your country?"

"Oui, Monsieur," I replied again with a wide grin on my face.

Ca c'est MERVEILLEUX, four voices chanted, "we shall try that next time."

"Good," I said, "you will like it."

"But Monsieur, you were kind to explain. Can we suggest something also?"

"Sure, go ahead."

"In France, we eat escargots much. We watched you. But we always take our baguette you know, bread? and dunk it in the garlic sauce after eating escargots. Tres bon! We don't like to waste good garlic and spices."

Ca c'est MERVEILLEUX, I chanted this time.

We all laughed and the men stretched out their hands. It was a perfect meeting of the minds between France and the United States.

The next day, I flew home to Atlanta on Delta's big bird. We had a lively, fun-loving group of about fifty French youngsters on board. They were in their late teens, perhaps exchange students on their way to a year in the US, under the AFS program. There was a lot of banter and laughter. But these kids were well-mannered and kept lovingly in line by one of Delta's flight attendants, a French woman in her thirties with a round, happy face and a warm, winning smile. So nobody minded the commotion in the cabin.

The plane touched down nine hours later at Atlanta's Hartfield International Airport on a sunny, warm afternoon. When the rumble of its landing gear indicated the touching of US soil, fifty young and clear voices chanted loudly in unison:

B O N J O U R , A T L A N T A !

followed by fifty pairs of hands clapping joyfully.

It took only a few seconds for everyone else on board to join in the applause. Even passengers in first class turned their heads and did likewise. Some 350 hands clapped!

What a spontaneous outburst of joy it was!

On the way to customs at the international terminal, I asked one of the kids, a lanky guy with a flattop, why they had saluted Atlanta upon touchdown.

"But you know, Monsieur, Andre from Calais won a gold medal here, last summer. Olympic games, right?"

Right. I had forgotten.

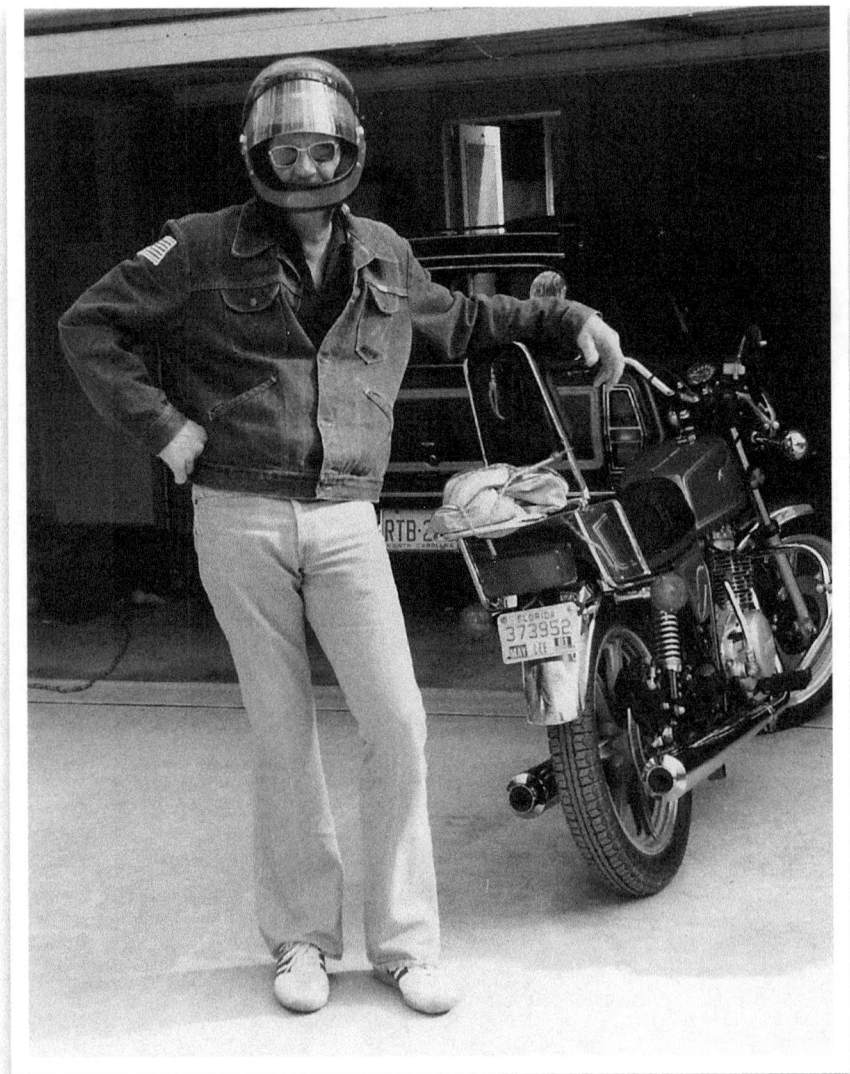

PETER WITH HIS YAMAHA.

Chapter Eleven:
ENTERING ANOTHER CENTURY

2001 OCTAVIO

In the high Andes of Argentina in March 2001, I arrived by car in Tilcara to meet my guide. His name was Octavio and his origins were pure Inca. For eight days, he guided me to the remote villages of the Andes, to visit small hamlets occupied by his brethren whose language he spoke. He was one of them, yet had left their villages at an early age and become the house man for a wealthy lady descended from Spanish conquistadores, who maintained a summer home in Tilcara.

Octavio spoke halting English, enough to carry on a sensible conversation with me, where I am completely void of any knowledge of Spanish. Octavio and I got along just fine.

Crossing over into Chile on a mountain pass some 5,100 meters (16,830 feet) in altitude, I jumped out of the car and ran up a short hill to take a photo of the magnificent mountain world of snow covered peaks around me. Halfway, I halted, bent over, and fought hard for air.

Later in the car again, Octavio said:

"Señor, you need pill."

"What pill? I haven't taken a pill since I was twelve years old. And I am not going to start now."

"But Señor, you do need pill."

"For heavens' sake, Octavio, I told you I don't need it. Stop pestering me with it."

"Señor, pill will make feel you better."

"Why is that?"

"Build up red blood cells is that what you call it?"

"What do red blood cells have to do with this pass we are on?"

"Will make you take altitude better, feel better," Octavio said with a grin. "Most people from lowlands suffer from lack of oxygen above 3,000 meter. Because we live here above 5,000 meter, we take the height better; we have larger lungs that have tiny sacs where oxygen is stored and transferred to blood. In our lungs these sacs are dilated forever so that we have maximum surface for transfer."

"Wow, that's miraculous of nature to provide."

"Yeah, and we have about two liter more blood than you do and our red blood cells are much larger. Also our heart is 20% larger than yours and pumps a lot slower. "

I became interested.

"What's this pill made of then?"

He grinned again, this time sheepishly, hesitated, then finally said,

"Garlic and..."

"And what?"

"COCA!"

Before I could really digest the magnitude of that word, he added:

"But garlic not stinky!"

I couldn't help but laugh out loud, slapped him on the shoulder and asked:

"Do you have any of these pills with you?"

He smiled now. He was happy because he felt he had won me over.

"Yes," he said, "here are two. Take one tonight, after supper, one tomorrow morning after eating. You then good for crossing other pass back to Argentina tomorrow."

I did as he told me. And indeed, I had no more trouble with the altitude of the next pass over 17,000 feet high.

Back in Buenos Aires two days before I flew home, I went into a Farmacia and showed the attendant the wrapper from Octavio's pill. Without hesitation, she reached behind herself onto a shelf, grabbed a packet and put it on the counter and commented in fluent English,, "there are twenty four pills in this pack. That will be 12.83 pesos, or if you prefer, 12.83 dollars."

I conveniently forgot to mention the pack when I came through customs in Miami.

Why did I buy them?

To have something to fight my empty headedness when I go out to Colorado to play on bikes and hiking trails at high altitudes. I am sure Customs would understand and agree to that reason.

2002: A NO-NAME ACTOR

The other day, I went to my neighborhood video shop to rent a movie for my Saturday night pastime. When I stepped into the store, I noticed a poster near the entrance, advertising a new comedy which had just entered the market place. The poster showed life-sized images of the movie's two main actors. I knew then that I had seen one of them somewhere. But when and where?

Next morning, while shaving, it all came back to me—on my last visit to Florida's Key West, barely a month ago. As on many previous occasions, I had gone to this often touristy but always charming place, to attend an annual literary seminar. It is held every year on the second weekend of January.

In Key West, everybody is from "up north." Everybody has to be, because Key West is the southernmost point of the United States.

The town offers numerous places of lodging. I prefer the bed and breakfast establishments—guest houses they are called there. Like all others, mine is an old Key West house well-renovated over the years. The abundant tropical vegetation helps to shield and transform the backyard, the swimming pool and Jacuzzi into a tranquil, deep and lush green sea of nature.

On one of my days in town, I returned from a seminar session in late afternoon and stopped off at the pier to watch Key West's most famous ritual, its spectacular sunset.

When the sun disappeared behind the edge of a crimson Gulf of Mexico and the ah's and oh's had subsided, I walked back to my guest house in the descending darkness. Once there, I changed into my swim trunks and went downstairs to soak in the Jacuzzi for a while, to relax and let the stress of the day escape. Six other guests were lounging there already. Three couples. Three guys with their wives or significant others. Who knows, who cares.

"Good evening," I said.

"Hi there," one of the men replied.

I stepped into the water slowly because it was hot. The thermometer at the pool's edge said it was 107 degrees. Very hot! Finally I sank down into a place near one of the high pressure nozzles pumping water into the oversized tub. I prefer these spots because I let the powerful water stream massage my back.

The usual pleasantries followed:

"Where are you from?"

"How cold was it back home when you left?"

"When did you get here?"

"How did you find this gorgeous place?"

"Have you discovered a good place to eat nearby?"

"How long will you be staying?"

My cohorts in the water were easygoing folks, in their late twenties or early thirties. Banter went back and forth. They laughed a lot. My type of people.

Fifteen minutes later, I sensed that my compatriots were becoming restless. The conversation had subsided. They moved around the small pool agitated, uncomfortable. Then one of the guys finally spoke up,

"Sir, we have been in here for a while now. It's beautiful, isn't it? But we are getting too hot."

"You'd better get out then," I said.

"Well, we want to, we need to. But, ahhh, we have a problem."

"What's your problem?"

"Well, uhmm, you see, we aren't wearing any clothes, that's our problem."

I was momentarily speechless. But then, after I realized what was going on, I started to laugh, pulled off my swim trunks under water, took them out and threw them like a sloshy ball yonder onto the wooden pool deck while happily telling my cohorts:

"That's grrrreat!"

They looked puzzled, then everyone burst out in boisterous laughter as they—in their birthday suits of course—started to climb up the stairs and out of the Jacuzzi. Once up, they grabbed their towels and left for their rooms. But the guy who had asked me, stopped, turned around and said to me down in the water,

"You sure are an okay guy, sir. Thanks."

"So are you," I said grinning.

Now, weeks later, in my video store, I knew I had seen him before. I knew he was the one who had talked to me in the Jacuzzi, who told me of their dilemma, and called me an okay guy.

So, now I can rightfully tell the world that I've met a Hollywood film star when we both weren't wearing any clothes!

I bought the video on the spot.

HANNA HILGER AT THE RETURN TO GERMANY
FROM THEIR HONEYMOON IN ITALY, TAKEN ON THE
MOTORCYCLE SHOWN, OCTOBER 1952.

Chapter Twelve:
FOREVER

1951–2000 MEETING HANNA

Chicago, August 1951, 98 degrees, a humid Wednesday.

I had been transferred to Chicago from Worcester, Mass. I was miserable. I missed my girlfriend Christine. She was enrolled at the prestigious Radcliffe College in Boston, for women only. She was gorgeous. During a short recess, she had asked me to come over to Wellfleet, Cape Cod, for a weekend. Her mother Anne owned a cottage there near the beach.

Yet now, I was drenched in sweat at Crane Company's home office, on South Kedzie Avenue in Chicago.

The stockyards to the east sent their stink drifting through our wide open windows, thanks to a breeze blowing in from the lake.

I was ready for a vacation. Everything in me screamed for it. Just two more days to endure. Then I would be out of there.

My buddy, Martin Renger, came in from Detroit by train Friday night,. He worked for Ford Motor Company and was volunteering as a park ranger in Wisconsin.

Early the next morning, we hopped into my Mercury convertible. The odometer read 192,000 miles. I purchased it for $25.00 the year before, in Washington DC. The trunk held the few things we owned: a tent, sleeping bags, some underwear, a couple of shirts, two pairs of jeans, sneakers. Packing took ten minutes. Then we roared out of town. We headed west on US 12.

In my duffel bag were 168 dollars in silver coins. I had saved them for as long as I worked for Crane. A year? I guessed that was about right. Because when we got paid weekly, any amount in excess of an even number was paid in silver dollars. $57.00 a week? Five tens, seven silvers!

I had never spent them and saved them for a trip someday. Now it was the treasure chest for my first journey west.

Through the Midwest to Colorado, then New Mexico and Arizona we went. We camped on the ground in the desert, ignorant of poisonous snakes who seek warmth during the cool nights by curling up next to warm human bodies.

In Las Vegas, it was 117 degrees. We wanted to go through Death Valley with the top down. Kind people told us we were nuts, we would die of a heat stroke.

"Pause now, drive it at night."

"Okay. But where do we park our car? It's full of our gear and I can't lock it. Can't even get the top up anymore," I asked them.

"You can park it in our garage, then go to the movies while it's hot. The theaters are air conditioned now," replied those friendly folks we'd never met before.

We did what they suggested. We drove through Death Valley at night during a full moon. It was mind-blowing. Still 101 degrees at midnight, but bone dry.

The following morning up in the Sierra Nevada, California's famous sun missed us. It was cloudy and cool. Yet we had to be on our way to San Francisco where earlier, we had made hotel reservations. It was still a stretch of 180 miles, half of them on narrow country roads. But we took it easy and detoured so we could spend a long time hanging around the beach of the Pacific Ocean at Half Moon Bay, seeing it for the first time. It looked majestic in spite of the fact that we could not be impressed by much anymore. We were almost overfed with the beauties of nature. But at least we could wash the filthy Mercury.

We arrived in San Francisco three weeks after we left Chicago.

We were ready for a big city now—street cars, noises, good eateries, hustle and bustle, jazz, fish restaurants galore—in short civilization as we knew it then. And then there it was, the white city on the Bay. The numerous outlying suburbs on the hills surrounding the city, the two monstrous bridges, the old and noisy cable cars. Fisherman's Wharf, Ghirardelli Place, The Opera. Then there was North Beach, the Mecca of original Jazz, with lots of life around us, straight and gay, with the majestic Fairmont and the venerable Mark Hopkins Hotels on Nob Hill. Sausalito on the other side of the Bay, the magnificent Golden Gate Park with its rich vegetation fed by moisture blowing in from the Pacific, with Museums and Twin Peaks overlooking the whole scene.

I fell in love with all of it. I just wanted to settle there until the end of my days. We debated checking in at the Mark Hopkins. But as usual, we had to stay in cheaper hotels. We drove down to the YMCA Hotel on Turk Street, where we had a reservation.

Howling with joy, we jumped under the shower, had our shirts washed and our suits cleaned and pressed. We felt like kings when we went out a few hours later, carefully shaved and cleaned. We were hardly comparable to those two guys in dirty Army slacks with more dirt on their faces than tan. We crossed the lobby heading for the street where my good ole Mercury rested from the 3,200 mile journey, still decorated with the motto

"California or Bust " that lost its meaning now since we didn't bust at all. We went to dinner at Fisherman's Wharf. We ate a huge meal, the way we had remembered good meals after weeks of frugal nourishments. And we had a lot of beer to wash it down.

Then Martin started to talk about Lois. And how much he missed her. And that he was already dreaming about her. And that he would ask her to marry him the minute he came back home. I just sat there and listened to my buddy's dreams. I knew Lois. She and Martin would make a good team. So Martin asked: "You've been so quiet—something wrong?"

That was the point where I lost it all. I rattled off to him my own worries of never finding a woman in my life. I had dates with a lot of girls but before I was allowed to kiss them, they wanted to make sure that I married them. Christine was one of them. But that was not in my book. I wanted someone who just loved me for who I am.

"You know, Martin, what I am talking about? You have that luck with Lois. I don't have anybody and at twenty-six I am getting to an age where I'd like to settle down."

Martin did not say anything to that. Except: "When I get married, you will be my best man."

"Yeah, I accept that. I will."

And then we hugged right in that restaurant even if people might think we were gay. Never mind people, the trip and our evening talk over sea bass in San Francisco brought us together closer than ever before.

The next morning, over a breakfast of eggs sunny side up, bacon and toasted San Francisco sour dough bread, I told him my plan:

"I have decided to go to my roots, to where my grandfather

came from—Remscheid in Germany. Maybe I can find a woman there."

"Are you nuts?"

"No seriously. I will put up the car up for sale today. I will go to Europe by way of Cape Cod, to ask Christine one last time if she wants to marry me."

"Wow, that's big time stuff."

"Yes, but I mean it."

"I know. You are serious, I can tell."

"I am homesick," I told Martin while we walked back from breakfast to the hotel.

"For Chicago? For Crane?" he asked.

"No, for Christine."

"Wow," said my buddy, "must be serious."

"It is."

"I know somebody who works in the legal department of Standard Oil of California. They are looking for grads to hire. Interested? We can go to their office tomorrow."

We did. They wanted me to start the next morning. Because of the languages I spoke. Great job. Fabulous company. I tossed it around in my mind.

"But I was looking for a woman," I told Martin.

I had decided to break off the trip and go back, soon. "You are crazy not to accept that job," said my pal.

Way back in my head, of course I agreed with him.

"How about your Mercury?"

"I will sell it."

"How?"

"Somehow."

When we came back to the hotel from dinner, a young guy

we'd seen before at the hotel admired my old Mercury parked on the street near the entrance. No wonder! It still shined.

"It's for sale," I told him.

"How much?"

"Doors don't lock anymore."

"How much?"

"Roof no longer goes up."

"HOW MUCH?"

Martin poked me in the ribs. I knew it meant 'say something'.

"Ninety dollars."

The guy paused, reflected, and then he said,

"It's a deal. But I don't have all the money. I can give you ten now, the rest later. Where can I send it to?"

"To my Uncle Gustav and Aunt Mary in Washington, DC," I told him, tearing a piece off the evening paper. I jotted the address down and handed it to my buyer friend.

GODSEND I thought.

"Can I count on the money?"

"Sure can. I promise. A deal, then?" he said again and stretched out his hand.

I gave him the key and title, then shook his hand. Within one year, he had sent Uncle Gustav eighty dollars in increments.

Next morning, Martin and I hopped on the "Chief" for Chicago. It took two days and two nights. In Denver, we switched engines. I walked up front and asked the engineer:

"We are forty minutes late. Will I make my connection in Chicago?"

"Sure thing, son. I have nothing but 1,100 miles of straight run in front of me. We'll pull in on the dot."

We were half a minute early at Chicago's La Salle Street Station.

Martin and I parted.

I called my boss at Crane and told him I'd be gone for a while longer.

"Don't be too long now, son," he reminded me.

Then I boarded a train for Boston. The next afternoon I took a Greyhound bus to Wellfleet on Cape Cod.

Christine was summering there at her mother's cottage. I knew it well. I'd been there before.

As I walked up to the front door through the pine forest and its soft needle floor, Christine appeared in a scant and tight fitting two-piece swim suit.

I had never seen one. She looked gorgeous.

I fell on my knees and asked her to marry me!

Her mother Anne heard it in the kitchen and rushed out.

"Peter, what are you doing here? I thought you were at the other end of the continent?"

"I was. But I came back because I am going to marry your daughter Christine."

"No, you are not," Christine snapped back.

"Why?"

"Because I am going to marry Jerry."

I knew Jerry. I thought he was the biggest oaf in the world.

And now this! I was out of Wellfleet within an hour. The hell with women! I had enough of them! For good! I was sure that was the end, that at my ripe age of twenty-six, I would not find anyone anymore. No more women! This is it!

I decided to lead a monk's life from now on. Saying under my breath to myself: don't ever try to latch on to another, it isn't worth it. Don't even look at them!

Maybe going back to my roots will help.

I rode the overnight Greyhound bus back to New York and checked myself into the YMCA Hotel on 34th Street in the morning. Then I walked over to the office of American Export Lines on Fifth.

"Do you have a bunk to Europe anytime soon?" I asked the clerk.

"Yes, we have one left. But it is in a four-bunk cabin. Is that all right with you?"

"When?"

"Tomorrow morning at nine."

"Which ship?"

"The 'SS Independence'."

"Where to?"

"Naples, then Genoa, Italy."

"I'll take it."

The ship sailed the next day at nine sharp. It was September 6.

Ten days later we docked at Genoa. I took the train from there to Remscheid, Germany. That's where my grandfather was born, and the place from which he emigrated, arriving in the US in 1876.

My family owned a steel plant there. Uncle Gustav in Washington had said they'd give me a job. I was sure he knew what he was saying. He also was from the same family from Remscheid.

"Because I am family?" I asked him.

"No. You will have to prove you can do the work required."

"Thanks, Uncle, I'll take it."

"Okay, I will write a letter and tell your Uncle Alfred about that while you are crossing the big pond."

So there I was, in a small industrial town where everyone

knew everyone, miles from nowhere. Surely different from glamorous San Francisco. Even Chicago looked like the Garden of Eden as seen from Remscheid! And here I had covered some 13,000 miles in six weeks to get to this godforsaken place.

I took a room in a private home, bought a brand new BMW R25 motorcycle for wet and windy transportation and lots of books for my leisure time. I was going to live like the Monks of Reus.

I went to work at seven and was home at five-thirty, six days a week. I avoided single bars. On Sundays, I took the Beemer out into the woods, alone. The rest of the time I read most of the books I had bought. I was desperately trying to be happy.

Was I ever homesick, though!

It lasted a bit over six months. Spring had arrived. My dad was sipping wine one Sunday evening in his club with an old buddy of his who had ten kids. Six were girls. By necessity, he had developed a keen interest in everyone who had sons, like my dad. Shortly thereafter, I was invited to a party, in Duesseldorf, some forty miles away.

"Informal. After dinner," the gold embossed invitation read.

Informal in my book meant grey flannel pants, wool sports jacket, a blue-striped shirt with matching tie and highly polished wing tips. I tried to matte down my golden red locks with a lot of Vitalis. It did not help much.

I arrived at eight. The maid opened the door. Twenty young couples all my age or younger were there. The men wore tuxedos, the women long evening gowns. With my crew-cut carrot top and street clothes I stood out like a hot dog at a formal banquet!

I told the maid, "No, I don't want this; I am not dressed for this, I don't belong here." But she had already grabbed my arm, probably thinking "I found a live one," to pull me along the foyer through all the tuxedos to knock on the living room door.

And there was Hanna!

Smiling! Tilting her head! Big blue eyes! Long blonde hair! Scandinavian features. It was her nineteenth birthday. Stunning! My heart raced.

See ya, monks, I murmured under my breath. I don't need you anymore 'cause I ran into a beautiful woman!

Three days later we were engaged. And as far as she and I were concerned, we would have married just that same day.

Our elders protested, though.

"Wait four months. Otherwise, what would the neighbors think?"

We didn't care much for what the neighbors might think. We weighed eloping. But we waited, in order to please our folks.

We were married on September 6, in a Protestant Church in Duessedorf, Germany, exactly one year to the day after I boarded the Independence in New York.

Was that, by chance, one of those encounters I mentioned in the title page of this book with the same title?

Hanna and I took the BMW to the boot of Italy on our honeymoon. We stopped along the way in small, inexpensive guest houses, Inns and Albergos. We also drank a lot of Chianti.

The Beemer worked fine. And, if we were both lying low out of the wind, on its tank, with me practically on the handlebars, Hanna clinging to my back, we could crank the two-wheeler up to almost seventy mph!

On the return trip to Remscheid, we stopped in Switzerland long enough to see my parents. When Hanna got off the bike and removed the goggles from her beautiful, youthful and suntanned face, my Mom asked her,

"How are you?"

"Fine, thank you."

My Mom weighed that answer in her mind for a couple of seconds. Then she probed further:

"Are you really fine?"

"Yes, I am okay," Hanna would mutter.

Whereupon my Mom turned to me and said in no uncertain tones, "You take that beautiful bride of yours off that motorcycle—NOW!"

I was stunned. "But why, Mom?"

"Because she is carrying your child!"

Oh Mom—my strict, stern, thrifty but deeply loving mother! She knew the signs. She was born and raised in the Dutch countryside, in lush forests and fields, among animals and neighboring farmers. She had given birth to four children herself, at home, with the help of a midwife—three of them sons ultimately riding and owning BMWs.

We went back to our apartment in Remscheid riding the BMW. But that was the last trip Hanna took on the Beemer. Not quite nine months later, Astrid was born. In reminiscing, we even remembered where it all happened, halfway between Venice and Bari.

Already during the dreary, wet and cloudy winter months living the Monk's life in Remscheid, I decided that the trip to Europe had been a vast mistake. So I had started to set small amounts of my paycheck aside in an old cigar box, for an ocean-going freighter trip back to New York.

But marrying Hanna doubled that effort overnight, and Astrid's birth delayed it even further. It took a while longer until the three of us could sail back to the States, on a Holland America Lines ship—First Class!

Hanna gave me three wonderful kids. And their eight kids, my grandchildren, are all grown up now. Also, a great-grandson, Nicholas, has been born in Santiago and a great-grand-daughter in Pebble Beach, California as well. Every one of them does constructive things. They are scattered around the world, as in Chile, England, China, Philippines, India, Hong Kong and assorted other places, among them a Trident nuclear submarine prowling the Pacific Ocean and adjacent North Pole ice masses.

When Hanna died in 2000 of the effects of her long road into the life-obliterating disease called multiple sclerosis, my life began to feel empty. But the kids and grandkids closed the ranks. Not hovering over me, no, I would not need or want it, but popping up next to me, whenever they think I need their helping presence.

So now, at ninety-one, I have a great many things to be thankful for.

THE END

EPILOGUE

Many of the people encountered in this tale vanished over the years, some not heard from likely by death, others by distance, other cultures, or busy lives. Still others are writing Christmas cards every year, although we might not have seen each other in decades.

A few I still have contact with. Take Sven for instance. I saw him in Stockholm on a business trip some nine years after we parted at Yukon's Dawson Creek at the southern end of the Dempster Highway. We started right where we left off all of those many years before. Older then and married to a very blonde Swede, Sven worked for the National Bank of Sweden. They had four boys in five consecutive years. Busy with family. I saw them last in 2003.

Eva succumbed to leukemia in 1999. Uncle Hermy is gone, so is Bambi.

Gustave Nobel died in Paris five years ago at the wise age of 101. I talk to Wendi when in Germany.

Klaus is still very much my buddy. It's been sixty-six years now since we first met. He lives on Spain's Mallorca Island. We regularly reunite when I am over there.

Rodin and I are still friends as well. We see each other almost every time I am in Paris and that is often, because I have a love affair with that city dating back to my years at the Sorbonne.

Mary Anne, Andre Gide, Bill, Dwight Eisenhower, Jacqueline, Alice, Paul Sartre, Emma, Todd, the Kayak Kid, Neil, and the numerous others in this book—allowed me to share in their lives as well.

And so it went.

—Sanibel Island, Florida, May 31, 2014